Research Reports on College Transitions | 9

2017 National Survey on the First-Year Experience:

LTSI

Creating and Coordinating Structures to Support Student Success

Dallin George Young, Editor

Cite as:

Young, D. G. (Ed.). (2019). *2017 National Survey on the First-Year Experience: Creating and coordinating structures to support student success.* Columbia, SC: University of South Carolina, National Resource Center for The First-Year Experience & Students in Transition.

ISBN: 918-1-942072-32-4
Published by:
National Resource Center for The First-Year Experience® and Students in Transition
University of South Carolina
1728 College Street, Columbia, SC 29208
www.sc.edu/fye

The First-Year Experience® is a service mark of the University of South Carolina. A license may be granted upon written request to use the term "The First-Year Experience." This license is not transferable without written approval of the University of South Carolina.

Production Staff for the National Resource Center:
Project Manager: Todd E. Money, Editor
Design and Production: Stephanie L. McFerrin, Graphic Artist
External Reviewers: Rachel Beech, Cal State San Bernardino
                            Stephanie Foote, Gardner Institute for Excellence in Undergraduate Education
                            Jodi Koslow-Martin, Triton College

LTSI

About the Publisher

The National Resource Center for The First-Year Experience and Students in Transition was born out of the success of University of South Carolina's much-honored University 101 course and a series of annual conferences on the first-year experience. The momentum created by the educators attending these early conferences paved the way for the development of the National Resource Center, which was established at the University of South Carolina in 1986. As the National Resource Center broadened its focus to include other significant student transitions in higher education, it underwent several name changes, adopting the National Resource Center for The First-Year Experience and Students in Transition in 1998.

Today, the Center collaborates with its institutional partner, University 101 Programs, in pursuit of its mission to advance and support efforts to improve student learning and transitions into and through higher education. We achieve this mission by providing opportunities for the exchange of practical and scholarly information as well as the discussion of trends and issues in our field through convening conferences and other professional development events, such as institutes, workshops, and online learning opportunities; publishing scholarly practice books, research reports, a peer-reviewed journal, electronic newsletters, and guides; generating, supporting, and disseminating research and scholarship; hosting visiting scholars; and maintaining several online channels for resource sharing and communication, including a dynamic website, listservs, and social media outlets. The National Resource Center serves as the trusted expert, internationally recognized leader, and clearinghouse for scholarship, policy, and best practice for all postsecondary student transitions.

Institutional Home

The National Resource Center is located at the University of South Carolina's (UofSC) flagship campus in Columbia. Chartered in 1801, the University's mission is twofold: (a) to establish and maintain excellence in its student population, faculty, academic programs, living and learning environment, technological infrastructure, library resources, research and scholarship, public and private support, and endowment; and (b) to enhance the industrial, economic, and cultural potential of the state. The Columbia campus offers 324 degree programs through its 15 degree-granting colleges and schools. In fiscal year 2018, faculty generated $258 million in funding for research, outreach, and training programs. UofSC is one of only 32 public universities receiving both Research and Community Engagement designations from the Carnegie Foundation.

Contents

Tables and Figures

Tables

Figures

Chapter 1

Introduction

Dallin George Young
National Resource Center for The First-Year Experience and Students in Transition

Jasmin K. Chung
Loyola Marymount University

Every three years from 1988-2012, the National Resource Center for The First-Year Experience and Students in Transition conducted a nationwide survey to collect data on first-year seminars in higher education. Throughout this process, our intent has been to understand a complex, diverse collection of curricular initiatives aimed at fostering active participation in learning and student development in the first college year. Over the past three decades, results of the National Survey of First-Year Seminars have refined the definition and typology of first-year seminars and provided information about the prevalence of these courses and their characteristics at U.S. institutions.

The survey has paved the way for an extensive body of research "establish[ing] the first-year seminar as one of the most important instructional vehicles for achieving the learning and developmental objectives of undergraduate education in the United States" (Padgett & Keup, 2011, p. 3). Further, the regular and ongoing research on the topic has allowed the National Resource Center to speak authoritatively about trends in changing structures, objectives, administration, instruction, and connection with other student success activities in the first year. Moreover, the results of these surveys have widely impacted the conversation on research and practice. A search of citations using Google Scholar at the time of writing revealed more than 500 publications that cite monographs showcasing the results from this research agenda. Given the nature of how these citations are identified, this is a conservative estimate of the reach and impact of this ongoing effort.

Nevertheless, our conversations with constituents have highlighted some of the shortcomings of research focusing solely on the first-year seminar. While the seminar continues to be a common structure for supporting first-year student success in higher education and warrants an ongoing focus, such seminars represent only one type of many first-year programs. The mission and core commitments of the National Resource Center explicitly state our responsibility to provide leadership in knowledge and practice related to first-year student transitions, and that our work should be inclusive of all first-year programs leading to student success.

Thus, we faced a dilemma: How to honor the heritage of our research efforts while charting a path to the future, and how to seek information useful to all those who are part of the first-year experience (FYE) movement?

Why the First-Year Experience Matters

The *first-year experience* has been put forward as a philosophy and movement for improving first-year student transitions for most of the past four decades (Hankin & Gardner, 1996; Upcraft & Gardner, 1989). The FYE, as advocated for by experts during this time, is not a single class, program, or even series of programs; it represents a comprehensive, coordinated, and wide-reaching effort designed to support first-year student success (Hankin & Gardner, 1996; Keup, in press; Koch & Gardner, 2006; Upcraft & Gardner, 1989; Young & Keup, 2019).

Colleges and universities have instituted many curricular and cocurricular efforts that might be called FYE programs or initiatives. These include the aforementioned first-year seminar, often (and somewhat mistakenly) referred to as an "FYE course," as well as summer bridge programs, new-student orientation, first-year academic advising, early-alert warning systems, residential programs, gateway courses, and developmental education (Feldman, 2018; Greenfield, Keup, & Gardner, 2013; Keup, in press). They may also include those student success initiatives labeled as *high-impact* or *promising practices*, including learning communities, service-learning, experiential learning beyond the classroom, supplemental instruction and tutoring, placement testing, common intellectual experiences, study abroad, and undergraduate research (CCSSE, 2012; Hatch, Crisp, & Wesley, 2016; Kuh, 2008).

These efforts are not always well designed, coordinated, or integrated, however. First-year programs often live in the margins of the academy and are vulnerable to threats of restructuring, resource reduction, or cancellation (Barefoot et al., 2005). The focus on the first year at many institutions has been characterized as piecemeal, not always formalized, rarely brought to scale, and often administered in isolation rather than in an integrated fashion (Barefoot et al., 2005; Greenfield et al., 2013). Thus, while these first-year student success initiatives might be similarly structured and work toward the same goals (Hatch, 2016; Hatch et al., 2016), they frequently suffer from the same organizational seclusion as much of higher education, operating in silos. Further, many campuses have placed the bulk of institutional support for first-year student transition on one educational activity, an unrealistic and untenable proposition. Barefoot et al. (2005) assert that "many faculty and administrators in American colleges and universities seem to labor under the false impression that somehow students can be prepared for the realities of college through a single programmatic initiative" (p. 4).

It is not enough for colleges and universities to simply increase the array of educational offerings aimed at first-year students. The FYE is not necessarily improved by the number of programs, but by the level of coordination and integration across them. Because first-year student success is not easily localized or specific to one functional area on campus (Young & Keup, 2019), efforts to bring newcomers from the periphery of the academy toward greater, more meaningful participation must include a cohesive, comprehensive, and campuswide mix of curricular and cocurricular initiatives (Barefoot et al., 2005; Greenfield et al., 2013; Hankin & Gardner, 1996; Keup, in press; Upcraft & Gardner, 1989). Coordination promises benefits such as improved communication and reduced duplication of services, while minimizing the chances that students will be overlooked (Young & Keup, 2019). These efforts must be deliberately and intentionally designed and include leadership from all institutional divisions in the academy (e.g., faculty, student services staff, senior administrators, and other campus professionals such as librarians, mental health counselors, financial aid officers, and institutional research staff; Greenfield et al., 2013). Moreover, the FYE represents a systematic onboarding process for first-year students that communicates a positive, assets-based approach grounded in respect between educators and new students (Hankin & Gardner, 1996). Thus, a well-constructed FYE represents a reversal of "a several hundred-year tradition of harassing new arrivals through intimidating rites of passage" (Hankin & Gardner, 1996, p. 10).

Such FYEs set the stage for student success, acting as a foundation for the rest of the undergraduate experience (Hankin & Gardner, 1996). To achieve the desired impact, a high-quality FYE includes assessment, focuses on learning and development, and responds to differences in backgrounds, abilities, and goals of a wide array of student groups (Barefoot et al., 2005; Upcraft & Gardner, 1989; Upcraft, Gardner, & Barefoot, 2005). The FYE should include monitoring systems to identify student success metrics and trigger responses when individual students are at risk for dropping out (Hankin & Gardner, 1996). However, evaluation should not focus on retention as the sole outcome of interest; rather, it should be part of a larger process leading to continuous improvement (Barefoot et al., 2005; Young & Keup, 2019).

Benefits of the FYE Approach

The maturity of the FYE movement and the concomitant proliferation of first-year programs have led to a robust base of research on the effectiveness of individual initiatives as well as a combining of efforts. The research literature on first-year programs, both individually and as a whole, can be grouped into two streams: *outcome studies* (i.e., those focusing on the effects of participation in certain first-year initiatives) and *landscape studies* (i.e., those that take stock of the national state of institutional practice).

Outcome Studies

Perhaps the most compelling studies on the FYE are those that investigate the impact and outcomes of students in first-year programs. First-year seminars are the most studied of these programs and may be the most researched course in the undergraduate curriculum (Padgett & Keup, 2011; Tobolowsky, Cox, & Wagner, 2005). Reviewing the research base on first-year seminars, Pascarella and Terenzini (2005) reported that these courses are related to "substantial and positive" (p. 403) outcomes such as the successful academic and social transition to college, as well as retention from the first to second year.

Although the first-year seminar might be one of the predominant first-year programs in the United States, research has demonstrated the benefits of other such initiatives. Living in on-campus residences has been found to be a consistent, positive factor contributing to a student's FYE (Mayhew, Rockenbach, Bowman, Seifert, & Wolniak, 2016). Similarly, academic advising and summer bridge programs offer valuable opportunities to connect students with their campus, faculty, staff, and peers (Kuh, Kinzie, Schuh, Whitt & Associates, 2005; Mayhew et al., 2016). These enriching experiences help students cultivate a positive FYE and contribute to their engagement on campus and within their community while also leading to high retention rates (Kuh et al., 2005; Mayhew et al., 2016).

Additionally, participation in first-year programs has been shown to improve academic and social adjustment (Blackhurst, Akey, & Bobilya, 2003; Braxton, Milem, & Sullivan, 2000; Eyler & Giles, 1999; Hoffman, Richmond, Morrow, & Salomone, 2002-2003; Logan, Salisbury-Glennon, & Spence, 2000; Mayhew, Stipeck, & Dorow, 2011; Nadler, Miller, & Dyer, 2004; Paul, Manetas, Grady, & Vivona, 2001; Wolf-Wendel, Tuttle, & Keller-Wolff, 1999). Summer bridge programs have been linked to improved confidence and self-efficacy throughout and beyond the first year (McLure & Child, 1998; Suzuki, Amrein-Beardsley, & Perry, 2012; Wolf-Wendel et al., 1999). Students who participate in service-learning, peer mentoring, and orientation in the first year have shown increased engagement (Kuh, 2008; Nadler et al., 2004; Pascarella & Terenzini, 1991, 2005). First-year residential communities, learning communities, and orientation have been shown to introduce the campus culture and build campus community (Blackhurst et al., 2003; Braxton et al., 2000; Brower & Inkelas, 2010; Jacobs, 2010; Nadler et al., 2004). Taking part in learning communities and common-reading experiences is linked to improved critical thinking, analytical thinking, and problem-solving skills (Goldfine, Mixson-Brookshire, Hoerrner, & Morrissey, 2011; Walker, 2003).

More promising is the evidence for improved outcomes when students engage in thoughtfully combined and coordinated first-year success programs. Studies show that coupling a first-year seminar with another course in a learning community leads to increased first-to-second-year retention, elevated perceived value of academic skills, and improved academic satisfaction (Crissman, 2001; Keup, 2005). Finley and McNair (2013) found that engaging in multiple high-impact practices, including programs typically connected with the FYE (e.g., first-year seminars, learning communities, common intellectual experiences), was associated with improved gains in deep learning, general education, practical competence, and personal and social development. Moreover, research has shown that participating in multiple high-impact practices benefits all students, including "larger boosts for particular groups that view their learning less positively in the absence of such practices" (Finley & McNair, 2013, p. 19), such as underrepresented minorities and first-generation students.

Landscape Studies

Another area in which empirical knowledge has developed is through landscape studies, which examine the current state of programs and initiatives offered for first-year students. The first such study is the aforementioned National Survey of First-Year Seminars. Its focus is to gather in-depth information about the purposes and structure of such seminars as well as other first-year programs frequently connected to or intentionally included in the seminar (e.g., learning communities, service-learning). Additionally, the John N. Gardner Institute for Excellence in Undergraduate Education (JNGI) has conducted a series of landscape studies examining the prevalence of a wide range of initiatives, courses, and academic structures for administering first-year programs. This series began with the National Survey of First-Year Curricular and Co-Curricular Practices (Barefoot, 2000), was soon followed up by the National Survey of First-Year Academic Practices (Barefoot, 2002), and most recently included the National Survey of Student Success Initiatives, administered separately to four-year and later to two-year colleges (Barefoot, Griffin, & Koch, 2012; Koch, Griffin, & Barefoot, 2014).

These two series of landscape studies have provided the most comprehensive national picture of institutional attention to the first year. Reports on the prevalence of key first-year programs are frequent and have found utility and prominence as benchmarks for these initiatives' adoption and success. Findings show that two such first-year programs, orientation and first-year seminars, are ubiquitous in American higher education. Nearly all institutions reported offering some form of orientation (Barefoot et al., 2012; Koch et al., 2014), while 80%-96% indicated at least one section of first-year seminars on their campuses (Barefoot et al., 2012; Koch et al., 2014; Young & Hopp, 2014). Other first-year programs offered by at least half of responding two-year institutions included developmental and remedial education programs, early warning or alert systems, and service-learning (Koch et al., 2014). Programs for students entering four-year colleges and universities included learning communities, early-alert systems, and service-learning (Barefoot et al., 2012).

Findings from these landscape studies also point to ways that first-year programs work across functional lines. Barefoot (2000) reported that research universities more frequently offered the greatest variety of first-year programs and worked "harder with more intentionality" (p. 2) to offer initiatives such as teaching courses in residence halls, learning communities, and supplemental instruction. In the 2002 study by JNGI, about half of all respondents said faculty were at least occasionally involved in first-year cocurricular activities on campus (Barefoot, 2002). Among four-year institutions, learning communities were offered far more frequently in the first year than at any other time in the undergraduate curriculum and were considered highly cost-effective interventions (Barefoot et al., 2012). Finally, Young and Hopp (2014) found that, on average, institutions reported intentionally connecting about three high-impact practices (e.g., diversity and global learning, collaborative assignments and learning, learning communities and common-reading experiences) to first-year seminars. Each of these examples requires coordination and work across organizational structures to support first-year student success.

2017 National Survey on the First-Year Experience

This brings us back to the decision of how to advance our research agenda at the National Resource Center. We decided on a bold move: to change the survey that has represented the backbone of the Center's research agenda for nearly all of its existence and move from a National Survey of First-Year Seminars to a National Survey on the First-Year Experience. This would allow us to (a) more closely align the Center's research with the breadth of the curricular and cocurricular efforts represented in the contemporary conversation on the FYE and (b) continue the good work done through the previous landscape studies on the topic. Thus, we expanded the focus of the survey to include a wider, more comprehensive range of first-year programs. Additionally, the move provided an avenue through which understanding these programs collectively in one survey could reveal linkages and shared purposes that our previous research efforts had not yet shown.

The 2017 National Survey on the First-Year Experience (NSFYE) builds on the previous research work from the National Survey of First-Year Seminars and includes a core set of questions about the course that allowed us to continue to track trends for this important program. We expanded the survey to include sections on overall institutional attention to the first year, as well as common first-year programs including academic advising, orientation, common readings, early-alert programs, learning communities, and residential programs.

Methods

The 2017 NSFYE was administered from February through August 2017. A total of 3,977 institutions were invited to participate. The number of campuses responding with information about the presence of "any program, initiative, and/or educational activity specifically or intentionally geared toward first-year students" was 537, representing an effective response rate of 13.5%. This rate is substantially lower than expected from a web-based education survey, which normally elicits about 25% participation (Gunn, 2002; Wang, Dziuban, & Moskal, 2000), and is less than the two previous online administrations of the NSFYS (Padgett & Keup, 2011; Young & Hopp, 2014). As a result, the low response rate presents a limitation in this research. The population for the NSFYE included chief academic officers (CAOs), chief executive officers (CEOs), and/or chief student affairs officers (CSAOs) at regionally accredited, undergraduate-serving institutions of higher education listed in the *Higher Education Directory*. The CAOs, CEOs, and/or CSAOs were contacted via email and asked to forward the invitation to participate if it would be more appropriate for another person on their campus to complete the survey.

The analyses of the sample data were primarily conducted at the descriptive level. Comprehensive frequency distribution and sample percentages for each item reported throughout the research brief were tabulated for the sample in the aggregate (total) across institutional type, control, and size. Because of the potential for small cell counts throughout the analyses, differences by institutional characteristics throughout the report were conducted and reported in comparative form only. No claim is being made that the reported differences are statistically significant unless specifically stated.

Because of the small number of private, for-profit institutions responding, comparisons between public and private institutions do not include for-profit institutions in the overall total for privates. We acknowledge important distinctions between private institutions that operate for profit and those that do not. However, there were so few responses from private, for-profit institutions that comparisons could not be made with any amount of confidence, and responses to many of the questions did not contain any representation from this sector. A full description of the survey methods and the sample of respondents can be found in Appendix A.

Organization of the Report

The structure of the 2017 NSFYE allowed for an approach that marks a change from previous reports on National Resource Center surveys. Recognizing that individual first-year programs are connected to extensive bodies of literature and practice, we chose to invite authors from those professional networks corresponding to the discrete first-year initiatives to discuss the analysis and presentation of the results. These authors were given the opportunity to contextualize and situate the findings in ways meaningful to the broader conversation about those respective programs. Therefore, because the web of choices made at an institutional level regarding structure, purpose, rationale, and resources are complex and frequently interrelated, many of the first-year programs represented in this research report are linked across many campuses. Responses highlighting these connections were analyzed and reported where it made sense to do so.

This report is organized around the following sections: (a) an overview of institutional attention to the first year and the prevalence and connections among first-year programs; (b) a review of results relating to selected first-year programs presented in alphabetical order by the main concept of the first-year initiative, namely first-year academic advising, common-reading programs, early-alert programs, the first-year seminar, learning communities, new-student orientation, and residential programs; and (c) a discussion of those results and their implications for practice and future research.

Throughout this chapter, we have advocated for institutions to move to a widespread, comprehensive, and coordinated approach to the FYE. This is captured explicitly in Chapter 2 and the conclusion

(Chapter 10). Nonetheless, we acknowledge that this review of the data describes discrete first-year programs in the remaining chapters in a way that focuses on those programs individually rather than collectively. Despite the present reality—that many of the approaches on campuses fall short of this recommended ideal—we encourage readers to engage with the findings presented with an eye toward discovering the linkages and opportunities to create a comprehensive and coordinated FYE on their campuses.

References

Barefoot, B. O. (2000). *National survey of first-year curricular practices: Summary of findings.* Brevard, NC: Policy Center on the First Year of College. Retrieved May 22, 2018, from http://www.jngi.org/wordpress/wp-content/uploads/2011/12/Final_Summary_Curricular.pdf

Barefoot, B. O. (2002). *Second national survey of first-year academic practices, 2002 responses.* Brevard, NC: Policy Center on the First Year of College. Retrieved May 22, 2018, from http://www.jngi.org/wordpress/wp-content/uploads/2011/12/2002_2nd_Nat_Survey_Responses_ALL.pdf

Barefoot, B. O., Gardner, J. N., Cutright, M., Morris, L. V., Schroeder, C. C., Schwartz, S. W., … Swing, R. L. (2005). *Achieving and sustaining institutional excellence for the first year of college.* San Francisco, CA: Jossey-Bass.

Barefoot, B. O., Griffin, B. Q., & Koch, A. K. (2012). *Enhancing student success and retention throughout undergraduate education: A national survey.* Brevard, NC: The John N. Gardner Institute for Excellence in Undergraduate Education. Retrieved from https://static1.squarespace.com/static/59b0c486d2b857fc86d09aee/t/59bad-33412abd988ad84d697/1505415990531/JNGInational_survey_web.pdf

Blackhurst, A., Akey, L., & Bobilya, A. (2003). A qualitative investigation of student outcomes in a residential learning community. *Journal of The First-Year Experience & Students in Transition, 15*(2), 35-60.

Braxton, J. M., Milem, J. F., & Sullivan, A. S. (2000). The influence of active learning on the college student departure process. *The Journal of Higher Education, 71*(5), 569-590.

Brower, A. M., & Inkelas, K. K. (2010). Living–learning programs: One high-impact educational practice we now know a lot about. *Liberal Education, 96*(2), 36-43.

Center for Community College Student Engagement (CCCSE). (2012). *A matter of degrees: Promising practices for community college student success: A first look.* Austin, TX: The University of Texas at Austin, Community College Leadership Program.

Crissman, J. L. (2001). Clustered and nonclustered first-year seminars: New students' first-year semester experiences. *Journal of The First-Year Experience & Students in Transition, 13*(1), 69-88.

Eyler, J., & Giles, D. E. Jr. (1999). *Where's the learning in service-learning?* San Francisco, CA: Jossey-Bass.

Feldman, R. S. (Ed.). (2018). *The first year of college: Research, theory, and practice on improving the student experience and increasing retention.* New York, NY: Cambridge.

Finley, A., & McNair, T. (2013). *Assessing underserved students' engagement in high-impact practices.* Washington, DC: Association of American Colleges and Universities.

Goldfine, R., Mixson-Brookshire, D., Hoerrner, K., & Morrissey, J. (2011). Using a common first-year book to promote reading, connections, and critical thinking. *Journal of The First-Year Experience & Students in Transition, 23*(2), 89-104.

Greenfield, G. M., Keup, J. R., & Gardner, J. N. (2013). *Developing and sustaining successful first-year programs: A guide for practitioners.* San Francisco, CA: Jossey-Bass.

Gunn, H. (2002, December). Web-based surveys: Changing the survey process. *First Monday, 7*(12). doi:10.5210/fm.v7i12.1014

Hankin, J. N., & Gardner, J. N. (1996). The freshman year experience: A philosophy for higher education in the new millennium. In J. N. Hankin (Ed.), *The community college: Opportunity and access for America's first-year students* (Monograph No. 19, pp. 1-10). Columbia, SC: University of South Carolina, National Resource Center for The First-Year Experience and Students in Transition.

Hatch, D. K. (2016). A brief history and a framework for understanding commonalities and differences of community college student success programs. In G. Crisp & D. K. Hatch (Eds.), *Promising and high-impact practices: Student success programs in the community college context* (New Directions for Community College, No. 175, pp. 19-31). San Francisco, CA: Jossey-Bass.

Hatch, D. K., Crisp, G., & Wesley, K. (2016). What's in a name? The challenge and utility of defining promising and high-impact practices. In G. Crisp & D. K. Hatch (Eds.), *Promising and high-impact practices: Student success programs in the community college context* (New Directions for Community College, No. 175, pp. 9-17). San Francisco, CA: Jossey-Bass.

Hoffman, M. B., Richmond, J. R., Morrow, J. A., & Salomone, K. (2002-2003). Investigating "sense of belonging" in first-year college students. *Journal of College Student Retention, 4*(3), 227-256.

Jacobs, B. C. (2010). Making the case for orientation. Is it worth it? In J. A. Ward-Roof (Ed.), *Designing successful transitions: A guide to orienting students to college* (Monograph No. 13, 3rd ed., pp. 29-39). Columbia, SC: University of South Carolina, National Resource Center for The First-Year Experience and Students in Transition.

Keup, J. R. (2005). The impact of curricular interventions on intended second year re-enrollment. *Journal of College Student Retention: Research, Theory, and Practice, 7*(1-2), 61-89.

Keup, J. R. (in press). First-year experience. In M.E. David & M. J. Amey (Eds.), *The SAGE encyclopedia of higher education.*

Koch, A. K., & Gardner, J. N. (2006). The history of the first-year experience in the United States: Lessons from the past, practices in the present, and implications for the future. In A. Hamana & K. Tatsuo (Eds.), *The first-year experience and transition from high school to college: An international study of content and pedagogy.* Tokyo, Japan: Maruzen.

Koch, S. S., Griffin, B. Q., & Barefoot, B. O. (2014). *National survey of student success initiatives at two-year colleges.* Brevard, NC: The John N. Gardner Institute for Excellence in Undergraduate Education. Retrieved from https://static1.squarespace.com/static/59b0c486d2b857fc86d09aee/t/59bad37251a584437bccc737/1505416079925/National-2-yr-Survey-Booklet_webversion.pdf

Kuh, G. D. (2008). *High-impact educational practices: What they are, who has access to them, and why they matter.* Washington, DC: Association of American Colleges and Universities.

Kuh, G. D., Kinzie, J., Schuh, J. H., Whitt, E. J., & Associates. (2005). *Student success in college: Creating conditions that matter.* San Francisco, CA: Jossey-Bass.

Logan, C. R., Salisbury-Glennon, J., & Spence, L. D. (2000). The Learning Edge Academic Program: Toward a community of learners. *Journal of The First-Year Experience & Students in Transition, 12*(1), 77-104.

Mayhew, M. J., Rockenbach, A. N., Bowman, N. A., Seifert, T. A., & Wolniak, G. C. (with Pascarella, E. T., & Terenzini, P. T.). (2016). *How college affects students (Vol. 3): 21st century evidence that higher education works.* San Francisco, CA: Jossey-Bass.

Mayhew, M., Stipeck, C., & Dorow, A. (2011). The effects of orientation programming on learning outcomes related to academic and social adjustment with implications for transfers and students of color. *Journal of The First-Year Experience & Students in Transition, 23*(2), 53-73.

McLure, G. T., & Child, R. L. (1998). Upward Bound students compared to other college-bound students: Profiles of nonacademic characteristics and academic achievement. *Journal of Negro Education,* 346-363.

Nadler, D. P., Miller, M. T., & Dyer, B. G. (2004). Longitudinal analysis of standards used to evaluate new student orientation at a case institution. *Journal of College Orientation and Transition, 11*(2), 36-41.

Padgett, R. D., & Keup, J. R. (2011). *2009 National Survey of First-Year Seminars: Ongoing efforts to support students in transition* (Research Report No. 2). Columbia, SC: University of South Carolina, National Resource Center for The First-Year Experience and Students in Transition.

Pascarella, E. T., & Terenzini, P. T. (1991). *How college affects students: Findings and insights from twenty years of research.* San Francisco, CA: Jossey-Bass.

Pascarella, E. T., & Terenzini, P. T. (2005). *How college affects students: Vol. 2. A third decade of research.* San Francisco, CA: Jossey-Bass.

Paul, E. L., Manetas, M., Grady, K., & Vivona, J. M. (2001). The transitions program: A precollege advising and orientation workshop for students and parents. *NACADA Journal, 21*(1&2), 76-87.

Suzuki, A., Amrein-Beardsley, A., & Perry, N. (2012). A summer bridge program for underprepared first-year students: Confidence, community, and re-enrollment. *Journal of The First-Year Experience & Students in Transition, 24*(2), 85-106.

Tobolowsky, B. F., Cox, B. E., & Wagner, M. T. (2005). *Exploring the evidence: Reporting research on first-year seminars, Vol. 3* (Monograph No. 42). Columbia, SC: University of South Carolina, National Resource Center for The First-Year Experience and Students in Transition.

Upcraft, M. L., & Gardner, J. N. (Eds.). (1989). *The freshman year experience: Helping students survive and succeed in college.* San Francisco, CA: Jossey-Bass.

Upcraft, M. L., Gardner, J. N., & Barefoot, B. O. (Eds.). (2005). *Challenging and supporting the first-year student.* San Francisco, CA: Jossey-Bass.

Walker, A. A. (2003). Learning communities and their effects on students' cognitive abilities. *Journal of The First-Year Experience & Students in Transition, 15*(2), 11-33.

Wang, M. C., Dziuban, C. D., & Moskal, P. D. (2000). A web-based survey system for distributed learning impact evaluation. *The Internet and Higher Education, 2*(4), 211-220. doi:10.1016/S1096-7516(00)00021-X

Wolf-Wendel, L. E., Tuttle, K., & Keller-Wolff, C. M. (1999). Assessment of a freshman summer transition program in an open-admissions institution. *Journal of The First-Year Experience & Students in Transition, 11*(2), 7-32.

Young, D. G., & Hopp, J. M. (2014). *2012-2013 National Survey of First-year Seminars: Exploring high-impact practices in the first college year* (Research Report No. 4). Columbia, SC: University of South Carolina, National Resource Center for The First-Year Experience & Students in Transition.

Young, D. G., & Keup, J. R. (2019). *Council for the Advancement of Standards (CAS) first-year experience cross-functional framework.* Fort Collins, CO: Council for the Advancement of Standards in Higher Education.

Chapter 2

Institutional Attention to and Integration of the First-Year Experience

Jennifer R. Keup
National Resource Center for The First-Year Experience and Students in Transition

As noted previously, the first-year experience (FYE) is a comprehensive, integrated, and intentional set of curricular and cocurricular initiatives organized into an approach to first-year student support, development, transition, and success that is appropriate to the mission, culture, student body composition, and desired learning outcomes at an institution (Barefoot et al., 2005; Greenfield, Keup, & Gardner, 2013; Koch & Gardner, 2006; Upcraft, Gardner, & Barefoot, 2005; Young & Keup, 2019). In addition, the various standards of best practice and conceptual frameworks for researching FYE highlight the importance of purposefulness, multiple approaches, and integration of initiatives. Further, "with a central goal of organizing or, often, reorganizing the academy with student success as critical to its mission, the power of partnerships and a collaborative approach to student success has become the standard of practice" (Greenfield et al., 2013, p. xxxii). Without this vision of FYE as a comprehensive, connected, and collaborative approach, individual first-year programs, courses, and support structures risk being implemented and administered in a piecemeal fashion, remaining tangential to the core work of educating and developing students, and undermining the sustainability of individual initiatives and the FYE program, writ large (Kuh, Kinzie, Schuh, Whitt, & Associates, 2005; Tinto, 2012).

Given these criteria for program development, implementation, evaluation, and success, it is vital to look at the scope of FYE efforts before examining various components of the overall initiative. Thus, this chapter will examine the objectives and myriad approaches that comprise the FYE at colleges and universities. In addition, I will use data from the 2017 NSFYE to discuss how these various elements fit together into a comprehensive approach to support and provide an education for new students.

Purpose and Objectives of a Focus on the First Year

A key element for any undergraduate initiative is its grounding in a firm sense of purpose as outlined by clear student learning outcomes or institutional objectives. Not only does this clarification help develop the initiative effectively, it may also generate buy-in and support, create a scaffolding for formative and summative assessment strategies, and enhance chances of sustainability, which are all hallmarks of FYE best practice (Barefoot et al., 2005; Greenfield et al., 2013; Young & Keup, 2019). As such, one of the first items on the 2017 NSFYE asked institutions to identify those campuswide objectives specific to the first year of college. Table 2.1 summarizes these responses for all 537 institutional participants.

Table 2.1

Campuswide Objectives for the First Year (*n* = 537)

Objectives	Freq.	%
Academic success strategies	432	80.4
Academic planning or major exploration	407	75.8
Knowledge of institution or campus resources and services	406	75.6
Connection with the institution or campus	403	75.0
Introduction to college-level academic expectations	375	69.8
Retention or second-year return rates	337	62.8
Common first-year experience	331	61.6
Student–faculty interaction	328	61.1
Career exploration and/or preparation	305	56.8
Writing skills	276	51.4
Introduction to a major, discipline, or career path	265	49.3
Analytical, critical-thinking, or problem-solving skills	264	49.2
Personal exploration or development	264	49.2
Social support networks (e.g., friendships)	262	48.8
Intercultural competence, diversity, or engaging with different perspectives	254	47.3
Developmental education, remediation, and/or review	235	43.8
Health and wellness	218	40.6
Information literacy	218	40.6
Introduction to the liberal arts	201	37.4
Oral communication skills	182	33.9
Civic engagement	178	33.1
Integrative and applied learning	132	24.6
Discipline-specific knowledge	122	22.7
Project planning, teamwork, or management skills	120	22.3
Digital literacy	113	21.0
Other	59	11.0
Graduate or professional school preparation	42	7.8
None	23	4.3

Note. The sum of the percentages is larger than 100% because of participants' ability to select more than one response.

Analyses of survey responses show that at least half of institutions in the sample most commonly identified 10 objectives for FYE initiatives and interventions. Perhaps surprisingly, given national attention on a completion agenda and persistence as a common focus of FYE discussions among campus leaders and decision makers, retention was not the most commonly cited objective for FYE programs. Fewer than two thirds of institutions indicated retention as an important reason for the FYE, which placed it sixth-highest among objectives. Instead, several of the top reasons for institutional interest in FYE were generally academic in nature and are important correlates of retention.

The two most commonly cited objectives across all colleges and universities in the sample were academic success strategies and academic planning/major exploration, and the fifth-most common goal was introduction to college-level academic expectations. Despite this interest in overall academic well-being, development of specific academic skills such as writing, analytical thinking, and information literacy, as well as integrative and applied learning, tended to be lower, priority-wise, as an institutional rationale and purpose for FYE. Further, a more specific introduction to particular disciplines and the attention to the knowledge therein was cited by only 23% of institutions in the sample and fell in the lowest quadrant of ranked responses.

Another category of commonly identified FYE objectives related to students' ability to forge a sense of community and create meaningful connections with the campus, its resources, and its key constituents. More specifically, these data show that three quarters of survey respondents rated knowledge of institutional resources and a connection with the campus as an important objective for their FYE. Further, 61% of institutions in the sample reported that interaction between students and faculty was a key purpose of their FYE efforts. However, it is notable that other interpersonal interactions, especially among social networks and with people who represented a diverse background or perspective, were not as high a priority for FYE as interactions with faculty. Thus, it appears that colleges and universities deem certain kinds of interpersonal interactions during the first year of college as more significant to student development, learning, and success than others.

As noted in the literature, careful selection of purpose, priorities, and outcomes of FYE is also related to institutional context. In fact, Barefoot et al. (2005) identify "evidence of an intentional, comprehensive approach to improving the first year that is *appropriate to an institution's type and mission*" (italics added for emphasis) as a criterion for FYE excellence (p. 6). Therefore, the data collected via the 2017 NSFYE were disaggregated by institutional type (two-year vs. four-year), control (public vs. private), and size of first-year student cohort divided into five groups: less than 500; 501-1,000; 1,001-2,000; 2,001-4,000; and more than 4,000. Comparative analyses for institutional objectives for FYE across these categories yielded the most substantial results for institutional type. Only one comparison yielded a difference of greater than 15%. Developmental education, remediation, and/or review was reported as one of the top FYE priorities at 61% of two-year campuses but at only 38% of four-year institutions in the sample. Conversely, 10 FYE objectives were reported at a rate of at least 15 percentage points higher for four-year than for two-year campuses in the sample: (a) introduction to the liberal arts; (b) writing skills; (c) retention; (d) civic engagement; (e) common first-year experience; (f) intercultural competence, (g) social support networks; (h) analytical, critical-thinking, or problem-solving skills; (i) health and wellness; and (j) student–faculty interaction. Differences between public and private institutions followed a very similar pattern to those between two-year and four-year campuses, but with less stark percentage-point differences. Comparisons across institutional size yielded no consistent patterns in the relationship between the number of entering students and campuswide objectives identified for first-year students.

First-Year Student Success Initiatives

Colleges and universities have a wide range of curricular and cocurricular options to help address campuswide FYE objectives. Nearly all (98%) of the responding sample reported offering at least one FYE program on their campus. Table 2.2 shows how respondents reported all first-year interventions in use at their institution, as well as the institutional FYE efforts that represented one of five primary programs for meeting first-year objectives at that campus.

One thing these data highlight is the large proportion of institutions offering a vast array of first-year initiatives on their campus, as noted by the high percentages for many of the student success programs, interventions, and courses in the first column. Table 2.2 shows that more than half of respondents identified one or more of 10 different initiatives as comprising their FYE. More than 70% reported that first-year academic advising, early-alert systems, pre-term orientation, or first-year seminars were included in their educational and support programs for new students, which were the most common FYE offerings among institutions in this sample. Several of the most common initiatives in the first year represent high-impact or promising educational practices as identified by the Association of American Colleges and Universities (AAC&U; Kuh, 2008) or the Center for Community College Student Engagement (CCCSE, 2012). However, it is also notable that many common responses represent other approaches, including peer support, general education, and student success centers. These data illustrate that institutions are leveraging a wide range of tactics to support the transition and success of first-year students that go beyond adherence to a prescriptive list of programs.

Table 2.2

First-Year Student Success Programs, Initiatives, or Courses (*n* = 525)

First-year programs	All FYE programs[a]		Primary FYE programs[b]	
	%	Rank	%	Rank
First-year academic advising	80.4	1	62.9	1
Early-alert systems	79.0	2	49.0	3
Pre-term orientation	75.4	3	36.9	4
First-year seminars	73.5	4	62.1	2
Placement testing	65.9	5	14.2	11
Peer education (e.g., SI, tutoring, peer-led team learning, peer mentoring)	62.3	6	26.5	5
Student success center	55.2	7	22.7	6
Developmental or remedial education	54.5	8	20.8	8
General education	54.1	9	19.2	9
Convocation	52.6	10	12.1	13
Residential programs or initiatives	48.8	11	16.5	10
Learning communities	46.7	12	21.9	7
First-year gateway courses	39.2	13	11.2	14
Common reading	38.3	14	13.8	12
Summer bridge	36.8	15	10.4	15
Writing-intensive coursework	35.4	16	7.7	17
Leadership programs	35.4	17	5.6	19
Service-learning	31.8	18	6.2	18
Mentoring by campus professionals	31.6	19	8.1	16
Experiential learning or learning beyond the classroom	31.0	20	5.4	20
Undergraduate research	21.1	21	1.9	22
Study abroad	19.4	22	0.8	23
Other	4.6	23	2.3	21

Note. The sum of the percentages is larger than 100% because of participants' ability to select more than one response.
[a]Represents institutions' responses for all FYE initiatives in use at their institution.
[b]Represents institutions' responses for FYE efforts that represent one of five primary programs intended to meet first-year objectives.

It is perhaps not surprising that the least common first-year approaches were undergraduate research and study abroad, both of which are historically associated with upper-division students. However, it is notable that these two practices, in particular, are growing in prevalence among first-year offerings as they become options for students earlier in their undergraduate career. Institutions also are intentionally engaging in activities to foreshadow and prepare student involvement in them at a later point in the curriculum (Bowman & Holmes, 2017; Kaul & Pratt, 2010; Rivard, 2010; Young & Hopp, 2014). Therefore, study abroad and undergraduate research may represent emergent areas of activity in the array of FYE offerings.

While the survey captured data on all of the FYE initiatives offered at each institution, it also collected data on the five primary first-year programs, courses, and interventions that responding campuses used to address their objectives for first-year students. Given that responses to this second set of questions represent more focused institutional attention, percentages for each FYE initiative decrease substantially compared with the proportion of campuses reporting on all FYE student success efforts (see Table 2.2). For instance, orientation is reported as one of the array of all FYE efforts among 75% of responding institutions but is identified as one of the five primary programs addressing FYE objectives in only 37% of the sample. Interestingly, the four most common programs across all FYE initiatives remain in their prominent positions despite comparatively lower percentages of their use as primary programs.

Only four FYE educational initiatives change rank order substantially from the data analyzed for all FYE programs offered and those that represent one of five primary programs intended to address first-year objectives at the campuses in the sample. For instance, placement testing moves from the fifth-most common initiative offered overall to the 11th-most frequent initiative identified as one of the five primary FYE programs. Conversely, learning communities represent the 12th-most commonly identified initiative among colleges and universities in the sample but move up to the seventh position when considering primary FYE approaches. Convocation falls three positions between the two rankings, showing that it is more often one of many FYE programs offered at respondent institutions but is not as frequently identified as a primary program. Conversely, mentoring of first-year students by campus professionals moved up three positions in the rank order between the two categories, illustrating that this tends to be a program of strategic intent rather than widespread use. While these changes are substantial, the overall data indicate that those programs offered as primary approaches are also the most commonly offered FYE initiatives overall, suggesting a fairly fixed set of programs and curricular components that are used as both overall and priority FYE initiatives.

Separating Differences: By Institutional Type

Much like with campuswide FYE objectives, institutional characteristics are a critical consideration with respect to the types of FYE initiatives offered at colleges and universities. As such, the data for all FYE interventions were disaggregated to compare the types of programs offered at two-year and four-year institutions, public and private campuses, and colleges and universities with various-sized cohorts of incoming students. Table 2.3 shows the differences in FYE offerings when evaluated separately by institutional type.

These analyses yield only one intervention that was a substantially more prominent FYE initiative in the two-year sector: developmental or remedial education. Conversely, the data show 12 FYE initiatives were offered at four-year campuses in this sample at substantially higher rates (20 percentage points or more). Comparisons across two-year and four-year campuses yield starkest differences for convocation (54 percentage-point difference) and residential programs (49 percentage-point difference), with greater frequency for these programs reported at four-year campuses. As such, these data show that four-year institutions offer a much wider array of FYE initiatives than their two-year counterparts. This finding has significance for understanding the transition of first-year students who begin at community colleges, as well as the FYE history for students who transfer from a two-year campus to a four-year setting, a group that includes historically underrepresented minorities, students from low socioeconomic status, international students, and part-time students. These student populations face historic and unique challenges to their transition and success (e.g., Brown, King, & Stanley, 2011; Poisel & Joseph, 2011), and by starting at a two-year campus with fewer FYE opportunities, they might not have adequate institutional support in their first year.

Separating Differences: By Institutional Control

Important differences also emerge among the comparisons between public and private institutions, although they are not as dramatic and are more equally distributed across the two categories than for institutional type (see Table 2.4). Five FYE programs yielded differences ranging from 10-20 percentage points higher at public institutions: (a) developmental or remedial education, (b) learning communities, (c) bridge programs, (d) gateway courses, and (e) placement testing. Four initiatives were more prominent at private institutions by 10-20 percentage points: (a) convocation, (b) residential life, (c) common-reading programs, and (d) writing-intensive coursework. Additionally, one program, peer education, yielded a 41 percentage-point difference in these comparative analyses: 87% of private institutions reported peer education as an FYE intervention, while only 46% of FYE programs at public institutions used peer education.

Table 2.3

All First-Year Student Success Programs, Initiatives, or Courses by Institutional Type (n = 525)

| | Institutional type | | |
| | Two-year | Four-year | Difference |
First-year programs	%	%	(%)
Percentages greater for two-year institutions			
Developmental or remedial education	68.3	50.2	−18.0
Placement testing	70.7	64.4	−6.3
Other	6.5	4.0	−2.5
Percentages greater for four-year institutions			
Convocation	11.4	65.2	53.8
Residential programs or initiatives	11.4	60.2	48.8
Common reading	16.3	45.0	28.8
Peer education	40.7	68.9	28.3
Writing-intensive coursework	16.3	41.3	25.0
Experiential learning or learning beyond the classroom	13.8	36.3	22.5
Pre-term orientation	58.5	80.6	22.1
Undergraduate research	4.9	26.1	21.2
Leadership programs	19.5	40.3	20.8
General education	38.2	59.0	20.7
Service-learning	16.3	36.6	20.3
First-year seminars	58.5	78.1	19.6
Early-alert systems	64.2	83.6	19.4
Learning communities	33.3	50.7	17.4
Study abroad	7.3	23.1	15.8
Summer bridge	26.0	40.0	14.0
Mentoring by campus professionals	22.0	34.6	12.6
First-year gateway courses	31.7	41.5	9.8
Student success center	52.0	56.2	4.2
First-year academic advising	78.0	81.1	3.0

Overall, these differences may be attributed to typical pathways of resource allocation, governance structures, and student populations served in these institutional environments. For example, public institutions are more likely to perform an access function, including the bulk of two-year institutions in this sample that are public, which could explain the greater prevalence of FYE programs relevant to students who are academically underprepared such as developmental education, bridge programs, placement testing, and gateway courses. Conversely, the liberal arts mission of many private institutions as well as the student populations more frequently found there (e.g., academically prepared, traditional, and residential), are more likely to use and expect peer education opportunities, live on campus, and engage in academic transition rituals such as convocation and common readings.

Table 2.4

All First-Year Student Success Programs, Initiatives, or Courses by Institutional Control (n = 525)

	Institutional control		
	Public	**Private**	**Difference**
First-year programs	**%**	**%**	**(%)**
Percentages greater for public institutions			
Developmental or remedial education	62.4	43.3	−19.1
Learning communities	54.5	36.9	−17.6
Summer bridge	42.6	29.5	−13.1
First-year gateway courses	44.6	32.3	−12.3
Placement testing	70.6	59.4	−11.2
Other	6.9	1.4	−5.5
Undergraduate research	23.4	18.4	−5.0
First-year academic advising	81.5	78.3	−3.2
Leadership programs	36.3	35.0	−1.3
Study abroad	19.8	19.4	−0.4
First-year seminars	73.9	73.7	−0.2
Percentages greater for private institutions			
Peer education	45.9	86.6	40.8
Convocation	44.9	64.1	19.2
Residential programs or initiatives	42.2	58.5	16.3
Common reading	33.7	45.2	11.5
Writing-intensive coursework	31.0	42.4	11.4
Service-learning	28.1	37.3	9.3
Mentoring by campus professionals	28.4	36.9	8.5
Experiential learning or learning beyond the classroom	28.4	35.5	7.1
Early-alert systems	77.2	82.0	4.8
General education	52.1	56.7	4.5
Pre-term orientation	74.6	77.0	2.4
Student success center	54.8	55.8	1.0

When data about FYE programs were analyzed by the five size categories for first-year cohorts, nine response options showed a consistent pattern (i.e., a positive relationship with size). Two programs more likely to be found at larger institutions, orientation and first-year seminars, are among the most common FYE programs overall and have longstanding roots in public institutions (Morris & Cutright, 2005). However, the six other programs that yielded discernible patterns across institutional size were less common FYE initiatives overall. More specifically, residential programs, summer bridge, leadership programs, and experiential learning were identified as FYE initiatives by less than half of the sample, and undergraduate research and study abroad were reported by less than 20% of respondents. These results suggest larger institutions support a wider array of first-year programs, a finding validated by a mean comparison of the number of FYE programs offered by the five size categories. Further supporting this assertion, larger institutions are even more likely to report the use of first-year programs not listed among the 22 response options on the survey, as noted by a positive relationship between institutions reporting "other" programs and size of first-year cohort. This proliferation of FYE programs on larger campuses could be partially explained by scale and resources but may also be related to the decentralized nature of larger organizations. In a loosely coupled environment such as a large university

(Birnbaum, 1988), it is highly plausible that various FYE programs are offered in pockets across campus rather than or in addition to a broad-based, centralized approach to the first year.

FYE Administration, Coordination, and Oversight

As noted in the most recent set of best-practice standards for FYE, "because supporting first-year student success is a topic that is not easily localized or specific to one functional area, an effectual first-year experience (FYE) requires campuswide coordination and cooperation" (Young & Keup, 2019). Thus, the FYE involves numerous units on campus, is one of the most horizontal structures in all of higher education, and can be a unifying structure for student success (Greenfield et al., 2013; Keeling, Underhile, & Wall, 2007). Several of the criteria for excellence and standards for best practice reference integration, involvement of a wide range of campus partners, effective collaboration among campus and community constituents, and intentionality. One key component of an FYE program's ability to meet these standards is successful coordination. The 2017 survey asked respondents to rate the coordination of first-year initiatives on a 7-point Likert-type scale.

The mean for the 511 responses to this question was 4.59 (SD = 1.54). These analyses indicate that FYE efforts are not completely decentralized and lack coordination between departments and units, but they also do not typically represent a tightly coupled, coordinated effort. Further, this pattern of responses is generally consistent across institutional type and control (see Figures 2.1 and 2.2) as well as for size of first-year student cohorts. Two-year institutions are slightly less coordinated in their FYE activities (see Figure 2.1) and private institutions slightly more so (see Figure 2.2), but the overall pattern for institutional responses norms toward the middle of the distribution.

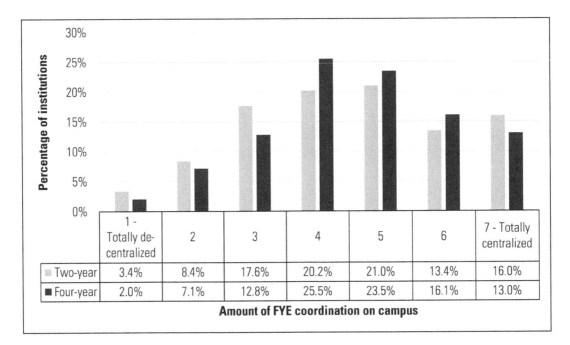

Figure 2.1. FYE program coordination by institutional type (*n* = 511).

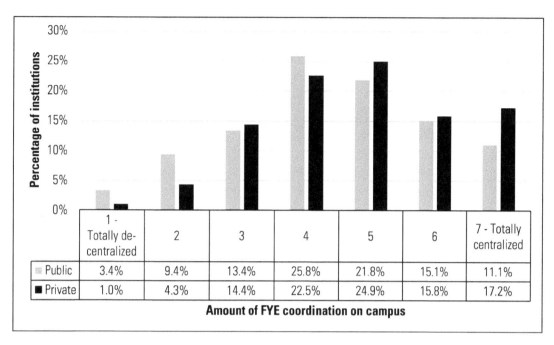

Figure 2.2. FYE program coordination by institutional control (*n* = 511).

The survey also inquired about organizational structures and reporting lines, both important components of FYE implementation and coordination. As noted in Table 2.5, 40% of institutions in the sample reported first-year program offices as their primary organizing structure, a finding that was more prominent for four-year campuses and public institutions. For these locations, FYE offices most commonly reside on the academic side of an institutional organizational chart, either in an academic affairs central office (37% of responding institutions), in an academic department (6%), or in a college or school (1%). However, student affairs offices are the primary division for housing the first-year program office for 29% of respondents, and enrollment management was the home for 7% of FYE program offices among institutions in this sample.

Table 2.5

Organizational Structures to Coordinate the First-Year Experience (n = 410)

Organizational structure	%
First-year program office	40.0
Cross-functional first-year team (e.g., team inclusive of curriculum and cocurriculum)	38.8
First-year program committee, task force, or advisory board	38.5
Other campuswide FYE coordination, please describe	31.0
First-year curriculum committee	15.1

Note. The sum of the percentages is larger than 100% because of participants' ability to select more than one response.

After accounting for FYE program offices, oversight was managed by an organizational structure not necessarily associated with a physical office or even an established place on the organizational chart. More specifically, 39% of institutions coordinated FYE through a cross-functional team overall, although this happened slightly more frequently for FYE activities at private institutions. Another 39% of colleges and universities in the overall sample were managed by a program committee, task force, or advisory board, and 15% engaged a first-year curriculum committee to oversee FYE. These campus structures benefit from engaging a wider array of campus partners and FYE constituents. However, as committee structures, they also risk (a) being less central to the institution and (b) being perceived as less permanent elements of the organizational structure. Survey responses also showed that coordination is not adequately captured by these categories, as nearly a third of respondents identified "other" organizational structures to coordinate FYE. This suggests oversight is an area of innovation for FYE.

Stars in a Constellation

As suggested throughout this chapter and stated by Greenfield and Associates, "a true first-year experience includes more than just one 'star' program and, instead, represents a constellation of support programs" (2013, p. xxxvi). Therefore, it is important not only to look at each program or to inventory the various programs that comprise an FYE, but also to understand how they fit together into an integrated approach. Figure 2.3 illustrates results of an empirical examination of the relationships between programs by drawing lines between the different initiatives that represent correlations with phi values greater than .25, which correspond to medium-size bi-variate categorical correlations (Cohen, 1988). Visualizing the data in this manner shows the connectivity of FYE initiatives at the colleges and universities responding to the 2017 NSFYE.

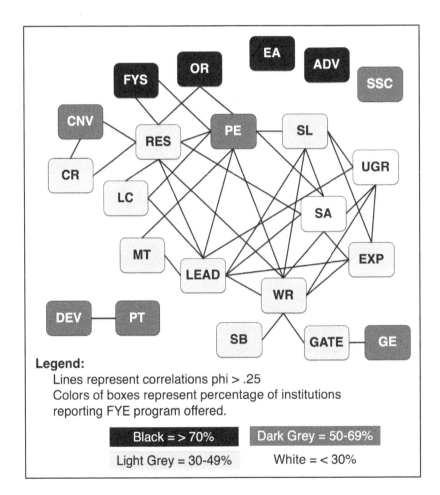

Figure 2.3. Bivariate categorical correlations between first-year programs (*n* = 525). ADV = first-year academic advising; CNV = convocation; CR = common reading; DEV = developmental or remedial education; EA = early-alert systems; EXP = experiential learning or learning beyond the classroom; FYS = first-year seminars; GATE = first-year gateway courses; GE = general education; LC = learning communities; LEAD = leadership programs; MT = mentoring by campus professionals; OR = pre-term orientation; PE = peer education; PT = placement testing; RES = residential programs or initiatives; SA = study abroad; SB = summer bridge; SL = service-learning; SSC = student success center; UGR = undergraduate research; WR = writing-intensive coursework.

As shown in Figure 2.3, several first-year initiatives are empirically illustrated as clusters with connected lines, which means that institutions in the sample tend to offer these programs, interventions, and courses together as part of the FYE. While it is not known whether these connections represent intentional integration among these programs, peer education, residential life, leadership programs, writing-intensive coursework, and study abroad have the greatest number of correlations. In addition, service-learning, experiential education, and undergraduate research are typically offered in combination with other FYE programs and often with one another. Correlations between other initiatives yield program couplets that make logical pairings but are less interconnected overall: placement testing and developmental education, gateway courses and general education, and convocation and common-reading programs. All of these programs are less tightly connected to a wide range of other FYE programs and remain on the edge of the constellation, however. Most peripheral to the constellation are the three FYE efforts that have no statistically significant correlation with any other initiative: early-alert systems, academic advising, and student success centers. Therefore, while these data show some evidence of an integrated approach to the first year, there is room to build more and stronger connections between these programs to yield optimal outcomes.

Perhaps even more interesting is the relationship between commonality of first-year initiatives and inter-connectedness. Overall, these correlations presented in this format show that the most frequently reported FYE initiatives (e.g., early-alert systems, academic advising, orientation, first-year seminars) tend to have the fewest intercorrelations and thus are the least-integrated "stars" in the constellation. In fact, as noted previously, early alert and academic advising are entirely unconnected from the cluster of programs. Conversely, several programs offered by fewer than 50% of the responding institutions—and both of the specific programs offered by fewer than one quarter of the sample—have numerous connections to other first-year programs, suggesting the potential for campuswide coordination and cooperation.

These relationships certainly present challenges in terms of understanding directionality. It is possible that the results represent the difficulty of scaling interconnected programs. Yet, it is just as likely that they illustrate the ease of connecting smaller FYE initiatives that may be situated in adjacent organizational pockets of the university. They may also be the result of institutional characteristics and the culture of campuses that tend to offer different programs. At any rate, these results highlight the need for institutions to continue to work toward drawing tighter connections between FYE programs to meet the criteria for excellence. In particular, these data suggest institutions should give attention to integrating some of their most frequently used programs and strategies to support new student transitions.

Finally, FYE programs need to take note of the strategies that undergird these efforts toward interconnection and integration in order to be sufficiently flexible to engage new partners and initiatives that may be common to the demography, interests, and needs of new cohorts of first-year students. Over the past few decades, new partners and programs have become key elements of FYE interventions, including librarians, student mental health counselors, admissions/enrollment management, and career services. Given the flexible nature of FYE and the changing composition of incoming students, future partners may include campus business services such as financial aid, the registrar, and the bursar, as well as assessment professionals and even community members. It is important to consider how new partners may be integrated into the existing stars of the constellation, as well as how new constellations may evolve in parallel to our existing first-year student support structures.

Conclusion

Overall, these results show that campuses are paying attention to first-year students and investing effort and resources into their transition, support, and learning. Several specific takeaways are worthy of special note.

First, the data show that the purpose of these FYE efforts is not solely focused on retention. Institutional FYE activities prioritize several other learning and development outcomes that represent key correlates of retention, most often with respect to academic adjustment and becoming part of the institutional community, but these are important student learning outcomes in their own right.

Second, these data show institutional flexibility and some signs of innovation with respect to FYE initiatives. Colleges and universities in the sample do draw upon established lists of high-impact educational activities, as shown by the large proportion of institutions in the sample offering them. However, analyses also show evidence of institutions going "off script" from lists of historic interventions, which suggests promising practice with respect to the identification and refinement of new tactics and strategies for FYE.

Third, results indicate that FYE efforts, whether traditional or innovative, are strongly connected to institutional type and control, and sometimes to size of the first-year cohort. Institutional context matters as we build, refine, assess, and examine FYE programs, and researchers and practitioners should heed the aspects of FYE best practice that acknowledge and address institutional type, mission, culture, and structure.

Finally, these results show some evidence of interconnection between FYE initiatives. However, the findings also represent a clarion call to campus leaders, policy makers, and researchers to further tend to issues of integration, particularly for large-scale common programs, in order to truly meet the standards of excellence that new students deserve as the foundation of their undergraduate experience.

References

Barefoot, B. O., Gardner, J. N., Cutright, M., Morris, L. V., Schroeder, C. C., Schwartz, S. W., … Swing, R. L. (2005). *Achieving and sustaining institutional excellence for the first year of college*. San Francisco, CA: Jossey-Bass.

Birnbaum, R. (1988). *How colleges work: The cybernetics of academic organization and leadership*. San Francisco, CA: Jossey-Bass.

Bowman, N. A., & Holmes, J. M. (2017). Getting off to a good start? First-year undergraduate research experiences and student outcomes. *Higher Education, 76*(1), 17-33. doi.org/10.1007/s10734-017-0191-4

Brown, T., King, M. C., & Stanley, P. (Eds.). (2011). *Fulfilling the promise of the community college: Increasing first-year student engagement and success* (Monograph No. 56). Columbia, SC: University of South Carolina, National Resource Center for The First-Year Experience and Students in Transition.

Center for Community College Student Engagement (CCCSE). (2012). *A matter of degrees: Promising practices for community college student success—A first look*. Austin, TX: The University of Texas at Austin, Community College Leadership Program.

Cohen, J. (1988). *Statistical power and analysis for the behavioral sciences* (2nd ed.). Hillsdale, NJ: Lawrence Erlbaum Associates.

Greenfield, G. M., Keup, J. R., & Gardner, J. N. (2013). *Developing and sustaining successful first-year programs: A guide for practitioners*. San Francisco, CA: Jossey-Bass.

Kaul, G., & Pratt, C (2010, Spring). Undergraduate research learning communities for first-year and lower-division students. *Peer Review, 12*(2). Retrieved from https://www.aacu.org/publications-research/periodicals/undergraduate-research-learning-communities-first-year-and-lower

Keeling, R. P., Underhile, R., & Wall, A. F. (2007). Horizontal and vertical structures: The dynamics of organization in higher education. *Liberal Education, 93*(4), 22-31.

Koch, A. K., & Gardner, J. N. (2006). The history of the first-year experience in the United States: Lessons from the past, practices in the present, and implications for the future. In A. Hamana & K. Tatsuo (Eds.), *The first-year experience and transition from high school to college: An international study of content and pedagogy*. Tokyo, Japan: Maruzen.

Kuh, G. D. (2008). *High-impact educational practices: What they are, who has access to them, and why they matter*. Washington, DC: Association of American Colleges and Universities.

Kuh, G. D., Kinzie, J., Schuh, J. H., Whitt, E. J., & Associates (2005). *Student success in college: Creating conditions that matter*. San Francisco, CA: Jossey-Bass.

Morris, L., & Cutright, M. (2005). University of South Carolina: Creator and standard-bearer for the first-year experience. In B. O. Barefoot, J. N. Gardner, M. Cutright, L. V. Morris, C. C. Schroeder, S. W. Schwartz, … R. L. Swing (Eds.), *Achieving and sustaining institutional excellence for the first year of college* (pp. 349-376). San Francisco, CA: Jossey-Bass.

Poisel, M. A., & Joseph, S. (Eds.). (2011). *Transfer students in higher education: Building foundations for policies, programs, and services that foster student success* (Monograph No. 54). Columbia, SC: University of South Carolina, National Resource Center for The First-Year Experience and Students in Transition.

Rivard, R. (2013, October 10). All the freshmen in Paris. *Inside Higher Ed*. Retrieved from https://www.insidehighered.com/news/2013/10/10/louisiana-college-plans-send-all-freshmen-paris-first-days-class

Tinto, V. (2012). *Completing college: Rethinking institutional action*. Chicago, IL: University of Chicago Press.

Upcraft, M. L., Gardner, J. N., & Barefoot, B. O. (Eds.) (2005). *Challenging and supporting the first-year student*. San Francisco, CA: Jossey-Bass.

Young, D. G., & Hopp, J. M. (2014). *2012-2013 National Survey of First-Year Seminars: Exploring high-impact practices in the first college year* (Research Report No. 4). Columbia, SC: University of South Carolina, National Resource Center for The First-Year Experience & Students in Transition.

Young, D. G., & Keup, J. R. (2019). *Council for the Advancement of Standards (CAS) first-year experience cross-functional framework*. Fort Collins, CO: Council for the Advancement of Standards in Higher Education.

Chapter 3

First-Year Advising

Wendy G. Troxel
NACADA: The Global Community for Academic Advising

Students enter higher education with intention. Regardless of age, background, or preparedness, the decision to go to either a community college or four-year institution comes with both purpose and trepidation (Kennett, 2011). There is much to consider when entering an academic program, and whether the individual has determined an initial major or is undecided, they will have access to and engage with an academic advisor.

The role of academic advisors—both faculty and those with advising as their primary role—is to provide guidance and support through a student's academic program from enrollment to graduation. The function of academic advising spans every discipline at an institution, during every season within a program of study, as well as transitions during critical junctures, such as decisions about a major, transfers between majors, and milestones leading to successful completion (Grites, Miller, & Voller, 2016). Academic advisors' activities can range from transactional duties (e.g., removing registration holds, tracking degree audits) to transformative conversations related to academic goal setting as well as personal joys and struggles. They have a bird's-eye view of a student's educational journey, particularly in the first year.

Decades of research suggest academic advising is critical to the educational experience (Gordon, 2007; Light, 2001; Mayhew et al., 2016). Further, Damminger and Rakes (2017) purport that "the first college year may prove the most crucial advising period for both advisors and students" (p. 23). As new students enter an institution's cultures and constructs, they search for both formal and informal resources to assist them. Academic advisors often serve as guides, providing valuable information and translation for navigating unfamiliar and uncomfortable new environments and academic processes (Drake, 2011). When advisement is integrated with other first-year programs and services, students have the best chance of transitioning to higher education, and academic advisors gain valuable knowledge and skills regarding the full scope of the curriculum and pathways for success (Poch, 2017). The research is clear that students who take advantage of these academic relationships reap benefits; however, there is inconsistency in the frequency and the quality of interactions that students have with advisors in the first year (Fosnacht, McCormick, Nailos, & Ribera, 2017).

The results of the academic advising portion of the 2017 National Survey on the First-Year Experience (NSFYE) reveal interesting differences in academic advising structures and practices across institutional type and size.

Academic Advising Approaches and Structures

As highlighted by Jennifer Keup in Chapter 2, respondents reported academic success strategies and academic planning or career exploration as the top two campuswide objectives (80.4% and 75.8%, respectively) specific to the first year of college. These results suggest first-year students at these institutions have access to important resources designed to support their success, including engagement with academic advisors. The extent to which students take advantage of these resources is unclear, however.

Before addressing participation in advising for first-year students, it is necessary to examine the extent that academic advising is required at the institution. Interestingly, only 59.1% of two-year institutions indicated it as a requirement for all first-year students. While advising is required for certain student subpopulations at some colleges and universities (e.g., student athletes, students on probation), 8.0% of two-year institutions said academic advising was not required for any first-year student.

By contrast, 85.7% of four-year institutions said academic advising is mandatory for all first-year students, with only 2.3% indicating that advising is not required for any first-year student. Private institutions in this group require advising for first-year students at a 91.0% rate, compared with 71.9% for publics. There is little difference in requirements for advising by enrollment size.

Researchers asked institutions to determine the approximate percentage of first-year students who participate in academic advising, whether required or not. Table 3.1 reveals a large disparity between two-year and four-year institutions, with 81.1% of four-year institutions reporting that the vast majority of students (91%-100%) see academic advisors in their first year, while just over a third of two-year institutions (37.5%) report the same. However, 81.9% of two-year institutions indicate that more than half of students overall participate in academic advising in the first year. More private institutions report that the vast majority (91-100%) of their students participate in academic advising than publics (89.0% vs. 59.7%; Table 3.2).

Table 3.1

Approximate Percentage of First-Year Students Who Participate in First-Year Academic Advising by Institutional Type (n = 389)

	Institutional type				
	Two-year		Four-year		Difference
% participating in first-year advising	Freq.	%	Freq.	%	(%)
10% or less	0	0.0	5	1.7	−1.7
11-20%	4	4.5	1	0.3	4.2
21-30%	2	2.3	0	0.0	2.3
31-40%	5	5.7	5	1.7	4.0
41-50%	5	5.7	3	1.0	4.7
51-60%	7	8.0	3	1.0	7.0
61-70%	8	9.1	6	2.0	7.1
71-80%	14	15.9	12	4.0	11.9
81-90%	10	11.4	22	7.3	4.1
91-100%	33	37.5	244	81.1	−43.6

Even though many institutions require first-year students to meet with an academic advisor, the way that requirement is managed varies considerably by institutional type and control. Respondents were asked to report how often first-year students were required to meet with their advisors. Table 3.3 reveals interesting differences in the frequency of these meetings, especially between two- and four-year institutions. Of those two-year institutions offering first-year advising initiatives, 35.2% reported requiring students to meet with their assigned advisors only once, during the first term, while 22.7% required students to meet at least once each term for the first year. Just under 15% indicated requiring students to meet with their assigned advisors two or more times each term. Just over 11% reported that first-year students are not required to meet with their academic advisors, even though they are assigned one.

Table 3.2

Approximate Percentage of First-Year Students Who Participate in First-Year Academic Advising by Institutional Control (n = 386)

| % participating in first-year advising | Institutional control | | | | Difference (%) |
| | Public | | Private | | |
	Freq.	%	Freq.	%	
10% or less	4	1.7	1	0.6	1.1
11-20%	4	1.7	1	0.6	1.1
21-30%	2	0.9	0	0.0	0.9
31-40%	7	3.0	3	1.9	1.1
41-50%	5	2.2	3	1.9	0.3
51-60%	9	3.9	1	0.6	3.3
61-70%	14	6.1	0	0.0	6.1
71-80%	21	9.1	3	1.9	7.2
81-90%	27	11.7	5	3.2	8.5
91-100%	138	59.7	138	89.0	−29.3

Table 3.3

Required Frequency of Meetings Between First-Year Students and Academic Advisors by Institutional Type (n = 389)

| Required frequency | Institutional type | | | | Difference (%) |
| | Two-year | | Four-year | | |
	Freq.	%	Freq.	%	
Only once, during the first term	31	35.2	35	11.6	23.6
Once during each term for the entire first year	20	22.7	135	44.9	−22.2
Two or more times each term for the entire first year	13	14.8	70	23.3	−8.5
First-year students are not required to meet with their first-year advisor	10	11.4	17	5.6	5.8
Other	14	15.9	44	14.6	1.3

For four-year institutions offering first-year advising initiatives, 44.9% required students to meet with their assigned advisors once each term, and 23.3% reported requiring first-year students to see their advisors at least twice each term. Only 11.6% of respondents require students to meet with advisors only once, during the first term. Just over 5% do not require first-year students to meet with their academic advisors, even though they are assigned one.

Table 3.4 highlights the level that first-year academic advising is required by institutional control. More private institutions than publics require first-year students to see an academic advisor multiple times during the year (72.3% vs. 54.6%; Table 3.4). A large number of respondents (*n* = 115) selected the "other" response, with 58 adding an explanation for the response. Of those 58, 22 added a response that should have been covered by the available response options; however, 15 respondents indicated a consistent version of "varies by program or student type." In some cases, respondents reported requiring students to see advisors three or more times during the semester (*n* = 6), and 13 participants explained that academic advisors also teach the first-year seminar and thus have weekly contact with students. They did not, however, specify whether each student meets weekly with an advisor in a meaningful, one-on-one setting. These results confirm the prevailing literature that

Table 3.4

Required Frequency of Meetings Between First-Year Students and Academic Advisors by Institutional Control
(n = 389)

| | Institutional control | | | | Difference |
| | Public | | Private | | |
Required frequency	Freq.	%	Freq.	%	(%)
Only once, during the first term	53	22.9	12	7.7	15.2
Once during each term for the entire first year	91	39.4	64	41.3	−1.9
Two or more times each term for the entire first year	35	15.2	48	31.0	−15.8
First-year students are not required to meet with their first-year advisor	19	8.2	7	4.5	3.7
Other	33	14.3	24	15.5	−1.2

shows both advising structures and practices varying widely across institutions and institutional type (Drake, Jordan, & Miller, 2013).

Advisor Types

Academic advisors may be faculty members who also have teaching and research responsibilities, or they can be staff members. Traditionally called professional advisors, the term primary role advisor is now more commonly used to refer to those individuals who serve full time in this capacity (Himes & Schulenberg, 2016). The 2017 NSFYE revealed that faculty are more likely to serve in advising roles at four-year private institutions than at publics (see Figure 3.1). Professional advisors (primary role) represent the majority of academic advisors at public institutions. About a third of two-year institutions indicate that faculty are most likely to serve in an advising role, while two thirds say advising is mostly conducted by those in the primary role.

Figure 3.2 explores the advising role by institutional size, showing that the larger the institution, the more likely that professional advisors, not faculty, serve first-year students. However, many institutions use a split model in which students are served by both faculty and professional advisors. (Note: Responses to "Other" indicated a combination of faculty and professional advisors [split model] or first-year seminar instructors.)

The split (shared) structure indicates that at most such institutions, academic advisors (both faculty and primary role) are likely to report to multiple supervisors across campus, even in the first year. Respondents in this survey confirmed that assumption, with only about 20% of institutions overall (20.5% and 23.3% for two-year and four-year institutions, respectively) reporting that first-year students are advised in a centralized unit. Just over 16% of four-year institutions and slightly less than 6% of two-year institutions report having no centralized advising for first-year students.

The extent of centralization also varied when exploring the differences between private and public institutions, with 26.5% of privates and 19.6% of publics reporting full centralization. Fewer than 1 in 4 private institutions (22.6%) reported no centralized advising for first-year students.

These results further confirm the challenge presented by both inter- and cross-institutional comparisons of effectiveness of advising practices and intended outcomes for students. Decentralization of advising, along with the differences in the roles of faculty and primary role advisors, also has implications for *advisor load.*

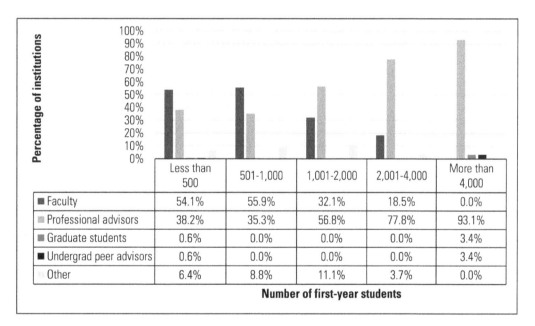

Figure 3.1. Most common professional role of first-year academic advisors by institutional type and control (*n* = 389).

	Two-year	Four-year	Public	Private
■ Faculty	33.0%	43.2%	24.2%	66.5%
▦ Professional advisors	56.8%	49.5%	67.5%	26.5%
▦ Graduate students	1.1%	0.3%	0.4%	0.6%
■ Undergrad peer advisors	1.1%	0.3%	0.4%	0.6%
Other	8.0%	6.6%	7.4%	5.8%

Institutional characteristics

	Less than 500	501-1,000	1,001-2,000	2,001-4,000	More than 4,000
■ Faculty	54.1%	55.9%	32.1%	18.5%	0.0%
▦ Professional advisors	38.2%	35.3%	56.8%	77.8%	93.1%
▦ Graduate students	0.6%	0.0%	0.0%	0.0%	3.4%
■ Undergrad peer advisors	0.6%	0.0%	0.0%	0.0%	3.4%
Other	6.4%	8.8%	11.1%	3.7%	0.0%

Number of first-year students

Figure 3.2. Most common professional role of academic advisors by institutional size (*n* = 389).

Advisor Load

The issue of student-to-advisor ratio (advisor load) is controversial, given the vast differences among disciplines, the stages of a student's academic journey, and the advising structures and approaches used at an institution. Other factors include advisor responsibilities and timelines (Robbins, 2013). Faculty members understandably tend to have fewer advisees than do primary role advisors, and the results typically vary across institutional type, as the results of this study confirm. Figure 3.3 indicates that four-year schools tend to have smaller advising loads than two-year institutions.

As shown in Figure 3.4, private institutions reported the lowest number of students per academic advisor, with 71.6% saying that advisors see 50 or fewer students. Public institutions, by contrast, reported the largest advising loads, with 28.7% indicating that their advisors see 251-500 students. With regard to delivery of advising services, institutions indicated whether their advising is done completely online, with 37.5% of two-year institutions and 11.3% of four-year institutions offering advising only online.

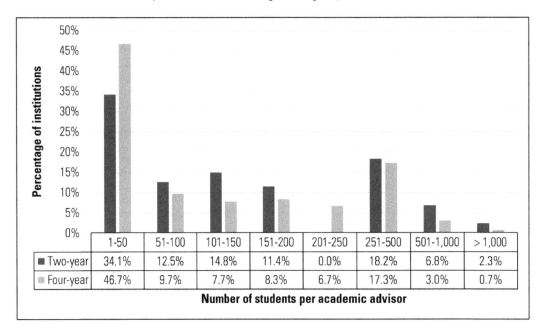

	1-50	51-100	101-150	151-200	201-250	251-500	501-1,000	> 1,000
■ Two-year	34.1%	12.5%	14.8%	11.4%	0.0%	18.2%	6.8%	2.3%
▨ Four-year	46.7%	9.7%	7.7%	8.3%	6.7%	17.3%	3.0%	0.7%

Number of students per academic advisor

Figure 3.3. Number of students per first-year academic advisor by institutional type (*n* = 388).

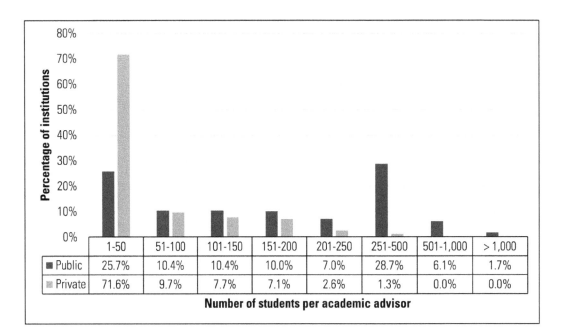

	1-50	51-100	101-150	151-200	201-250	251-500	501-1,000	> 1,000
■ Public	25.7%	10.4%	10.4%	10.0%	7.0%	28.7%	6.1%	1.7%
▨ Private	71.6%	9.7%	7.7%	7.1%	2.6%	1.3%	0.0%	0.0%

Number of students per academic advisor

Figure 3.4. Number of students per first-year academic advisor by institutional control (*n* = 388).

Reporting Structure for Academic Advising

Table 3.5 indicates the administrative division where institutions house their first-year advising. As advising is an academic function, combining responses for academic affairs central office, academic department, and college or school into a more general "academic affairs" umbrella reveals that 54.7% of four-year institutions and 26.4% of two-year schools operate first-year advising under academic affairs. By contrast, just over half (57.5%) of two-year institutions indicated their first-year advising function reports to a student affairs central office, while only 11.3% of four-year institutions reported the same.

Table 3.5

Administrative Division Where First-Year Advising is Housed (n = 387)

| Administrative division | Institutional type | | | | Institutional control[a] | | | |
| | Public | | Private | | Public | | Private | |
	Freq.	%	Freq.	%	Freq.	%	Freq.	%
Academic affairs central office	14	16.1	92	30.7	45	19.7	60	38.7
Academic department	7	8.0	34	11.3	21	9.2	20	12.9
College or school	2	2.3	38	12.7	23	10.0	17	11.0
First-year advising office	4	4.6	17	5.7	13	5.7	8	5.2
First-year program office	1	1.1	11	3.7	4	1.7	8	5.2
Student affairs central office	50	57.5	34	11.3	63	27.5	20	12.9
University college	0	0.0	8	2.7	7	3.1	1	0.6
Other	9	10.3	66	22.0	53	23.1	21	13.5

Note. Responses to "Other" included different titles, such as "academic success centers" and "centers for academic advising."
[a] Because private, for-profit institutions were not included in analysis by control, *n* = 384.

Text responses to the "Other" category revealed additional institutional reporting structures for first-year advising (e.g., academic success centers, centers for academic advising). Most indicated that these units report to academic affairs, while some have a dual appointment to both academic and student affairs.

When asked about the perceived "return on investment for the campus's approach to first-year student advising," a slight majority of institutions provided responses that were above the median on a 7-point Likert-type scale (64.3% and 67.1% of two- and four-year institutions, respectively). A higher percentage of public institutions (66%) than privates (50.8%) were relatively pleased with the educational benefits attained given their human and fiscal resources. About 10% of respondents in all categories registered responses below the median (1-3). The concept of return on investment assumes that academic leaders use evidence (institutional and student data) to evaluate efficiency and impact. Respondents turned next to items inquiring about their assessment processes and practices.

Assessment/Evaluation

To determine the effectiveness of strategies and processes used to advise students regardless of advisor type or structure, purposeful assessment of intended outcomes must be conducted systematically. While some institutions indicated formally assessing the impact of their advising programs as part of an accreditation cycle or as an ongoing process, Figure 3.5 shows most reporting that either their academic advising programs have not been assessed since Fall 2013, or the respondents were not aware of a formal process for evaluation. Across institutional type, most of the conducted assessments comprised analyses of institutional data and survey instruments, though other types of assessment were also used (see Tables 3.6 and 3.7).

It is unclear whether the institutions that reported no assessment or evaluation since Fall 2013 have gathered at least some data and feedback on their academic advising programs. Across all categories, *student satisfaction* and *academic planning or major exploration* were the outcomes most commonly assessed.

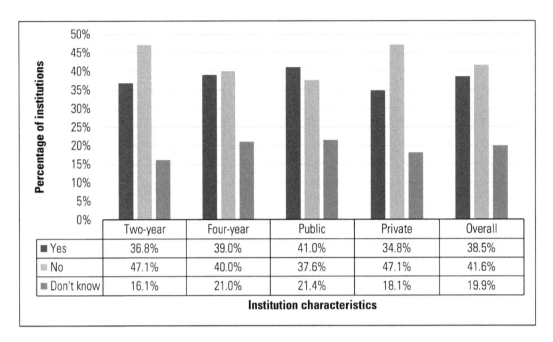

	Two-year	Four-year	Public	Private	Overall
■ Yes	36.8%	39.0%	41.0%	34.8%	38.5%
■ No	47.1%	40.0%	37.6%	47.1%	41.6%
■ Don't know	16.1%	21.0%	21.4%	18.1%	19.9%

Institution characteristics

Figure 3.5. Assessment or evaluation of first-year academic advising since Fall 2013 by institutional type and control (*n* = 387).

Table 3.6

Assessment or Evaluation of First-Year Academic Advising Since Fall 2013 by Institutional Type (*n* = 149)

	Institutional type				Difference
	Two-year		Four-year		
Type of assessment	Freq.	%	Freq.	%	(%)
Analysis of institutional data	20	62.5	82	70.1	−7.6
Direct assessment of student learning outcomes	8	25.0	33	28.2	−3.2
Focus groups with advisors	9	28.1	30	25.6	2.5
Focus groups with students	8	25.0	28	23.9	1.1
Individual interviews with advisors	4	12.5	15	12.8	−0.3
Individual interviews with students	1	3.1	10	8.5	−5.4
Program review	10	31.3	39	33.3	−2.0
Student course evaluation	5	15.6	24	20.5	−4.9
Survey instrument	18	56.3	81	69.2	−12.9
Other	2	6.3	7	6.0	0.3

Table 3.7

Assessment or Evaluation of First-Year Academic Advising Since Fall 2013 by Institutional Control (n = 149)

| | Institutional control | | | | Difference |
| | Public | | Private | | |
Type of assessment	Freq.	%	Freq.	%	(%)
Analysis of institutional data	67	71.3	35	64.8	6.5
Direct assessment of student learning outcomes	23	24.5	18	33.3	−8.8
Focus groups with advisors	20	21.3	19	35.2	−13.9
Focus groups with students	18	19.1	18	33.3	−14.2
Individual interviews with advisors	13	13.8	6	11.1	2.7
Individual interviews with students	5	5.3	6	11.1	−5.8
Program review	29	30.9	20	37.0	−6.1
Student course evaluation	16	17.0	13	24.1	−7.1
Survey instrument	66	70.2	32	59.3	10.9
Other	4	4.3	5	9.3	−5.0

Discussion

The function of academic advising touches all students at all stages. First-year experience programming works best when it is seamless, integrated, and systematic. While some functions of advising (e.g., goal setting, enculturation into campus life) are addressed by other entities at institutions, some processes and activities (e.g., academic planning) are primary to the advising interaction. Given the vast differences in institutional type, size, and mission, generalizing some survey results is challenging. As these findings show, respondents report a wide range of structures, focuses, and formats, and most, but certainly not all, of the institutions indicated focusing specifically on an academic advising program for first-year students.

There seems to be a disconnect between requirements and purpose when an institution requires and assigns academic advisors to students but does not require those students to be seen by an academic advisor even once during the first semester. It is likely that institutions that ignore the value of academic relationships intended to support students and encourage academic planning will continue to find themselves with low retention and completion rates (Fosnacht et al., 2017).

For both faculty and primary role academic advisors, to be informed and effective, institutions must commit to professional development and training. Quite often, the curriculum is complex and dynamic, so advisors must be well-versed in institutional policy and procedures. They must also be continually aware of the resources available to students in order to make appropriate referrals. Increasingly, individuals choose academic advising as a professional role, and many faculty commit as much energy to their advisees as they do their teaching, research, and service. Interestingly, while a large majority of institutions include academic advising as part of orientation, far fewer indicate that first-year academic advising accomplishes their objectives for the first year. This may be a result of the transactional nature of many advising approaches, and the inconsistencies with which academic advising is situated within the teaching and learning mission of the institution.

Professional organizations such as NACADA: The Global Community for Academic Advising encourage institutions to approach the work of academic advisors (both faculty and primary role) in a much deeper, transformational way. That organization's new *Core Competencies Model*, for example, identifies a broad range of skills, knowledge, and understanding that underpin the contributions to student development, progress, and success (NACADA Academic Core Competencies Model, 2017, para. 1). Three content categories provide a framework for the foundational aspects of academic advising interaction:

- The ***conceptual*** component provides context for the delivery of academic advising. It covers the ideas and theories that advisors must understand to effectively advise their students.

- The ***informational*** component provides the substance of academic advising. It covers the knowledge advisors must gain in order to guide students at their institution.

- The ***relational*** component provides the skills that enable academic advisors to convey concepts and information from the other two components to their advisees (NACADA, 2017, para. 4).

Intentional professional development, directly linked to articulated expectations of an approach to academic advising that acknowledges a transformative relationship, will bring consistency to academic advisors' role in influencing student success. Joslin (2018) states that "The best advising system is the system that reflects the campus culture, meets institutional and student learning outcomes, and is supported by campus personnel, resources, and infrastructure to the fullest extent" (p. 16).

Future research should further explore the differences between two- and four-year institutions, advising for transfer students, the influence of organizational structure (reporting lines and degree of centralization) on advising-related outcomes, and the benefits and challenges inherent in faculty and primary-role advising strategies.

Institutions that articulate academic advising as a top priority for the first year are challenged to make adequate resources available to effectively support students, ensuring that learning is at the center of the educational process, in and out of the classroom.

References

Damminger, J., & Rakes, M. (2017). The role of the academic advisor in the first year. In J. R. Fox & H. E. Martin (Eds.), *Academic advising and the first college year* (pp. 19-42). Columbia, SC: University of South Carolina, National Resource Center for The First-Year Experience and Students in Transition and NACADA: The Global Community for Academic Advising.

Drake, J. K. (2011). The role of academic advising in student retention and persistence. *About Campus, 16*(3), 8-12.

Drake, J. K., Jordan, P., & Miller, M. A. (2013). *Academic advising approaches: Strategies that teach students to make the most of college.* San Francisco, CA: Jossey-Bass.

Fosnacht, K., McCormick, A. C., Nailos, J. N., & Ribera, A. K. (2017). Frequency of first-year student interactions with advisors. *NACADA Journal, 37*(1), 74-86.

Gordon, V. N. (2007). *The undecided student* (3rd ed.). Springfield, IL: Charles C. Thomas.

Grites, T. J., Miller, M. A., & Voler, J. G. (2016). *Beyond foundations: Developing as a master advisor.* Hoboken, NJ: John Wiley & Sons.

Himes, H., & Schulenberg, J. (2016). The evolution of academic advising as a practice and as a profession. In T. J. Grites, M. A. Miller, & J. G. Voler (Eds.). *Beyond foundations: Developing as a master advisor* (pp. 1-20). Hoboken, NJ: John Wiley & Sons.

Joslin, J. E. (2018). The case for strategic academic advising management. In W. G. Troxel & J. E. Joslin (Eds.), *Academic advising re-examined* (New Directions for Higher Education, No. 184, pp. 11-20). Hoboken, NJ: John Wiley & Sons. doi:10.1002/he.20299

Kennett, D. J. (2011). The importance of directly asking students their reasons for attending higher education. *Issues in Educational Research, 21*(1), 65-74.

Light, R. (2001). *Making the most of college: Students speak their minds.* Cambridge, MA: Harvard University Press.

Mayhew, M. J., Rockenbach, A. N., Bowman, N. A., Seifert, T. A., & Wolniak, G. C., with Pascarella, E. T., & Terenzini, P. T. (2016). *How college affects students: 21st century evidence that higher education works, Volume 3.* San Francisco, CA: Jossey-Bass.

NACADA: The Global Community for Academic Advising. (2017). *NACADA academic core competencies model.* Retrieved from https://www.nacada.ksu.edu/Resources/Pillars/CoreCompetencies.aspx

Poch, S. (2017). Advisors' tools, resources, and partnerships. In J. R. Fox & H. E. Martin (Eds.), *Academic advising and the first college year* (pp. 181-198). Columbia, SC: University of South Carolina, National Resource Center for The First-Year Experience and Students in Transition and NACADA: The Global Community for Academic Advising.

Robbins, R. (2013). Implications of advising load. In Carlstrom, A., *2011 national survey of academic advising.* (Monograph No. 25). Manhattan, KS: National Academic Advising Association. Retrieved from NACADA Clearinghouse of Academic Advising Resources website: http://www.nacada.ksu.edu/tabid/3318/articleType/ArticleView/articleId/94/article.aspx

Chapter 4

Common-Reading Programs

Krista M. Soria
University of Minnesota

Common-reading experiences represent richly diverse opportunities to engage new students within higher education, and an emerging body of research points to the potential impact of such programs on students' outcomes. For instance, Goldfine, Mixson-Brookshire, Hoerrner, and Morrissey (2011) discovered that students who engaged in a common reading within a learning community reported greater ability in seeing multiple sides of issues—a form of critical thinking—and a greater connection with their peers. Soria (2015) found that students in common-reading programs reported greater development in academic skills and multicultural appreciation and competence compared with peers who did not participate.

The hallmark of such programs is a common book assigned to students either before they arrive on campus or during their first semester or first year of enrollment. It may be assigned in individual classes (e.g., first-year seminar courses), in new-student orientation, in learning communities, within an academic major program, or across an entire institution. The reading is often accompanied by a wide variety of programmatic opportunities, including library exhibits, theatrical performances, cultural events, discussions, film series, campus visits by authors, accessory library reading and research material, yearlong themes tied to the primary text, art exhibits, or class assignments (Ferguson, 2006; Goldfine et al., 2011; Laufgraben, 2006; Thorne, 2015).

While some common-reading programs are unique to the institution where they are implemented, they are often designed with similar goals. Many seek a foundation for students to explore their values; read literature beyond textbooks; raise awareness and appreciation for intercultural differences; grapple with political and social issues; orient themselves to the academic expectations of higher education; and build a community through increased interaction with peers, staff, and faculty (Fister, 2008). In a review of 239 common-reading programs, Thorne (2015) discovered the majority of programmatic goals fell into five categories: building community, setting academic expectations, starting conversations, encouraging social activism among students, and inspiring critical thinking. Similarly, Lewin (2007) wrote that such programs aim to develop a sense of community and engage students intellectually.

Although common readings are conspicuous in many colleges' first-year experience programs, few researchers have investigated their nature, the frequency they are implemented at institutions nationally, or the benefits of what is considered a high-impact practice (Kuh, 2008). Additionally, the extant scholarship lacks clear insights into the various components of common readings, the primary groups of students engaging in them, or the return on investment (ROI) for the practice, especially from a national perspective. Soria's (2015) study was one of the more robust on the subject, as it examined those outcomes while controlling for students' demographic variables, collegiate experiences, and participation in first-year seminars or learning communities. However, it was also limited because its nature prohibited a deeper examination of various components embedded in the common reading at participating institutions.

The negligible research related to common readings may contribute to college staff or faculty members' hesitancy to invest in such programs, a reduction in funds dedicated to the programs, or non-renewal of programs, as referenced in Chapter 5. The purpose of this chapter is to fill a few of those gaps in scholarship by providing an overview of common readings using data from the 2017 National Survey on the First-Year Experience (NSFYE). I aim to analyze the frequency of common-reading programs and their experiential components to discover whether they differ substantially given institutional type, control, and size. Finally, I will investigate how often institutions assess or evaluate the ROI of their common-reading programs and how they rank them overall. Administrators, practitioners, and scholars may find this information useful as they seek to organize common readings for the first time on their campuses, develop new initiatives for existing programs, or discover the wide variety of experiential components involved in order to assess their effectiveness.

Results

Institutional Prevalence

The results suggest that 38.3% of institutions in the NSFYE sample offer a common reading as a part of their student success programs, initiatives, or courses specifically or intentionally geared toward first-year students, while 20.7% offer a common reading within pre-term orientation. The majority of institutions offer common-reading programs to 91%-100% of their first-year students (Figure 4.1). Two-year colleges are less likely than four-year colleges to offer common readings (16.3% vs. 45.0%) and common-reading programs within pre-term orientation (4.5% vs. 24.3%). Four-year colleges are also more likely to offer common-reading programs to greater proportions of their students (Figure 4.2). Public institutions are less likely than privates to offer common-reading programs to first-year students (33.7% vs. 45.2%) or embed such programs in pre-term orientation (14.8% vs. 29.1%; Figure 4.3).

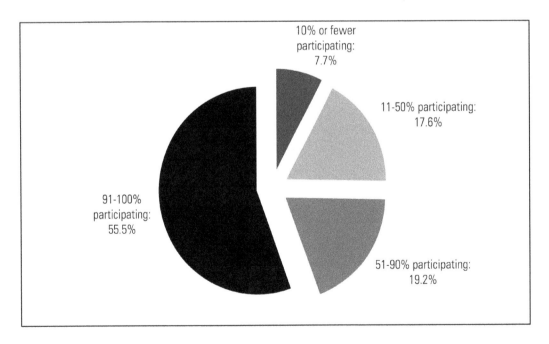

Figure 4.1. Approximate percentage of first-year students participating in a first-year common-reading program, all institutions (*n* = 182).

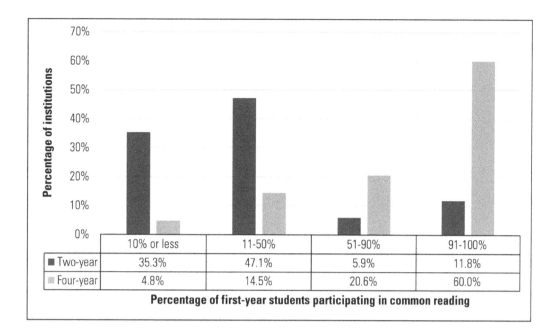

Figure 4.2. Approximate percentage of first-year students participating in a first-year common-reading program, by institutional type (*n* = 182).

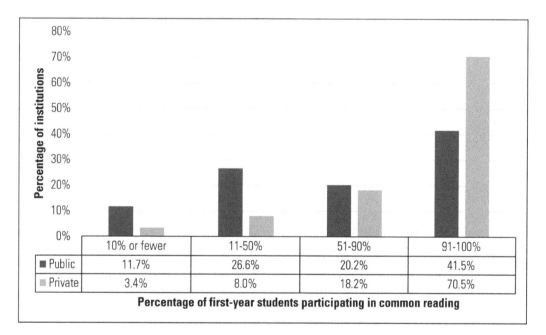

Figure 4.3. Approximate percentage of first-year students participating in a first-year common-reading program, by institutional control (*n* = 182).

In general, schools with higher populations of first-year students are more likely to offer common readings than schools with smaller first-year cohorts (e.g., 61.0% of schools with first-year populations greater than 4,000 offered the programs, compared with 34.9% of schools with fewer than 500 entering first-year students; Figure 4.4). There are some exceptions to this trend; for instance, only 30.0% of schools with 2,001-4,000 entering first-year students offered common readings (Figure 4.4).

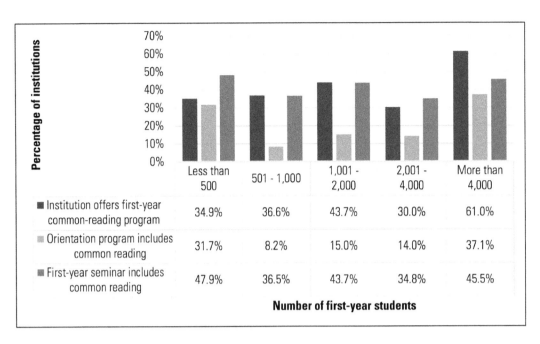

Figure 4.4. First-year common-reading programs by size of first-year student enrollment at institutions (*n* = 182).

These findings are complex: It appears that institutional control, type, and size yield independent effects on whether institutions offer a common reading and whether those programs reach the majority of first-year students. Private and four-year institutions are most likely to offer them to the majority of first-year students, for example, while institutions with higher numbers of first-year students are more likely to offer a common reading but less likely to reach the majority of their first-year students with those programs.

The results of the 2017 NSFYE present one of the few overall estimates of the prevalence of the form. Previous estimates of this prevalence were based on questions from surveys that asked respondents to indicate whether a common-reading program was offered in connection with some other first-year program, such as orientation or the first-year seminar (e.g., Barefoot, Griffin, & Koch, 2012; Koch, Griffin, & Barefoot, 2014; Young & Hopp, 2014). Those previous estimates placed the prevalence of common-reading programs connected to orientation and first-year seminars at between 43-46% for four-year institutions and between 8-15% at two-year colleges (Barefoot et al., 2012; Koch et al., 2014; Young & Hopp, 2014). Responses to the NSFYE about the prevalence of common-reading programs reveals a more complete and nuanced picture than before. Table 4.1 presents the overall and relative prevalence of common-reading programs among the respondents on campus.

Table 4.1

Estimates of Prevalence of Common-Reading Programs Overall and by Connection to Other First-Year Programs

2017 NSFYE item	%
Institution offers common-reading programs for first-year students (*n* = 525)	38.3
Institution's orientation program includes common reading (*n* = 376)	20.7
Institution's first-year seminar includes common reading (*n* = 368)	42.9

These results suggest that common-reading programs are frequently offered in connection with or embedded in other first-year programs and thus may represent an opportunity for many institutions to coordinate first-year efforts. However, on their own, only 13.8% of respondents indicated that common-reading programs were among the primary programs by which first-year objectives are met. This presents yet another complex picture: While common-reading programs tend to be conspicuous first-year activities, they seem to play more of a supporting role, serving as the glue to strengthen collaborations or as content that facilitates student engagement in other, more institutionally central first-year programs (e.g., orientation, the first-year seminar).

Experiential Components

The three most common experiential components incorporated into common-reading programs include bringing text-related speakers to campus (74.7%), creating discussion groups (67.0%), and incorporating the text into first-year seminars (62.6%). Noteworthy differences appear in the experiential components by institutional characteristics. For instance, two-year colleges and private colleges are less likely to incorporate any experiential components for common-reading programs compared with four-year or public colleges (Table 4.2). Public institutions were more likely to include all components compared to private institutions, with the exception of discussion groups (Table 4.3). Further, close to 96% of institutions with a first-year student enrollment greater than 4,000 brought speakers to campus, compared with 62.7% of institutions with first-year student enrollment of less than 500 (Table 4.4). The variety of experiential components employed may be associated with the diversity of campus units tasked with administering the programs: Across all institutions, 39.0% of common readings are administered by first-year programs, 30.2% are administered by academic affairs central offices, and 12.6% are administered by student affairs units. The location of those units within institutions likely affects how the programs are implemented, including their experiential components.

Assessment and Value of Common-Reading Programs

Finally, the ROI associated with common-reading programs is somewhat nebulous, likely because so few institutions have engaged in assessing these programs. Among all of the institutional respondents to the NSFYE, only 27.5% have formally evaluated or assessed their common-reading programs since 2013. Only 13.8% indicated these programs as a primary vehicle for meeting their objectives. Additionally, on a scale from 1 (lowest) to 7 (highest),

- 8.8% rated their ROI for the programs as 1 (lowest),
- 24.7% selected the 2-3 range (lower),
- 14.3% selected 4 (medium),
- 27.5% selected the 5-6 range (higher),
- 14.7% selected 7 (high), and
- the remaining 10.4% were unable to judge the ROI.

The mixed results were relatively consistent across institutional type, control, and enrollment size; however, public institutions and institutions with 501-1,000 first-year students enrolled were most likely to rate their ROI for common readings as high (17% and 21.6%, respectively). Given that so many first-year seminars and new-student orientation experiences incorporate a common reading, perhaps some of these programs' potentially beneficial programmatic components are mediated by the programs' other components (e.g., engaging subject material, academic and social integration).

Table 4.2

Experiential Components of Common-Reading Programs by Institutional Type (n = 182)

| Component of common-reading program | Institutional type | | | | Difference |
| | Two-year | | Four-year | | |
	Freq.	%	Freq.	%	(%)
Bringing speakers related to text to campus	11	64.7	125	75.8	−11.1
Discussion groups	10	58.8	112	67.9	−9.1
Incorporating text in first-year seminar	6	35.3	108	65.5	−30.2
Campus programming throughout academic year	6	35.3	85	51.5	−16.2
Film adaptations of or films related to common-reading text	6	35.3	57	34.5	0.8
Structured interaction with faculty	3	17.6	58	35.2	−17.6
Incorporation of text in English and writing courses	2	11.8	57	34.5	−22.7
Campus–community engagement	5	29.4	51	30.9	−1.5

Table 4.3

Experiential Components of Common-Reading Programs by Institutional Control (n = 182)

| Component of common-reading program | Institutional control | | | | Difference |
| | Public | | Private | | |
	Freq.	%	Freq.	%	(%)
Bringing speakers related to text to campus	77	81.9	59	67.0	14.9
Discussion groups	60	63.8	62	70.5	−6.7
Incorporating text in first-year seminar	62	66.0	52	59.1	6.9
Campus programming throughout academic year	58	61.7	33	37.5	24.2
Film adaptations of or films related to common-reading text	37	39.4	26	29.5	9.9
Structured interaction with faculty	32	34.0	29	33.0	1.0
Incorporation of text in English and writing courses	35	37.2	24	27.3	9.9
Campus–community engagement	36	38.3	20	22.7	15.6

Table 4.4

Experiential Components of Common-Reading Programs by First-Year Student Enrollment (n = 182)

Component of common-reading program	Number of entering first-year students									
	Less than 500		501 - 1,000		1,001 - 2,000		2,001 - 4,000		More than 4,000	
	Freq.	%	Freq.	%	Freq.	%	Freq.	%	Freq.	%
Bringing speakers related to text to campus	42	62.7	28	75.7	31	81.6	13	76.5	22	95.7
Discussion groups	41	61.2	29	78.4	22	57.9	14	82.4	16	69.6
Incorporating text in first-year seminar	40	59.7	22	59.5	21	55.3	12	70.6	19	82.6
Campus programming throughout academic year	24	35.8	16	43.2	23	60.5	9	52.9	19	82.6
Film adaptations of or films related to common-reading text	21	31.3	11	29.7	13	34.2	8	47.1	10	43.5
Structured interaction with faculty	23	34.3	11	29.7	11	28.9	7	41.2	9	39.1
Incorporation of text in English and writing courses	19	28.4	11	29.7	12	31.6	5	29.4	12	52.2
Campus–community engagement	13	19.4	12	32.4	15	39.5	6	35.3	10	43.5

Discussion

The results from the NSFYE suggest that common-reading programs are present at about two fifths of the campuses surveyed but are most likely to be implemented at four-year colleges, private institutions, and schools with more than 4,000 first-year students. Private institutions, four-year institutions, and those with smaller first-year enrollments are more likely to reach the majority of their first-year students through common readings, possibly because of lower programming costs associated with a smaller first-year student cohort. The results also confirm the ancillary nature of common-reading programs. While these programs spur the creation of attendant programming, such as inviting speakers to campus or organizing discussion groups around the reading, the frequency that institutions offer such experiential components varies considerably by institutional size, control, and type.

There is also a lack of consensus on whether these programs meet institutional objectives for the first-year experience. Very few institutions have formally assessed the effectiveness of their common readings, and most do not rate their ROI very highly. Even with high numbers of students participating, these programs were infrequently identified as a primary vehicle for meeting institutional objectives for the first year. Instead, the top two programs that colleges and universities identified as meeting those objectives were first-year seminars (62.1%) and first-year academic advising (62.9%). Common readings are likely to complement—or be embedded within—first-year seminars, new-student orientation programs, or learning communities; therefore, institutional representatives may perceive them as less impactful than other components of those more holistic programs. However, common readings can affect students' development above and beyond their participation in first-year seminars or learning communities, providing support for their efficacy (Soria, 2015).

Finally, the results point to a longstanding imperative to investigate the potential benefits of students' participation in common-reading programs, especially if so many institutions offer them and their administrators either do not assess them or do not see them as producing a high ROI. The institutional context and culture related to common readings may also affect the outcomes of their implementation. Therefore, researchers and program administrators should continue to consider the impact of environmental conditions (e.g., institutional control, type, and size) on the outcomes of students' participation in these programs. As common readings are rife with potential to influence students' development, institutions should undertake more concerted efforts to uncover the components with the greatest potential impact on students.

References

Barefoot, B. O., Griffin, B. Q., & Koch, A. K. (2012). *Enhancing student success and retention throughout undergraduate education: A national survey.* Brevard, NC: The John N. Gardner Institute for Excellence in Undergraduate Education. Retrieved from https://static1.squarespace.com/static/59b0c486d2b857fc86d09aee/t/59bad-33412abd988ad84d697/1505415990531/JNGInational_survey_web.pdf

Ferguson, M. (2006). Creating common ground: Common reading and the first year of college. *Peer Review, 8*(3), 8-10.

Fister, B. (2007). One book, one campus: Exploring common reading programs. *E-Source for College Transitions, 5*(1), 1, 3, 5.

Goldfine, R., Mixson-Brookshire, D., Hoerrner, K., & Morrissey, J. (2011). Using a common first-year book to promote reading, connections, and critical thinking. *Journal of The First-Year Experience & Students in Transition, 23*(2), 89-104.

Koch, S. S., Griffin, B. Q., & Barefoot, B. O. (2014). *National survey of student success initiatives at two-year colleges.* Brevard, NC: The John N. Gardner Institute for Excellence in Undergraduate Education. Retrieved from https://static1.squarespace.com/static/59b0c486d2b857fc86d09aee/t/59bad37251a584437bc-cc737/1505416079925/National-2-yr-Survey-Booklet_webversion.pdf

Kuh, G. D. (2008). *High-impact educational practices: What they are, who has access to them, and why they matter.* Washington, DC: Association of American Colleges and Universities.

Laufgraben, J. L. (Ed.). (2006). *Common reading programs: Going beyond the book* (Monograph No. 44). Columbia, SC: University of South Carolina, National Resource Center for The First-Year Experience and Students in Transition.

Lewin, T. (2007, August 8). Summer reading programs gain momentum for students about to enter college. *The New York Times.* Retrieved from http://www.nytimes.com/2007/08/08/education/08books.html?_r=0

Soria, K. M. (2015). Common reading, learning, and growing: An examination of the benefits of common book reading programs for college students' development. *Journal of The First-Year Experience and Students in Transition, 27*(1), 29-47.

Thorne, A. (2015). Common reading programs: Trends, traps, tips. *Academic Questions, 28*(2), 135-146.

Young, D. G., & Hopp, J. M. (2014). *2012-2013 National Survey of First-Year Seminars: Exploring high-impact practices in the first college year* (Research Report No. 4). Columbia, SC: University of South Carolina, National Resource Center for The First-Year Experience and Students in Transition.

Chapter 5

Early-Alert Programs

Stephanie M. Estrada
San Diego State University

Jennifer A. Latino
Ellucian

A key component of retention-focused student success initiatives is the early identification of students at risk of academic struggle or attrition. This is particularly important in the first year, when students experience social and academic transitions as well as new learning environments. Thus, many first-year experience programs have implemented early-alert or early-warning efforts to allow for early identification of and intervention with struggling students. Such efforts have become widespread in the United States, with 79% of respondents to the 2017 National Survey on the First-Year Experience (NSFYE) reporting their institutions hosted early-alert initiatives; in a previous survey, 93% of a sample of four-year institutions indicated using these systems on their campus (Barefoot, Griffin, & Koch, 2012).

The body of literature surrounding the expansion and success of early-alert programs is growing. Koch and Gardner (2014) identified these programs as a structure benefitting first-year students, emphasizing the need to intervene early on and positing that many programs do not identify at-risk students early enough to help right their path. Rudmann (1992) also voiced the notion of the earlier the identification, the better, saying that by the time some students show concerning behavior, it is too late. More recently, Greenfield, Keup, and Gardner (2013) highlighted the importance of such initiatives throughout the first year—not just at the beginning.

Key to early intervention is identifying the behaviors that contribute to success, then implementing a systematic method to intervene when students fall short of those behaviors. One factor often used as an alert is class attendance. A plethora of literature supports the impact of attendance on academic success, including performance on exams (Clump, Bauer, & Whiteleather, 2003) and overall grades (Kuh, Kinzie, Schuh, Whitt, & Associates, 2005; Richie & Hargrove, 2005). Thus, any early patterns of absences should trigger an intervention so the behavior can be changed before academic repercussions result.

Another trigger for an alert is academic performance. Students who perform below the expectations of the institution can be at risk of attrition. One common early-alert method is to collect midterm grades for first-year students and intervene with those who are falling short of institutional standards (Greenfield et al., 2013). This practice is usually coupled with creating a plan to use academic support resources and change study habits to reach more desirable outcomes by the end of the term.

Behavioral differences or changes in academic engagement may also trigger an alert. Perhaps a student who has regularly contributed to class and submitted assignments seems to be withdrawing from class participation or is underperforming on or missing assignments, for example (Kuh et al., 2005; Rudmann, 1992). These behavioral changes can be an early sign of disengagement and, ultimately, attrition.

An effective early-alert program includes a systematic approach to early identification of student need, appropriate intervention, and meaningful connections with the student, including referral to appropriate resources. These steps are aimed at positively impacting behavior and increasing engagement and persistence.

Key Components of Early Alert

An early-alert action is a "systematic initiative designed to identify and support students at risk of attrition in order to improve student success, retention, and persistence" (Lynch-Holmes, Troy, & Ramos, 2012, p. 2). The initiative is supported by two factors: (a) the *alert* and (b) the *intervention*.

The alert, or "red flag" (Cuseo, n.d.) is signaled by a faculty or staff member who has observed a concerning behavior or event that may hinder a student's success. The subsequent intervention is critical to correcting this behavior and can be either *proactive* or *reactive*. A proactive intervention may come in the form of an engagement effort focusing on a historically at-risk population. An example is summer bridge, either for students in highly rigorous academic programs or for first-generation students. Summer bridge programs allow students time to acclimate to the social and academic nature of their institution by supporting them through initial transition challenges. Another example of an intervention is a mentoring program for minority students who tradition-ally have a lower rate of engagement and, thus, retention. More often, the intervention is reactive, based on a referral from a peer or faculty or staff member who observes concerning behavior (e.g., absences, academic performance, disengagement).

The most impactful interventions include intrusive, personalized outreach that demonstrates to students that they are important to the institution and that staff and faculty are committed to helping them succeed (Varney, 2008). Intervention should also connect students with appropriate resources to assist with their cur-rent needs as well as future challenges. When done meaningfully, intervention not only helps students with immediate needs but also arms them with the information to succeed throughout college.

While each institution is different, a few key features for any early-alert or intervention initiative exist. When building such programs, it is important to start small, with a pilot population, and grow as the process is established and refined (Lynch-Holmes, 2015). Well-executed early-alert programs include (a) a clearly defined alert process that faculty and staff can easily access and (b) detailed, personalized messages for student groups as well as individual students. Messages should be designed and delivered for varied formats (e.g., phone, text, email) as well as residence hall or affiliate group outreach. Further, those tasked with outreach should consider multiple points of contact, including providing broad access to alerts among faculty, staff, and administrators as appropriate. Ongoing assessment is essential and should consider gathering evidence on reasons for alerts and tracking outreach, as well as identifying repeat alerts, use of resources, behavior changes, and long-term student success. Most importantly, to achieve success, early alert and interventions must become part of the institutional culture.

Challenges

Establishing and maintaining a successful early-alert or intervention initiative presents challenges. Demonstrating evidence of success is one obstacle. Tracking alerts and interventions can be cumbersome, especially as students are referred to resources and take advantage of them. Establishing clear objectives for an early-alert initiative is critical, as is developing a systematic way to collect alerts and track interventions and follow-up efforts to determine whether student behavior changes. Many technology tools connected to the student information system can help with tracking and assessment efforts. For instance, NACADA hosts a list of common technology tools and some considerations for vetting those products (NACADA, n.d.). When a technology tool is used to support the alert and intervention processes, it often requires training and develop-ment of faculty and staff users. This can be an additional challenge for implementation.

Another challenge is gaining faculty and staff buy-in. Early-alert initiatives that include cross-campus collaboration are most successful (Kuh, Kinzie, Buckley, Bridges, & Hayek, 2006). Many in institutional roles (e.g., faculty, staff, administrators, peer educators) observe student behavior, yet few have in-depth, daily contact with individual students. As such, allowing multiple parties to create an alert or post a red flag in a student's interest is critical. Generally, faculty observe the academic behaviors of new students while other staff (e.g., advisors, residence hall staff, and student life personnel) observe out-of-class behaviors. All of these behaviors can warrant an alert, however, and faculty and staff should be diligent in their observations and flagging of student behavior. This further enforces the need for buy-in from all areas and embedding early alert into the institution's culture.

Such collaboration can make the communication flow between the alerting party and the responder challenging. However, this communication is critical for success, as those who create the alert need to be informed about next steps. Also, closing the loop on communication helps build buy-in. As faculty and staff see changes in student behavior, they can better understand the value of the initiative and continue to make alerts.

To provide further information about how early-warning and academic alert systems are structured to support first-year student success, the 2017 NSFYE included questions about the reach, characteristics, perceived value, and assessment of these programs. The following sections present results from each of these areas and contextualize how various institutions administer early-warning systems by providing comparisons based on institutional characteristics.

Results

First-Year Students Reached by Early-Warning/Academic Alert Systems

Respondents to the NSFYE were asked what percentage of first-year students were reached by early-warning/academic alert systems at their institution. Figure 5.1 represents the percentage disaggregated by institutional type (two-year vs. four-year). Of 383 respondents who reported on an early-alert initiative, about 47% of four-year institutions reported that their early-warning/academic alert systems reached 81% or more of their first-year students, compared with 22.5% of two-year institutions. At the other end of the spectrum, nearly 27% of two-year institutions reported that 20% or fewer of their first-year students were reached by early-alert programs, while only 18% of four-year institutions said so.

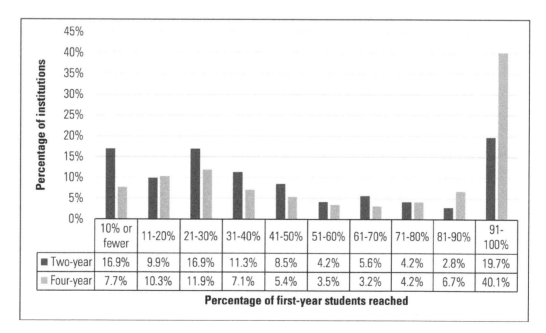

Figure 5.1. Percentage of first-year students reached by early-warning/academic alert systems (*n* = 383).

Figure 5.2 presents program reach disaggregated by institutional control (public vs. private). Nearly 54% of private institutions reported that more than 80% of their first-year students were reached by early-warning/academic alert systems, while only 34% of public institutions reported the same. The results show that four-year and private institutions have a higher chance of reaching first-year students with early-warning/academic alert programs than two-year and public institutions.

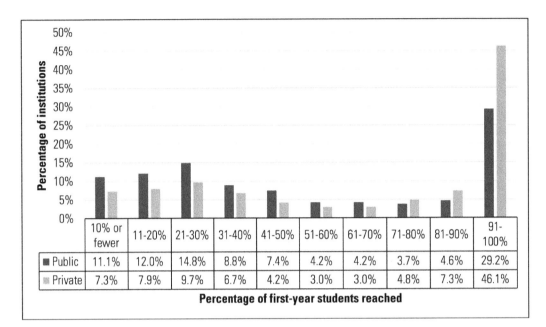

Figure 5.2. Percentage of first-year students reached by early-warning/academic alert systems by institutional control (*n* = 383).

First-Year Students Monitored Through Early Warning/Academic Alert

Survey respondents were asked which types of students are monitored through an early-warning/academic alert system. Overwhelmingly, all first-year students were the group most heavily monitored at two-year (nearly 60%) and four-year (nearly 81%) institutions. This held true for public (65.7%) and private institutions (89.1%). No other student group was listed at more than 10% in any of the four classifications (at two-year institutions, students enrolled in developmental or remedial courses came in at nearly 10%, while students on probation were monitored most heavily at 6.4% of four-year institutions). These results make sense considering the focus on retention from the first to the second year at both two- and four-year institutions.

Characteristics of First-Year Early Alert/Academic Warning

When examining the components of an early-alert system, many factors warrant consideration. For this study, we considered how various institutions execute these systems, when early-alert monitoring and/or responses occur, the types of interventions possible, and the types of professional staff associated with early alert.

Using early alert. Respondents were asked to describe the early-warning system most prevalent at their institution on a scale ranging from 1 to 7, with 1 representing an entirely technology-based warning system and 7 signifying a system that is entirely human-based and relies on faculty, staff, or fellow students. Overall, 1.3% said their early-warning tools were entirely technology-based, while 30.5% said their systems were entirely human-based. We saw little variation by institutional type or control.

When responses occur. Asked when their early-alert monitoring and/or responses go into effect, respondents at two-year institutions most often reported their systems are ongoing throughout the term (46.5%), while more than half of four-year institutions (57.4%) said monitoring and responses are ongoing throughout the first year (Figure 5.3). Additionally, 28.2% of public institutions said their response systems are ongoing throughout the term, while 59.4% of private institutions said they are ongoing throughout the first year (Figure 5.4). The trend shows two-year institutions putting a larger focus on monitoring from term to term, while four-year institutions monitor the first year at a higher rate.

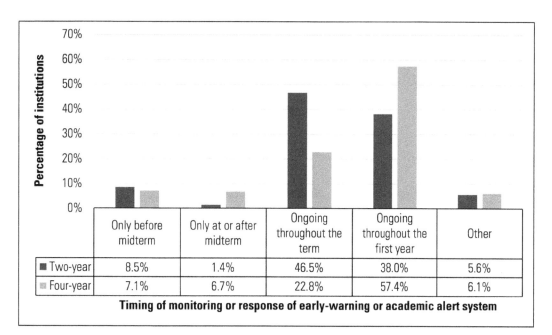

	Only before midterm	Only at or after midterm	Ongoing throughout the term	Ongoing throughout the first year	Other
■ Two-year	8.5%	1.4%	46.5%	38.0%	5.6%
▨ Four-year	7.1%	6.7%	22.8%	57.4%	6.1%

Timing of monitoring or response of early-warning or academic alert system

Figure 5.3. Timing of early-warning/academic alert systems for first-year students by institutional type (*n* = 383).

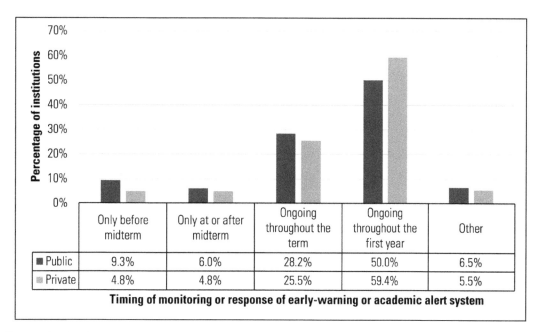

	Only before midterm	Only at or after midterm	Ongoing throughout the term	Ongoing throughout the first year	Other
■ Public	9.3%	6.0%	28.2%	50.0%	6.5%
▨ Private	4.8%	4.8%	25.5%	59.4%	5.5%

Timing of monitoring or response of early-warning or academic alert system

Figure 5.4. Timing of early-warning/academic alert systems for first-year students by institutional control (*n* = 383).

The types of interventions occurring, and which staff members participate. The three most frequent types of intervention reported in the survey were: (a) contacting students via phone, letter, or electronic means (96.6%); (b) informing students of opportunities to seek assistance (82.5%); and (c) in-person contact (62.9%; Figure 5.5). Moreover, respondents were asked which employees participate in some aspect of early-alert/academic warning systems. The three types of professional staff most frequently reported were (a) faculty/instructors (89.6%), (b) academic advisors (88.3%), and (c) academic support personnel (68.4%). It is noteworthy that student affairs staff (64.0%) and athletics department staff (54.8%; Figure 5.6) were also highly involved in these systems.

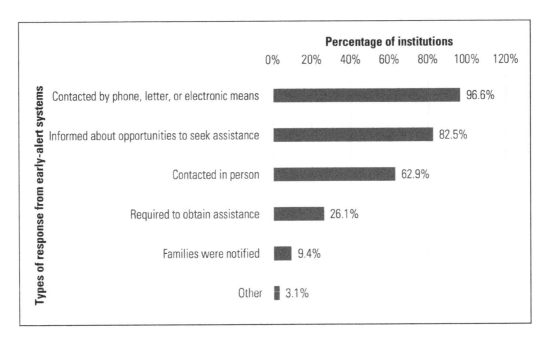

Figure 5.5. Types of interventions that occur in early-alert/academic warning systems (*n* = 383).

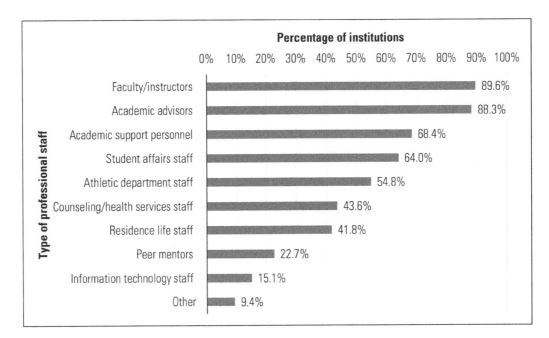

Figure 5.6. Types of professional staff participating in early-alert/academic warning systems (*n* = 383).

Often, those who think about early alert tend to link the responsibility for such programs to academic advisors. However, the NSFYE data make the case that early alert falls on a variety of staff from different departments. With this in mind, departments and staff across institutions should work together to ensure that early alert is effective and that affected students are more successful.

Return on Investment for Early-Alert/Academic Warning Systems

Survey respondents were asked to consider staff time and resources (cost) and educational benefits to measure the return on investment for the early-alert/academic warning system at their respective campuses. The scale ranged from low (1-3) to high (5-7), with 4 signifying a medium return, and an additional option of "unable to judge." As displayed in Figure 5.7, 42.2% of two-year institutions rated return on investment for early-alert initiatives as high, while 26.7% rated their return as low. Respondents at four-year institutions were much more likely to rate their return on investment as high (58%) than low (13.2%).

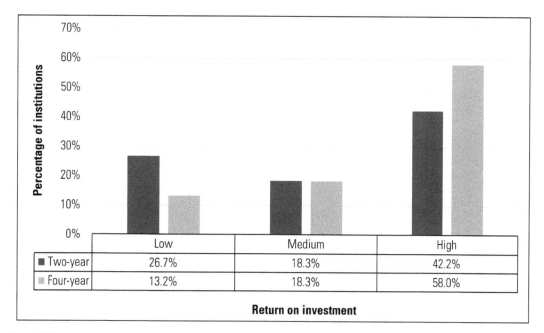

Figure 5.7. Return on investment for first-year early-alert/academic warning systems by institutional type (*n* = 383).

Assessing First-Year Student Early-Alert/Academic Warning Systems

As part of the survey, participants were asked whether their early-alert/academic warning system had been formally assessed or evaluated since Fall 2013 (Tables 5.1 and 5.2). Nearly 47% of those from public institutions indicated their programs had not been evaluated in that period, while 20.8% were not sure. Similarly, 45.5% of respondents from private institutions said their programs had not been evaluated in the previous four years, while 26.1% did not know. Two-year institutions indicated their programs had not been evaluated recently at the highest rate of the groups considered (52.1%), while four-year institutions reported this at 44.6%. There was a large discrepancy between those unsure about assessment at two-year institutions (11.3%) and four-year institutions (25.6%).

Table 5.1

Assessment of First-Year Early-Alert/Academic Warning Systems by Institutional Control

| | Institutional control | | | | Difference |
| | Public | | Private | | |
Assessment of programs	Freq.	%	Freq.	%	(%)
Yes	70	32.4	47	28.5	3.9
No	101	46.8	75	45.5	1.3
Unsure	45	20.8	43	26.1	−5.3

Table 5.2

Assessment of First-Year Early-Alert/Academic Warning Systems by Institutional Type

| | Institutional type | | | | Difference |
| | Two-year | | Four-year | | |
Assessment of programs	Freq.	%	Freq.	%	(%)
Yes	26	36.6	93	29.8	6.8
No	37	52.1	139	44.6	7.5
Unsure	8	11.3	80	25.6	−14.3

Conclusion

Early-alert initiatives can be valuable components of a comprehensive first-year experience. By identifying students who show at-risk behavior academically or socially early on, institutions can intervene and direct them toward more positive outcomes. While a large proportion of early-alert programs are offered across institutions of all types (see Tables 2.3 and 2.4), there is a need for institutions to provide evidence of these programs' impact. Early-alert efforts should be tied in with desired outcomes of the overall first-year experience, and the impact of these interventions should be shared broadly.

The NSFYE data demonstrate that the approach to early-alert initiatives and the value placed on them differs by institutional type. We found that two-year institutions tend to focus more on early-alert monitoring from term to term, while such measures at four-year institutions tend to be ongoing throughout the first year. Further, four-year institutions see a higher return on investment for their early-alert initiatives. This might be a byproduct of how resource-intensive these programs can be and the limited funding available at two-year colleges. Future research should look at how these early-alert systems might impact students depending on their part-time or full-time status.

References

Barefoot, B. O., Griffin, B. Q., & Koch, A. K. (2012). *Enhancing student success and retention throughout undergraduate education: A national survey.* Brevard, NC: The John N. Gardner Institute for Excellence in Undergraduate Education. Retrieved from https://static1.squarespace.com/static/59b0c486d2b857fc86d09aee/t/59bad-33412abd988ad84d697/1505415990531/JNGInational_survey_web.pdf

Clump, M. A., Bauer, H., & Whiteleather, A. (2003). To attend or not to attend: Is that a good question? *Journal of Instructional Psychology, 30,* 220-224.

Cuseo, J. (n.d). *Red flags: Behavioral indicators of potential student attrition.* [White paper]. Retrieved from http://listserv.sc.edu/wa.cgi?A0=FYE-LIST

Greenfield, G. M., Keup, J. R., & Gardner, J. N. (2013). *Developing and sustaining successful first-year programs: A guide for practitioners.* San Francisco, CA: Jossey-Bass.

Koch, A. K., & Gardner, J. N. (2014). Perspectives on a history of the first-year experience in the United States during the twentieth and twenty-first centuries: Past practices, current approaches, and future directions. *The Saudi Journal of Higher Education, 11*, 11-44.

Kuh, G. D., Kinzie, J., Buckley, J. A., Bridges, B. K., & Hayek, J. C. (2006). *What matters to student success: A review of the literature.* Commissioned report for the National Symposium on Postsecondary Student Success: Spearheading a dialog on student success. Washington, DC: National Postsecondary Education Cooperative. Retrieved from http://nces.ed.gov/npec/pdf/kuh_team_report.pdf

Kuh, G. D., Kinzie, J., Schuh, J. H., Whitt, E. J., & Associates (2005). *Student success in college: Creating conditions that matter.* San Francisco, CA: Jossey-Bass.

Lynch-Holmes, K. L. (2015). *Early alerts as a tool for student success: Defining what "good" looks like.* [White paper]. Fairfax, VA: Ellucian. Retrieved from https://www.ellucian.com/assets/en/white-paper/whitepaper-early-alerts-tool-student-success.pdf

Lynch-Holmes, K. L., Troy, A. B., & Ramos, I. (2012). *Early alert & intervention: Top practices for retention.* [White paper]. Boston, MA: ConnectEdu. Retrieved from https://issuu.com/connectedu/docs/early_alert_white_paper

NACADA: The Global Community for Academic Advising. (n.d.). *Early alert systems and resource links.* Retrieved from https://www.nacada.ksu.edu/Resources/Clearinghouse/View-Articles/Early-alert-systems-and-resource-links.aspx

Richie, S. D., & Hargrove, D. S. (2005). An analysis of the effectiveness of telephone intervention in reducing absences and improving grades of college freshmen. *Journal of College Student Retention: Research, Theory & Practice, 6*(4), 395-412.

Rudmann, J. (1992). *An evaluation of several early alert strategies for helping first semester freshmen at the community college and a description of the newly developed early alert retention system (EARS) software.* Irvine, CA: Irvine Valley College. Retrieved from ERIC database. (ED 349055)

Varney, R. A. (2008). *Study of early alert intervention on first-year, nondevelopmental community college freshmen* (Doctoral dissertation). Available from ProQuest Digital Dissertations. (UMI No. 3302988)

Chapter 6

First-Year Seminars

Dallin George Young
National Resource Center for The First-Year Experience & Students in Transition

Jason Skidmore
Northeastern University

A discussion of the first-year experience (FYE) would be incomplete without a look at the first-year seminar (FYS), a group of courses "intended to enhance the academic and/or social integration of first-year students" (Barefoot, 1992, p. 49). The FYS has been one of the most durable success initiatives for first-year students, present in American higher education since the late 19th century (Drake, 1966; Fitts & Swift, 1928; Gordon, 1989). The curricular structures that were the antecedents of the FYS were among the earliest forms of first-year student orientation (Drake, 1966; Fitts & Swift, 1928). A renewed and focused interest in the FYS concept led to the FYE movement and the establishment of a national organization focused on the first year of college, to wit the National Resource Center for The First-Year Experience and Students in Transition. In addition, as was presented in Chapter 2 and throughout the research record, the FYS is one of the most prevalent programs on U.S. campuses aimed at supporting the first-year transition (see Barefoot, Griffin, & Koch, 2012; Young & Hopp, 2014). Finally, the FYS might be the most researched course in the undergraduate curriculum (Tobolowsky, Cox, & Wagner, 2005).

FYS: A Brief History

Numerous sources have chronicled the origins of what we would now recognize as the FYS (Drake, 1966; Dwyer, 1989; Fitts & Swift, 1928; Gordon, 1989). The advent of the Internet and the extent that information has been cataloged and can be easily searched allows us to shed greater light on the history of the FYS in ways unavailable to authors of previous histories of the course. This has allowed us to investigate further the possible origins of the form, the historical prevalence of the course, and the development of structures of the FYS.

Possible Origins

Fitts and Swift (1928) identified a course with the specific goal of orienting first-year students at Boston University in 1888, what we would now identify as an FYS. In the same report, the first orientation course for credit was initiated at Reed College in 1911 (Fitts & Swift, 1928). The significance of this claim may be an artifact of what "for credit" means. The Carnegie unit—an attempt to standardize the academic experience of students across U.S. colleges and universities and to define what counted as progress toward completion—was not adopted in higher education until 1910, becoming the basis of the term *for credit* (Shedd, 2003).

Additionally, an early administration of the National Survey of First-Year Seminars found evidence of an FYS at Lee College in Kentucky in 1882 (Barefoot & Fidler, 1996). However, an exhaustive historical search could not find evidence of a Lee College in Kentucky. There was a Lees College in Kentucky, but it was not founded until 1883 and did not start offering postsecondary education until 1891 (Lees College, n.d.). Seeking an explanation for this potential mix-up based on similarity of names yields problems with the timeline, as Lee University (Tennessee) was not founded until 1918 and Lee College (Texas) was founded in 1934.

Prevalence Through the Years

From the initial establishment of orientation courses, the format began to be adopted widely, and by 1926, about 3 in 10 colleges and universities in the United States offered such a course (Fitts & Swift, 1928). The popularity of the course in U.S. higher education increased in the next several decades; in 1958, an estimated 44% of a sample of colleges offered an orientation course (Plutchik & Hoffmann, 1958). Estimates from this era show the distribution of orientation courses was not uniform across institutional type. For example, in 1926, 54% of the membership of the Association of American Universities, a group of elite research institutions, offered orientation courses (Fitts & Swift, 1928). Similarly, one study in the 1950s found that about 70% of colleges in the mid-Atlantic states offered these courses (Plutchik & Hoffmann, 1958), while another study during the same timeframe found that slightly more than half of small colleges (i.e., those with enrollment of 2,000 or less) did so (Greene, 1954).

Many commentators (see Barefoot & Fidler, 1996; Drake, 1966; Gordon, 1991) highlight a decline in the prevalence of orientation courses during the 1960s, to the point that they practically disappeared from the landscape. This is based on a 1966 estimate by Kronovet (1969) that put the prevalence of the course at just under 15%. However, a deeper reading of Kronovet's findings indicates an additional 20% of institutions reported "combin[ing] an approach of meetings before classes begin with regular meetings spread over the freshman year" (Kronovet, 1969, p. 204), resulting in a total of 34% of institutions offering what would now be considered some combination of different types of FYS. Moreover, Kronovet (1969) described a difficulty in tracking trends in the prevalence in the FYS through the late 1960s "because of a lack of systematic research in this field" (p. 205).

The first attempt to gather information systematically on this subject came with the 1988 administration of the National Survey of Freshman Seminar Programming. This first version of a triennial survey that spanned nearly 25 years placed the prevalence of FYS at 69% (Fidler & Fidler, 1991).[1] The first four administrations of the survey reported a fairly steady percentage of institutions offering FYS, ranging between 65%-72% of respondents (Tobolowsky & Associates, 2008). Between the 2000 and 2012-2013 administrations, however, the prevalence climbed steadily, from 73% to nearly 90% of respondents indicating one or more FYS on their campuses (Padgett & Keup, 2011; Tobolowsky & Associates, 2008; Young & Hopp, 2014). Estimates from other surveys during this timeframe are in general agreement with these figures; a 2010 survey of four-year institutions found that 84% reported offering FYS (Barefoot et al., 2012), and a 2012 follow-up survey of two-year colleges found that 80% offered the course (Koch, Griffin, & Barefoot, 2014).

Structures of the FYS

Even from their earliest days, the curricular structures that we now identify as FYS took various shapes and formats (see Fitts & Swift, 1928). In their overview of the history and structure of orientation courses in 1926, Fitts and Swift (1928) described the first typology of FYS, which consisted of three types: (a) Type I, adjustment to college life, (b) Type II, introduction to the methodology of thinking and study, and (c) Type III, adjustment to the social and intellectual world. In addition to variations in course format, the authors described

---

[1]The name of the survey evolved throughout its history, with National Survey of First-Year Seminars being adopted for the 2003 administration.

key differences in other aspects, including organization (predominantly lecture vs. lecture and instruction mixed with small-group work) and purpose (college resources, adjustment, and personal development vs. an introduction to academic content and important ideas of the time).

When the National Resource Center took up the study of FYS, one of the earliest outcomes was the development of a classification scheme that remains largely unchanged more than a quarter century later. Using results from the 1991 administration of the NSFYS, Barefoot (1992) outlined a scheme that described five types of FYS:

1. extended orientation seminars;

2. academic courses with uniform content across all sections;

3. academic courses with varying content across sections;

4. preprofessional, discipline-linked, or major-specific courses; and

5. seminars with a focus on basic study skills.

Further, Tobolowsky and Associates (2008) described a sixth type, hybrid courses, containing elements of two or more of the types outlined above. Young and Hopp (2014) observed an increase in the prevalence of academic seminars across the administrations of the NSFYS, including those seminars with varying topics and those with uniform content across sections, and a decrease in the percentage of institutions offering extended orientation courses. Moreover, they predicted if the trend continued, academic seminars would overtake extended orientation courses as the most common type of seminar offered in the United States by spring 2017, the next planned administration of the survey.

Contemporary Conversations on the FYS

The FYS continues to be a source of much discussion and interest in higher education research and practice. A review of the conference proceedings from the 2018 Annual Conference on The First-Year Experience showed the FYS continues to be the predominant first-year structure discussed in that space. This is likely because (a) the seminar has a long history in the FYE conversation and (b) extensive research has demonstrated its effectiveness as an initiative supporting student success (see Brownell & Swaner, 2010; Pascarella & Terenzini, 2005; Permazadian & Crede, 2016).

This body of research and the impact of the FYS on student outcomes has landed it on both the list of *promising practices* identified by the Center for Community College Student Engagement (CCCSE, 2012) and the Association of American Colleges and Universities' (AAC&U) list of high-impact practices (HIPs; Kuh, 2008). With its inclusion on these lists of practices, the FYS has continued to receive attention in contemporary higher education. As noted earlier, it is widespread in the field and may be the most common promising or high-impact practice on campuses (Skipper, 2017). Moreover, there is evidence the FYS might be a hub or key structure through which other promising and high-impact practices are offered to students in the first year (Young & Hopp, 2014). On the other hand, the extensive adoption of such practices has led to concern about the quality and implementation fidelity of HIPs such as the first-year seminar, with many asking, Just how high-impact is the FYS? (Johnson & Stage, 2018; Keup & Young, 2018; Kuh & Kinzie, 2018; Skipper, 2017; Young & Hopp, 2014; Young & Keup, 2016).

Flexibility of the FYS to meet the needs of a wide variety of institutional contexts is a feature seen as part of its widespread success (Greenfield, Keup, & Gardner, 2013; Hunter & Linder, 2005). As a result, however, there is a tension between the promise of the format's flexibility and findings that suggest varying course structures may lead to different outcomes. For example, recent work has found that academic first-year seminars with varying topics are the seminar types structured to include most elements of HIPs (Keup & Young, 2018; Skipper, 2017) and most closely fit the definition offered by AAC&U (Kuh, 2008; Skipper, 2017). However, the research record is unclear about which seminar types have greater impact on student outcomes (Clouse, 2012;

Friedman & Marsh, 2009; Ryan & Glenn, 2004; Young, 2015). Even a meta-analysis of the extant research on FYS by Permazadian and Crede (2016) found that variations in seminar types were associated with differences in outcomes. Their study showed that extended orientation seminars were significant and positive predictors of first-to-second-year retention, while other seminar types were not. On the other hand, the same study found that academic seminars were positive predictors of first-year GPA, while other seminar types were not.

Recent research on the FYS, particularly around student success courses in the two-year sector, has explored questions on how courses are structured and how they might deliver on pedagogical effectiveness (Hatch, 2017; Hatch, Garcia, Mardock-Uman, Rodriguez, & Young, 2019; Hatch, Mardock-Uman, Garcia, & Johnson, 2018). In other words, how are these courses being constructed, realized, delivered, and experienced?

"Benefits of student success programs are often presupposed, and ... unquestioned assumptions undergirding their implementation can lead to students experiencing undesirable outcomes" (Hatch et al., 2018, p. 117). This line of inquiry seeks to understand more about the effective educational experiences of these and other related student success initiatives. Findings suggest the way the educational environment is structured and carried out (e.g., greater focus on participation, increased group work, connecting the coursework to the campus community) matters more to overall engagement and success than the more practical aspects such as study skills, time management, and basic academic planning (Hatch, 2017; Hatch et al., 2018).

Organization of the Chapter

This chapter is organized to shed some light on the current status of the practice related to first-year seminars using selected findings from the FYS section of the 2017 NSFYE. First, we will present information about the seminar's prevalence, given its history, widespread adoption, and continued interest. Second, we will detail the types of FYS offered, particularly as the comparative frequency of the academic and extended orientation seminars have trended toward convergence for several administrations of the NSFYS. Third, as there continues to be interest in how seminars are structured, administered, and carried out, we will highlight those features. Finally, the role of the FYS as a hub for educationally purposeful activities (i.e., HIPs) remains an area of interest. After presenting these results, we will discuss the findings and their implications for future research and practice.

Results

Prevalence of the FYS

Overall, 73.5% of respondents in the 2017 survey reported offering an FYS on campus, a substantially lower percentage compared with the 2012-2013 data (89.7%). Figure 6.1 depicts the overall trend of such seminars from 1988 to 2017. Responses to previous administrations of the NSFYS show a steady increase every year since 1997 and an overall increase since 1988. There were dips before (1988 to 1991; 1994 to 1997) but nothing as pronounced as from 2012 to 2017. Even with this noticeable decrease, however, almost three quarters of higher education institutions still offer the FYS.

This drop in FYS prevalence led us to investigate potential reasons for the decline. Some possible explanations include (a) measurement or researcher error, (b) previous overestimation, or (c) a measured drop in the actual prevalence of the seminar. We will address these three potential influential factors in order.

First, a case could be made for attributing the drop to a change in how the question was asked on previous administrations of NSFYS versus the most recent administration of the NSFYE. In the former, respondents answered whether an FYS was offered on their campus. In the latter, respondents indicated which first-year programs were offered and were asked to select the FYS from a list of more than 20 potential initiatives. This might have led to fewer institutions identifying the presence of the FYS on campus.

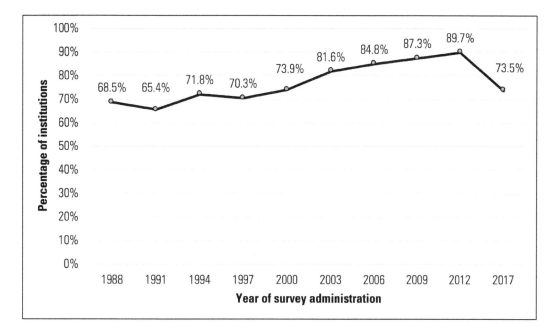

Figure 6.1. Overall response rate of institutions offering a first-year seminar, 1988-2017.

Second, the argument for overestimation has to do with self-selection in the research. In other words, some might argue that institutions with first-year seminars are more likely to respond to a survey on the topic than institutions without one. To investigate this possibility, we created a matched dataset including responses to the 2009, 2012-2013, and 2017 administrations of the NSFYS and NSFYE to track how institutions responded at multiple data collection points. If institutions responding to previous surveys reported offering the FYS at comparatively higher levels than those that did not respond, there is evidence for overestimation due to self-selection. As reported earlier, the overall prevalence of the FYS in the 2017 sample was 73.5%. Among those institutions that responded to both the 2012 and 2017 surveys, the overall percentage offering FYS in 2017 was 79.8%, a slightly higher figure.

We saw a similar but less striking trend for those institutions that responded in both 2009 and 2017, where 75.3% reported offering an FYS, as well as campuses that participated in all three administrations (77.5%). Additional comparisons were made to investigate potential overestimation in previous administrations of the survey, and the differences in percentages were consistently positive and ranged between 1.3 and 6.1 percentage points. In addition, the previous estimates were compared to responses gathered by surveys of student success programs conducted by the John N. Gardner Institute (JNGI). In 2010, the institute's survey of four-year institutions found that 84% of respondents offered a FYS (Barefoot et al., 2012), compared with 87% of four-year colleges and universities in the 2009 NSFYS. The pattern was similar when comparing estimates of prevalence at two-year colleges. JNGI reported that 80% of two-year institutions offered FYS in 2012 (Koch et al., 2014), compared with 86% of two-year respondents to the 2012-2013 NSFYS. This indicates some degree of overestimation was likely, but not to the extent that would explain the 16-point drop in prevalence.

Third, to investigate whether the newest estimate represented a measured decrease in the overall prevalence of the FYS, responses from participants in the past three administrations were tracked over time. This allowed us to compare similar sets of institutions across time to see whether the percentage with FYS dropped consistently. Perhaps the most illustrative example of both overestimation and the potential drop in prevalence came with the set of 151 institutions that responded to all three surveys. Among these respondents, the percentage that reported offering an FYS in 2009 was 93.4%. For 2012-2013 the figure was 94.1%, and in 2017 it was 77.5%, a drop of 16.6 percentage points, nearly equal to the difference in prevalence in the overall estimates.

These analyses suggest ample evidence that the overall proportion of institutions offering an FYS has decreased since the 2012-2013 administration of the NSFYS by a conservative estimate of nearly 10%. In addition, when disaggregating the data by institutional type, about 78% of four-year institutions offered an FYS, about 19 percentage points lower than in 2012-2013. It is notable that two-year institutions offering an FYS have decreased 27.7 percentage points from 2012-2013; however, most such institutions still offer a seminar course (58.5%). Examining institutional control showed comparable percentages between public and private institutions: 73.9% and 73.7%, respectively.

Seminar Type

As previously mentioned, the FYS may exist on campus in one or more forms: (a) extended orientation seminars, (b) academic courses with uniform content across all sections, (c) academic courses with content that varies across sections, (d) preprofessional, discipline-linked, or major-specific courses, (e) seminars with a focus on basic study skills, and (f) a hybrid seminar encompassing elements from two or more of the other seminar types. The 2017 data indicated a large number of institutions classify the FYS as extended orientation (47.6%; Figure 6.2). However, this figure is down about 13 percentage points from the 2012-2013 implementation of the NSFYS (see Figure 6.2). Concurrently, increases were seen in the reported prevalence of seminars as academic with uniform content (31.4%) and academic seminars on various topics (33.0%). For the first time since the National Resource Center started using this typology in 1991, the sum percentage of those two academic categories combined (64.4%) was greater than that for extended orientation (47.6%). Figure 6.3 compares prevalence of extended orientation seminars and academic seminars (combined) from 1991 to 2017.

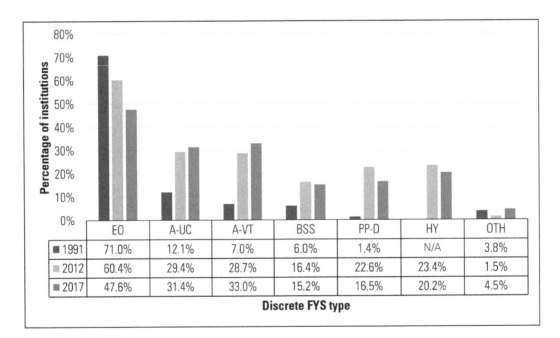

	EO	A-UC	A-VT	BSS	PP-D	HY	OTH
1991	71.0%	12.1%	7.0%	6.0%	1.4%	N/A	3.8%
2012	60.4%	29.4%	28.7%	16.4%	22.6%	23.4%	1.5%
2017	47.6%	31.4%	33.0%	15.2%	16.5%	20.2%	4.5%

Discrete FYS type

Figure 6.2. Percentage of discrete types of first-year seminars offered by institutions in 1991, 2012, and 2017. EO = Extended orientation seminar; A-UC = Academic seminar with generally uniform content; A-VT = Academic seminar on various topics; BSS = Basic study skills seminar; PP-D = Preprofessional or discipline-linked seminar; HY = Hybrid; OTH = Other. The sum of the percentages is higher than 100% because of participants' ability to select more than one response.

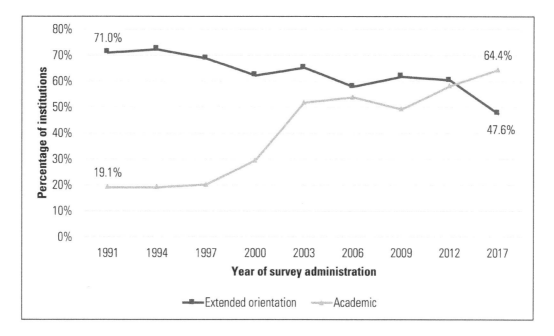

Figure 6.3. Percentage of institutions offering extended orientation seminars and academic seminars combined, 1991-2017. The sum of the percentages is higher than 100% because of participants' ability to select more than one response.

When the data are disaggregated by institutional control, certain patterns emerge (see Figure 6.4). A larger percentage of private institutions (40.5%) than publics (27.8%) described the seminar on their campus as academic on various topics. When the two academic classifications are consolidated, about 70.9 of private institutions identified their programs as academic, compared with 59.6% of publics. Public institutions were more likely than privates to say their seminars could be identified as preprofessional (discipline-linked), focused on basic study skills, or as hybrid courses (those with elements from two or more types listed).

Figure 6.5 displays the differences in responses disaggregated by institutional type. A much larger percentage of four-year institutions (37.9%) reported offering academic seminars on various topics than did two-year institutions (11.3%). Similarly, four-year institutions more frequently indicated the presence of hybrid seminars (22.5%) than two-year campuses (9.9%). Two-year institutions more often reported offering academic seminars with uniform content (39.4% two-year; 29.6% four-year), extended orientation seminars (57.7% two-year; 45.3% four-year), and basic study skills seminars (21.1% two-year; 13.8% four-year).

Disaggregated by size of the incoming first-year class, results show institution size was correlated with the type of FYS offered. A greater proportion of larger institutions (> 4,000 entering students) reported offering preprofessional or discipline-linked seminars than smaller institutions. These larger institutions also indicated being more likely to offer a hybrid model of the FYS.

Primary seminar types. The survey asked participants to identify which seminar type had the highest student enrollment at their institution. Overall, responses indicated extended orientation (28.5%) as the most popular type of FYS (Figure 6.6). When the academic seminar with generally uniform content across sections (24.1%) and the academic seminar on various topics (22.3%) are combined to create an overall academic category, they make up 46.4% of the highest enrolled seminar type. The remaining 25.1% is composed of basic study skills (2.9%), preprofessional or discipline-linked (3.4%), hybrid (15.2%), and other (3.7%).

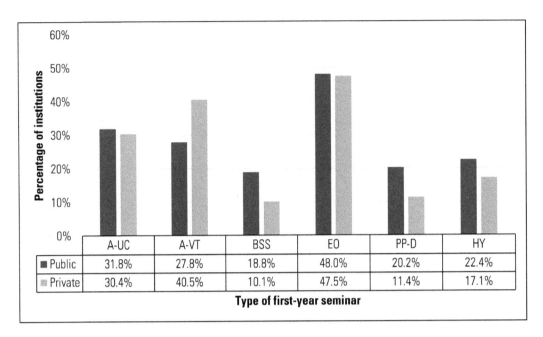

Figure 6.4. Comparison of first-year seminars offered by institutional control (*n* = 382). A-UC = Academic seminar with generally uniform content; A-VT = Academic seminar on various topics; BSS = Basic study skills seminar; EO = Extended orientation seminar; PP-D = Preprofessional or discipline-linked seminar; HY = Hybrid.

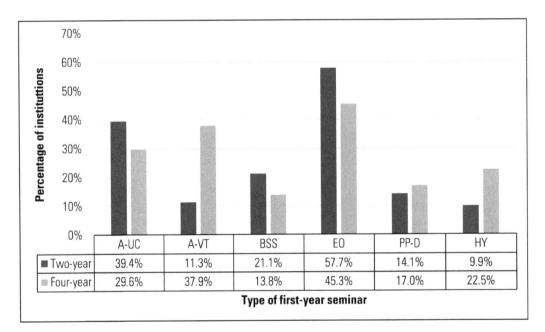

Figure 6.5. Comparison of first-year seminars offered by institutional type (*n* = 382). A-UC = Academic seminar with generally uniform content; A-VT = Academic seminar on various topics; BSS = Basic study skills seminar; EO = Extended orientation seminar; PP-D = Preprofessional or discipline-linked seminar; HY = Hybrid.

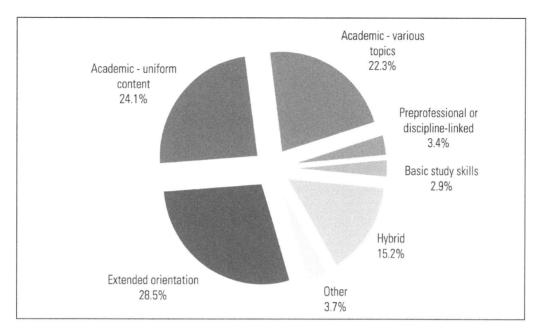

Figure 6.6. First-year seminar type with highest student enrollment (*n* = 382).

Looking at differences by level of instruction, extended orientation was the most prevalent primary seminar type at both two-year (36.6%) and four-year (26.7%) colleges and universities (see Figure 6.7). Comparatively, academic seminars with uniform content across sections, basic study skills, and extended orientation formats were more common among two-year respondents, while academic seminars with variable content were more than six times more common at four-year than two-year institutions. In addition, hybrid seminars were more frequent at four-year colleges and universities. When broken down by institutional control, private institutions selected the academic seminar on various topics (30.4%) as most prevalent, while public institutions indicated the extended orientation seminar (30.5%). Academic seminars on various topics were nearly twice as prevalent among private institutions as publics. Conversely, all other seminar types were reported to include higher percentages of students on public campuses than privates, except for academic seminars with uniform content, which were listed with nearly the same frequency of institutions from both categories of institutional control.

Features of the FYS

Credits and credit classification. It has become nearly standard for FYS courses to offer credit in order to contribute to students' academic achievement. Of institutions that reported offering an FYS, about 96% did so for credit. A majority indicated that the course carries either one credit (39.2%) or three credits (32.8%). Both public (43.8%) and private (32.9%) schools indicated commonly offering a one-credit version of the seminar. Two-year (40.3%) and four-year institutions (39.0%) reported offering one credit at nearly the same rate. However, more two-year colleges reported offering the course for three credits (41.8%) than for any other amount and more frequently than their four-year counterparts (30.8%).

We also sought insight about where the academic credit from FYS was applied during the student's time at the institution. Figure 6.8 illustrates how academic credit has been classified at institutions. Most colleges indicated the FYS credit applied toward the general education requirement (57.1%) or as an elective (32.5%). Comparing the 2017 NSFYE data to the previous 2012-2013 NSFYS reveals a trend about the classification of credit: Figures for each component of credit (general education, elective, and major requirement) have decreased. We inferred that this is because the question requires a select-all-that-apply response. With this response option, we assumed less overlap in where institutions are choosing to apply the seminar credit for students, meaning that at an institution where the seminar previously counted for either an elective or general education requirement, it now only counts for the latter.

When considering institutional type, the application of credit is split. For two-year institutions, elective credit (50.8%) was selected most frequently. However, at four-year colleges and universities, the credit is usually applied toward the general education program (61.8%). We observed a similar but more pronounced difference between public and private schools; the credit was most commonly used as an elective by slightly less than half of public institutions (47.1%), while more than 8 in 10 private institutions reported applying credit for the FYS toward general education requirements (82.2%).

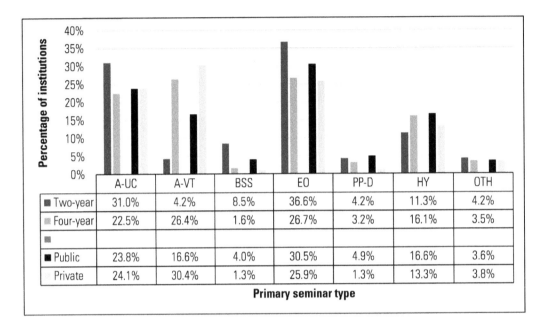

	A-UC	A-VT	BSS	EO	PP-D	HY	OTH
■ Two-year	31.0%	4.2%	8.5%	36.6%	4.2%	11.3%	4.2%
▨ Four-year	22.5%	26.4%	1.6%	26.7%	3.2%	16.1%	3.5%
▨							
■ Public	23.8%	16.6%	4.0%	30.5%	4.9%	16.6%	3.6%
▨ Private	24.1%	30.4%	1.3%	25.9%	1.3%	13.3%	3.8%

Primary seminar type

Figure 6.7. Primary first-year seminar type by institutional type and control (*n* = 382). A-UC = Academic seminar with generally uniform content; A-VT = Academic seminar on various topics; BSS = Basic study skills seminar; EO = Extended orientation seminar; PP-D = Preprofessional or discipline-linked seminar; HY = Hybrid; OTH = Other.

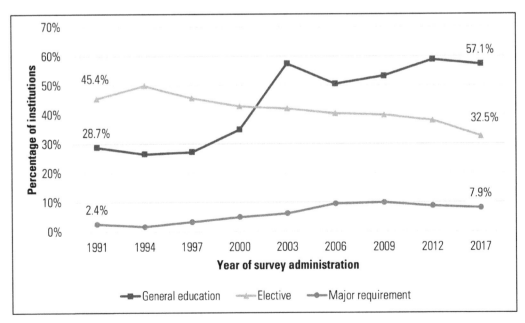

Figure 6.8. Comparison of institutional application of first-year seminar credit, 1991-2017.

Seminar instructor. As illustrated in Figure 6.9, most responding institutions indicated that tenure-track (69.3%) and full-time, non-tenure-track faculty (68.2%) are instructors of the FYS. Student affairs professionals (53.0%), academic advisors (46.2%), and adjunct faculty (52.7%) were also well represented. Other campus professionals (22.8%), graduate students (8.7%), and undergraduate students (4.6%) were reported as teaching the seminar less often.

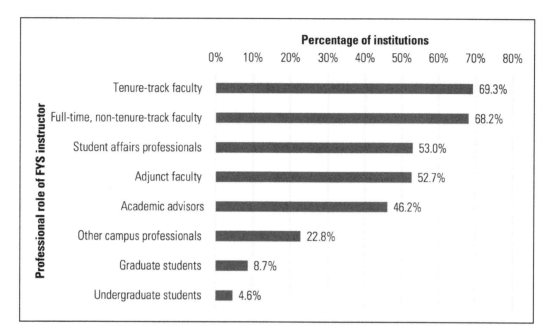

Figure 6.9. Professional role of FYS instructors (*n* = 368). Institutions could select multiple responses; therefore, percentages will add up to more than 100%.

Public (58.4%) and two-year institutions (57.6%) indicated more frequently than private (29.2%) and four-year (43.7%) colleges that academic advisors teach the FYS. Similarly, public (62.1%) and two-year schools (77.3%) reported using adjunct faculty more than private (39.6%) and four-year institutions (47.4%). Full-time faculty on the tenure track and non-tenure track were more frequently reported by four-year institutions (73.8% tenure track; 70.9% full-time, non-tenure) than two-year (48.5% tenure track; 56.1% full-time, non-tenure). Student affairs professionals were more commonly listed as FYS instructors at public institutions (59.3%) than privates (44.2%).

Undergraduate student role. To better understand the use of undergraduate students as peer educators in the FYS, a question was proposed to delineate how they assist in the delivery of the course. More than half of institutions reported using undergraduate students in some manner to assist in the FYS (53.3%). Some responses indicated that students assist the instructor but do not teach during the seminar (29.8%), while others show that these students teach as part of a team (19.9%). The use of peer leaders in the FYS was more common at four-year institutions; almost twice as many two-year (63.6%) as four-year institutions (33.3%) reported not using undergraduate students to assist with the seminar.

Students in FYS. Many institutions require specific groups or even all first-year students to enroll in the FYS. Slightly more than half (51.8%) of institutions made it a requirement for all first-year students. At the institutions that did not do so, the top populations of students required to take the course were

- students enrolled in developmental or remedial courses (33.1%),

- honors students (31.6%),

- first-generation students (30.8%), and

- provisionally admitted students (30.1%).

A large number of institutions required "other" first-year student populations to take the course (39.1%). These groups could include students below a certain number of credits (e.g., those who had earned fewer than 30 semester hours), traditional-age first-year students, students in specific academic programs on the responding campus, students in specific scholarship or grant programs, students in residential programs, and even students with academic risk factors such as late registration or low incoming GPA. Considering institutional type, the subpopulations of students selected most frequently at two-year colleges were those enrolled in developmental or remedial courses (28.9%) and "other" (36.8%). By contrast, at four-year institutions, provisionally admitted students (41.1%) and "other" students (40.0%) were required to participate in an FYS.

When disaggregating by institutional control, private institutions required students to take the FYS more than twice as frequently as publics (79.1% private, 32.4% public). Of those private institutions that did not require the seminar, more than half (59.3%) required first-generation students to take the course (see Table 6.1). Meanwhile, more than a quarter of public institutions required students enrolled in developmental or remedial courses (27.4%) to take the seminar. Moreover, when we compare the difference in percentages of private and public institutions, some student populations stand out. Six groups show a difference of more than 30 percentage points, indicating that not only are private colleges more frequently requiring all first-year students to participate, when they do not do so, they more frequently require a greater variety of student subpopulations to take the seminar than public colleges.

Table 6.1

Categories of Students Required to Enroll in a First-Year Seminar by Institutional Control (n = 133)

| Students required to participate in the first-year seminar | Institutional control | | | | Difference (%) |
| | Public | | Private | | |
	Freq.	%	Freq.	%	
Percentages larger for private institutions					
Preprofessional students (e.g., pre-law, pre-med)	14	51.9	17	16.0	35.8
First-generation students	16	59.3	25	23.6	35.7
Students residing within a particular residence hall	11	40.7	10	9.4	31.3
Students on academic probation	12	44.4	14	13.2	31.2
Student athletes	14	51.9	22	20.8	31.1
Science, technology, engineering, and math (STEM) students	13	48.2	19	17.9	30.2
International students	13	48.2	21	19.8	28.3
Students enrolled in developmental or remedial courses	15	55.6	29	27.4	28.2
Honors students	14	51.9	28	26.4	25.4
Provisionally admitted students	13	48.2	27	25.5	22.7
Students from low-income backgrounds	10	37.0	16	15.1	21.9
Students participating in dual-enrollment programs	8	29.6	9	8.5	21.1

Table continues on page 75

Table continued from page 74

Categories of Students Required to Enroll in a First-Year Seminar by Institutional Control (n = 133)

Students required to participate in the first-year seminar	Public		Private		Difference (%)
	Freq.	%	Freq.	%	
Students eligible for federal or state equal-opportunity programs	12	44.4	25	23.6	20.9
Undeclared students	9	33.3	21	19.8	13.5
Transfer students	4	14.8	6	5.7	9.2
Learning community participants	9	33.3	27	25.5	7.9
Students within specific majors	6	22.2	19	17.9	4.3
Students with at-risk factors (e.g., GED, low ACT scores)	7	25.9	23	21.7	4.2
Other	11	40.7	41	38.7	2.1

Disaggregating by level of instruction, four-year institutions more frequently reported requiring students to take the FYS. Four-year colleges and universities required the course for all students at nearly twice the rate of two-year institutions (56.9% four-year; 29.0% two-year). Comparing percentages between two- and four-year institutions (see Table 6.2) revealed seven groups with a difference of more than 20 percentage points by institutional type. This indicates that not only do four-year colleges more frequently make the seminar a requirement, but when they do not require it, they require a greater variety of student subpopulations to participate at a higher level than two-year schools do.

Objectives. The five most frequently identified objectives for the FYS overall were to (a) teach academic success strategies (48.1%); (b) develop a connection with the institution or campus (34.7%); (c) cultivate a knowledge of campus resources (30.4%); (d) foster analytical, critical-thinking, or problem-solving skills (24.7%); and (e) provide an introduction to college-level academic expectations (24.2%; see Table 6.3).

The objectives of the seminar are consistent with previous recent administrations of the NSFYS. Table 6.3 compares the most frequently identified objectives with previous administrations. The relative importance of the top three objectives has remained fairly consistent over the past three administrations. Two objectives from the previous administrations that consistently placed in the top 10 but fell lower in the list for this survey were developing a support network and improving retention or sophomore return rates. Improving retention ranked 11th (8.3%), and developing a social support network ranked 18th (5.4%) among respondents to the 2017 NSFYE.

Comparing the relative focus of FYS at two-year and four-year institutions revealed that academic success strategies (71.6% two-year, 43.0% four-year), academic planning or major exploration (35.0% two-year, 18.0% four-year), and knowledge of campus resources (44.8% two-year, 27.2% four-year) were more frequently identified as objectives by two-year colleges. Analytical, critical-thinking, or problem-solving skills (16.4% two-year, 26.6% four-year), writing skills (3.0% two-year; 11.1% four-year), and intercultural competence, diversity, or engaging with different perspectives (1.5% two-year; 8.9% four-year) were more often reported as important course objectives by four-year schools. The pattern for public institutions is similar to two-year colleges, where academic success strategies (59.4% public, 32.3% private), academic planning or major exploration (28.6% public, 11.0% private), and knowledge of campus resources (37.3% public, 20.6% private) were more commonly reported objectives of the seminar. Private colleges and universities were more likely to report introduction to the liberal arts (0.0% public, 14.2% private), common FYE (8.3% public, 19.4% private), and writing skills (5.5% public, 15.5% private) as important objectives for the FYS.

Assessment. A critical component of any educational activity is evaluating its quality. This is particularly true of FYS during a time when the course's prevalence is retrenching. Of respondents to the NSFYE, nearly two thirds reported formally assessing or evaluating their course at some point in the three years before the administration of the survey (see Figure 6.10). This figure is up slightly since the 2012-2013 NSFYS, when 59.4% of respondents reported having assessed their seminars in the same timeframe. Among those respondents who indicated assessing their FYS, more than half reported using student course evaluations (81.1%), analysis of institutional data (72.2%), and direct assessment of student learning outcomes (63.4%) to carry out their evaluative activities.

Table 6.2

Categories of Students Required to Enroll in a First-Year Seminar by Institutional Type (n = 133)

	Institutional type				Difference
	Two-year		Four-year		
Students required to participate in the first-year seminar	**Freq.**	**%**	**Freq.**	**%**	**(%)**
Percentages larger for two-year institutions					
Transfer students	4	10.5	6	6.3	4.2
Percentages larger for four-year institutions					
Provisionally admitted students	1	2.6	39	41.1	−38.4
Honors students	5	13.2	37	38.9	−25.8
Preprofessional students (e.g., prelaw, premed)	2	5.3	29	30.5	−25.3
First-generation students	5	13.2	36	37.9	−24.7
Learning community participants	4	10.5	32	33.7	−23.2
Student athletes	4	10.5	32	33.7	−23.2
Science, technology, engineering, and math (STEM) students	3	7.9	29	30.5	−22.6
Students residing within a particular residence hall	1	2.6	20	21.1	−18.4
International students	5	13.2	29	30.5	−17.4
Students eligible for federal or state equal-opportunity programs	6	15.8	31	32.6	−16.8
Students participating in dual-enrollment programs	1	2.6	16	16.8	−14.2
Undeclared students	5	13.2	25	26.3	−13.2
Students from low-income backgrounds	4	10.5	22	23.2	−12.6
Students with at-risk factors (e.g., GED, low ACT scores)	6	15.8	24	25.3	−9.5
Students within specific majors	5	13.2	20	21.1	−7.9
Students enrolled in developmental courses	11	28.9	33	34.7	−5.8
Other	14	36.8	38	40.0	−3.2
Students on academic probation	7	18.4	19	20.0	−1.6

Table 6.3

Concordance of Top 10 First-Year Seminar Objectives from 2017 NSFYE with Objectives Identified in Previous Surveys on First-Year Seminars

Seminar objectives	2009 NSFYS		2012-13 NSFYS		2017 NSFYS	
	%	Rank	%	Rank	%	Rank
Academic success strategies	54.6	1	36.3	3	48.1	1
Connection with the institution or campus	50.2	2	44.9	1	34.7	2
Knowledge of or orientation to campus resources and services	47.6	3	37.8	2	30.4	3
Analytical, critical-thinking, or problem-solving skills	a	a	23.3	4	24.7	4
Introduction to college-level academic expectations	a	a	a	a	24.2	5
Academic planning or major exploration	a	a	a	a	21.2	6
Self-exploration or personal development	28.5	4	17.0	6	14.8	7
Common first-year experience	23.3	5	21.6	5	12.9	8
Student–faculty interaction	16.9	7	12.4	9	10.5	9
Writing skills	11.9	9	11.6	10	9.7	10

Note. Table is sorted by rank order of top 10 objectives identified by respondents to the 2017 NSFYE. Figures for 2009 and 2012-2013 NSFYS are from Padgett and Keup (2011) and Young and Hopp (2014), respectively.

[a] Objective was not included among the response set in this survey administration.

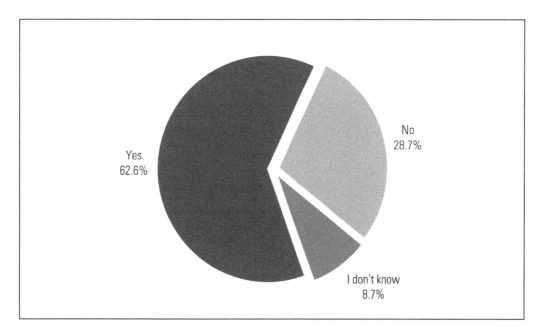

Figure 6.10. Percentage of institutions reporting assessment of first-year seminars (*n* = 366).

When asked about the outcomes of the seminar that were measured through assessment efforts, more than half of respondents reported measuring student satisfaction (61.2%) and retention or second-year return rates (50.7%). Further, more than a third reported measuring academic success strategies (42.7%), connection with the institution or campus (41.9%), knowledge of institution or campus resources and services (41.9%), student–faculty interaction (38.8%), analytical, critical-thinking, or problem-solving skills (37.0%), and introduction to college-level academic expectations (35.2%). Despite the most frequent assessment activities measuring broad outcomes such as satisfaction and retention, a fair amount of alignment exists between the reported course objectives and the outcomes measured through assessment, with the top five course objectives listed among the top eight assessment outcomes. Indeed, once the three outcomes of satisfaction, retention, and student–faculty interaction are removed, the outcomes measured rank in the same order as the most frequently stated objectives for the seminar.

Promising and High-Impact Practices Connected to the FYS

The 2017 NSFYE was designed to allow for continued investigation of the role of the FYS as a hub for promising or high-impact practices in the first year. Young and Hopp (2014) found that the FYS was a key delivery or connection point for several of the AAC&U's HIPs for first-year students (Kuh, 2008) including (a) writing-intensive courses, (b) collaborative assignments and projects, (c) diversity and global learning, (d) service-learning, (e) learning communities, (f) common-reading experiences, and (g) undergraduate research. The 2012-2013 NSFYS did not include internships and senior capstones, as these were determined to be either outside the first year definitionally, in the case of senior capstones, or less likely to be part of a first-year student's experience. The 2017 NSFYE included questions aimed at getting at these HIPs and added the option for institutions to report whether the first-year seminar was intentionally connected to first-year internship opportunities. In addition, two other response options were included in the set that came from the CCCSE's list of 13 promising practices for two-year colleges: goal setting and monitoring class attendance (CCCSE, 2012). Because of the overlap in the list of high-impact and promising practices, this meant the NSFYE now directly asked about how four of the promising practices were intentionally connected to the seminar.

Table 6.4 presents the promising and high-impact practices reported by institutions as connected to the FYS. The most frequently reported practices were goal setting and planning (70.9%), diversity and global learning (67.9%), collaborative assignments (66.0%), monitoring of student class attendance (64.1%), and writing-intensive coursework (42.9%). This is in line with the results of the 2012-2013 NSFYS (see Young & Hopp, 2014). Similarly, the top promising and high-impact practices intentionally connected to the FYS were pedagogical exercises that could easily be managed within each section by an instructor or instructional team. Less frequently reported were those practices that required some coordination with other first-year programs beyond the course itself.

A disaggregation of the specific promising and high-impact practices by institutional type is found in Table 6.5. Four-year institutions were more likely to report intentionally including all but one of the promising and high-impact practices in the FYS: goal setting and planning. It is not surprising that this practice was reported more frequently by two-year institutions, as it was listed among the promising practices for community colleges by CCCSE. Notwithstanding, the other option added from the list of promising practices for community colleges, monitoring of student class attendance, was comparatively more common at four-year institutions.

When the promising and high-impact practices were broken down by institutional control, public institutions were more likely to report including goal setting and planning, learning communities, collaborative assignments and projects, monitoring of student class attendance, and diversity and global learning in the FYS than private institutions (Table 6.6). Private colleges, on the other hand, were more likely to report including service-learning, common-reading experiences, writing-intensive projects, internships, and undergraduate research. These findings are consistent with results of the 2012-2013 NSFYS (see Young & Hopp, 2014).

Table 6.4

Promising or High-Impact Practices Connected to First-Year Seminars (n = 368)

Promising or high-impact practice	Freq.	%
Goal setting and planning	261	70.9
Diversity, global learning, or experiences with difference	250	67.9
Collaborative assignments and projects	243	66.0
Monitoring of student class attendance	236	64.1
Writing-intensive	158	42.9
Common-reading experience	158	42.9
Learning community	151	41.0
Service-learning	116	31.5
Undergraduate research	48	13.0
Internships	8	2.2

Note. The NSFYE contained two separate questions on promising or high-impact practices (see Appendix B).

Table 6.5

Promising or High-Impact Educational Practices Connected to First-Year Seminars by Institutional Type (n = 368)

	Institutional type				Difference
	Two-year		Four-year		
Promising or high-impact practice	Freq.	%	Freq.	%	(%)
Percentages larger for two-year institutions					
Goal setting and planning	59	89.4%	202	66.9%	22.5%
Percentages larger for four-year institutions					
Common reading experience	18	27.3%	140	46.4%	−19.1%
Diversity, global learning, or experiences with difference	35	53.0%	215	71.2%	−18.2%
Writing-intensive	19	28.8%	139	46.0%	−17.2%
Service-learning	12	18.2%	104	34.4%	−16.3%
Monitoring of student class attendance	36	54.5%	200	66.2%	−11.7%
Undergraduate research	3	4.5%	45	14.9%	−10.4%
Collaborative assignments and projects	41	62.1%	202	66.9%	−4.8%
Internships	0	0.0%	8	2.6%	−2.6%
Learning community	27	40.9%	124	41.1%	−0.2%

Note. The NSFYE contained two separate questions on promising or high-impact practices (see Appendix B).

Table 6.6

Promising or High-Impact Educational Practices Connected to First-Year Seminars by Institutional Control
(*n* = 368)

| Promising or high-impact practice | Institutional control | | | | Difference (%) |
| | Public | | Private | | |
	Freq.	%	Freq.	%	
Percentages larger for public institutions					
Goal setting and planning	176	82.2%	85	55.2%	27.0%
Learning community	108	50.5%	43	27.9%	22.5%
Collaborative assignments and projects	147	68.7%	96	62.3%	6.4%
Monitoring of student class attendance	139	65.0%	97	63.0%	2.0%
Diversity, global learning, or experiences with difference	146	68.2%	104	67.5%	0.7%
Percentages larger for private institutions					
Service-learning	55	25.7%	61	39.6%	−13.9%
Common-reading experience	84	39.3%	74	48.1%	−8.8%
Writing-intensive	85	39.7%	73	47.4%	−7.7%
Internships	0	0.0%	8	5.2%	−5.2%
Undergraduate research	26	12.1%	22	14.3%	−2.1%

Note. The NSFYE contained two separate questions on promising or high-impact practices (see Appendix B).

Discussion and Conclusion

The 2017 NSFYE provided a useful snapshot on practice related to the FYS on campuses. It allowed us to identify a few key themes related to our research questions, specifically providing information on (a) the prevalence of the FYS as a curricular intervention used in the first college year in the United States, (b) trends in how the FYS is being structured, and (c) its role as a key mechanism for connecting students to multiple promising or high-impact practices on campus.

Perhaps the most noteworthy finding is the decrease in the overall percentage of institutions offering the FYS on campuses. Despite the potential overestimation in previous administrations of the NSFYS, this survey saw a measurable and consistent overall decrease of approximately 10 percentage points. After two decades of steady increases, further research is warranted to understand this decrease. We suggest two potential contributing factors that might be investigated.

First, a review of the responses to this and previous surveys has demonstrated evidence revealing that first-year seminars exhibit a lifecycle, or as Barefoot and Fidler (1996) described it, "as [first-year] seminars are born, others die an untimely death" (p. 5). As institutional populations change, the seminar course evolves with the developing student body, causing adjustments in implementation or structure. An initial review of the responses to this survey administration about the age of the FYS suggests the seminars are not being replaced at the same rate they were previously.

Second, compounding this cyclic nature of seminars, a potential contributing factor is that universities have not simply focused on one single aspect of the FYE to support first-year students. Instead, institutions use a breadth of initiatives to inform students of resources and provide support during the first year. During orientation, students actively learn about the transition to collegiate life; within housing and residence life, they engage in social interaction to develop interpersonal skills; and during academic advising, students evaluate how to progress academically toward graduation. Looking at the FYE from a wider perspective, multiple units impact the first year and thus contribute to a successful student transition. It is possible that many institutions were relying on the FYS as a primary or sole first-year support program. However, as institutions adopt a broad and more coordinated approach to the FYE, this expanded focus could contribute to a decrease in first-year seminars and their slow replacement at institutions. Most concerning is the magnitude of the decrease among respondents in the two-year sector, where there is evidence that students might not have access to as many promising and high-impact practices as those at four-year institutions (Young & Hopp, 2014; Young & Keup, 2016).

Along with the decline in overall prevalence, we saw a sharp decrease in extended orientation seminars, suggesting that these are the type of FYS not being reintroduced on campuses. As previous commentators have stated, this decline and the steady climb of academic seminars might be in response to significant pressures from faculty. Such criticism might characterize extended orientation as lacking in academic rigor and the features that have been shown to support student success (Padgett & Keup, 2009; Young & Hopp, 2014). Additional research and institutional assessment should be carried out to identify the connection of seminar structure to student outcomes, despite strong internal institutional pressures to format the course in a particular way. As Young and Hopp (2014) commented, "Research and assessment continue to be important for the future of first-year seminars, as these evidence-gathering activities can help set all types of seminars down the right path toward long-term success" (p. 3).

Additionally, the findings reiterate the importance institutions place on the objectives of connecting first-year students to the academic community. More promising is the finding that a greater percentage of institutions are assessing the seminar, and that their outcomes are strongly and almost directly connected to the seminar's stated objectives. A clear connection between objectives, practice, and assessment holds the promise of achieving the goals of the seminar and engaging in institutional change processes, by interpreting the results and identifying and acting on ways that the practice can be improved.

Finally, results of the survey show that the FYS continues to be an important hub in the first year for connecting students to promising and high-impact practices. However, the opportunities continue to be more plentiful at four-year institutions, even for some of those items considered promising practices for community colleges. The equity implications in this finding are strong, as community college students are disproportionately from historically underserved populations in higher education. Thus, they are precisely the group standing to benefit the most from participating in promising and high-impact practices, including the FYS.

References

Barefoot, B. O. (1992). *Helping first-year college students climb the academic ladder: Report of a national survey of freshman seminar programming in American higher education* (Unpublished doctoral dissertation). College of William and Mary, Williamsburg, VA.

Barefoot, B. O., & Fidler, P. P. (1996). *The 1994 national survey of freshman seminar programs: Continuing innovations in the collegiate curriculum* (Monograph No. 20). Columbia, SC: University of South Carolina, National Resource Center for the Freshman Year Experience and Students in Transition.

Barefoot, B. O., Griffin, B. Q., & Koch, A. K. (2012). *Enhancing student success and retention throughout undergraduate education: A national survey.* Brevard, NC: The John N. Gardner Institute for Excellence in Undergraduate Education. Retrieved from https://static1.squarespace.com/static/59b0c486d2b857fc86d09aee/t/59bad-33412abd988ad84d697/1505415990531/JNGInational_survey_web.pdf

Brownell, J. E., & Swaner, L. E. (2010). *Five high-impact practices: Research on learning outcomes, completion, and quality.* Washington, DC: Association of American Colleges and Universities.

Center for Community College Student Engagement (CCCSE). (2012). *A matter of degrees: Promising practices for community college student success: A first look.* Austin, TX: The University of Texas at Austin, Community College Leadership Program.

Clouse, W. A. (2012). *The effects of non-compulsory freshman seminar and core curriculum completion ratios on post-secondary persistence and baccalaureate degree attainment.* (Doctoral dissertation). Retrieved from ProQuest Dissertations Publishing. (3523633)

Drake, R. (1966). *Review of the literature for freshman orientation practices in the United States*. Fort Collins, CO: Colorado State University.

Dwyer, J. O. (1989). A historical look at the freshman year experience. In M. L. Upcraft & J. N. Gardner (Eds.), *The freshman year experience* (pp. 25-39). San Francisco, CA: Jossey-Bass.

Fidler, P. P., & Fidler, D. S. (1991). *First national survey on freshman seminar programs: Findings, conclusions, and recommendations* (Monograph No. 6). National Resource Center for The Freshman Year Experience. Columbia, SC: University of South Carolina.

Fitts, C. T., & Swift, F. H. (1928). The construction of orientation courses for college freshmen. *University of California Publications in Education, 1897-1929, 2*(3), 145-250.

Friedman, D. B., & Marsh, E. G. (2009). What type of first-year seminar is most effective? A comparison of thematic seminars and college transition/success seminars. *Journal of The First-Year Experience and Students in Transition, 21*(1), 29-42.

Gordon, V. N. (1989). Origins and purposes of the freshman seminar. In M. L. Upcraft & J. N. Gardner (Eds.), *The freshman year experience* (pp. 183-197). San Francisco, CA: Jossey-Bass.

Gordon, V. N. (1991). The evolution of a freshman seminar course: A case study. *Journal of The Freshman Year Experience, 3*(2), 107-117.

Greene, G. H. (1954). Freshman orientation courses in small colleges. *Personnel and Guidance Journal, 32*(8), 480-482.

Greenfield, G. M., Keup, J. R., & Gardner, J. N. (2013). *Developing and sustaining successful first-year programs: A guide for practitioners*. San Francisco, CA: Jossey-Bass.

Hatch, D. K. (2017). The structure of student engagement in community college student success programs: A quantitative activity systems analysis. *AERA Open, 3*(4), 1-14.

Hatch, D. K., Garcia, C. E., Mardock-Uman, N., Rodriguez, S., & Young, D. G. (2019). What works: Learning outcomes due to design variations in community college student success courses. *Teachers College Record, 121*(7). Advance online publication.

Hatch, D. K., Mardock-Uman, N., Garcia, C. E., & Johnson, M., (2018). Best laid plans: How community college student success courses work. *Community College Review, 46*(2), 115-144.

Hunter, M. S., & Linder, C. W. (2005). First-year seminars. In M. L. Upcraft, J. N. Gardner, B. O. Barefoot & Associates (Eds.), *Challenging and supporting the first-year student: A handbook for improving the first year of college* (pp. 275-291). San Francisco, CA: Jossey-Bass.

Johnson, S. R., & Stage, F. K. (2018). Academic engagement and student success: Do high-impact practices mean higher graduation rates? *Journal of Higher Education, 89*(5), 1-29. doi:10.1080/00221546.2018.1441107

Keup, J. R., & Young, D. G. (2018). Investigating the first-year seminar as a high-impact practice. In R. S. Feldman (Ed.), *The first year of college: Research, theory, and practice on improving the student experience and increasing retention* (pp. 93-125). New York, NY: Cambridge.

Koch, S. S., Griffin, B. Q., & Barefoot, B. O. (2014). *National survey of student success initiatives at two-year colleges*. Brevard, NC: The John N. Gardner Institute for Excellence in Undergraduate Education. Retrieved from https://static1.squarespace.com/static/59b0c486d2b857fc86d09aee/t/59bad37251a584437bccc737/1505416079925/National-2-yr-Survey-Booklet_webversion.pdf

Kronovet, E. (1969). Current practices in freshman orientation. *Improving College and University Teaching, 17*(3), 204-205.

Kuh, G. D. (2008). *High-impact educational practices: What they are, who has access to them, and why they matter*. Washington, DC: Association of American Colleges and Universities.

Kuh, G. D., & Kinzie, J. K. (2018, May 1). What really makes a "high-impact" practice high impact? *Inside Higher Ed*. Retrieved from http://www.insidehighered.com

Lees College. (n.d.). *In America's lost colleges*. Retrieved from http://www.lostcolleges.com/lees-college

Padgett, R. D., & Keup, J. R. (2011). *2009 National Survey of First-Year Seminars: Ongoing efforts to support students in transition* (Research Report No. 2). Columbia, SC: University of South Carolina, National Resource Center for The First-Year Experience and Students in Transition.

Pascarella, E. T., & Terenzini, P. T. (2005). *How college affects students: Vol. 2. A third decade of research*. San Francisco, CA: Jossey-Bass.

Permzadian, M., & Crede, V. (2016). Do first-year seminars improve college grades and retention? A quantitative review of their overall effectiveness and an examination of moderators of effectiveness. *Review of Educational Research, 86*(1), 277-316.

Plutchik, R., & Hoffmann, R. W. (1958). The small-group college orientation program. *Journal of Higher Education, 29*(5), 278-279.

Ryan, M. P., & Glenn, P. A. (2004). What do first-year students need most: Learning strategies instruction or academic socialization? *Journal of College Reading and Learning, 34*(2), 4-28.

Shedd, J. M. (2003). The history of the student credit hour. In J. V. Wellman & T. Ehrlich (Eds.), *How the student credit hour shapes higher education: The tie that binds* (New Directions for Higher Education, No. 122, pp. 5-12). San Francisco, CA: Jossey-Bass. Retrieved from https://doi.org/10.1002/he.106h

Skipper, T. L. (2017). *What makes the first-year seminar high impact? An exploration of effective educational practices.* (Research Reports No. 7). Columbia, SC: University of South Carolina, National Resource Center for The First-Year Experience and Students in Transition.

Tobolowsky, B. F., & Associates. (2008). *2006 National Survey of First-Year Seminars: Continuing innovations in the collegiate curriculum* (Monograph No. 51). Columbia, SC: University of South Carolina, National Resource Center for The First-Year Experience & Students in Transition.

Tobolowsky, B. F., Cox, B. E., & Wagner, M. T. (Eds.). (2005). *Exploring the evidence: Reporting research on first-year seminars, Vol. 3* (Monograph No. 42). Columbia, SC: University of South Carolina, National Resource Center for The First-Year Experience and Students in Transition.

Young, D. G. (2015, November). *First-year seminar characteristics predicting institutional retention rates*. Paper presented at the 2015 ASHE Annual Conference, Denver, CO.

Young, D. G., & Hopp, J. M. (2014). *2012-2013 National Survey of First-Year Seminars: Exploring high-impact practices in the first college year* (Research Report No. 4). Columbia, SC: University of South Carolina, National Resource Center for The First-Year Experience and Students in Transition.

Young, D. G., & Keup, J. R. (2016). Using hybridization and specialization to enhance the first-year experience in community colleges: A national picture of high-impact practices in first-year seminars. In G. Crisp & D. K. Hatch (Eds.), *Promising and high-impact practices: Student success programs in the community college context* (New Directions for Community College, No. 175, pp. 57-69). San Francisco, CA: Jossey-Bass.

Chapter 7

First-Year Learning Communities

Jean M. Henscheid
National Resource Center for The First-Year Experience & Students in Transition

Building and sustaining undergraduate learning communities has never been easy (Fink & Inkelas, 2015; Smith, 2001). Whether in the form of a single course taken by a cohort of students in one residence hall or as a completely coordinated curriculum, learning communities require institutions to relinquish autonomy of one or more components of the curriculum or cocurriculum to allow those components to intersect (Dunlap & Sult, 2013). The elimination of walls between courses and other student experiences is a hallmark of the integrated first-year experience approach advocated for in Chapter 1 of this volume and has been a tough sell since Alexander Meikeljohn opened his Experimental College in 1927 and closed it five years later (Fink & Inkelas, 2015). Despite the struggles, respondents to the 2017 National Survey on the First-Year Experience (NSFYE) indicate that learning communities continue to offer a high rate of return on institutions' investment in them. Also, the interdependence of learning communities and first-year seminars has never been higher. More than 40% of this survey's respondents reported that the primary feature of the learning community enrolling the most students was a link with a seminar. That figure was 17.2% in 1994, when the first count was taken (Barefoot & Fidler, 1996). This chapter explores these and other findings and begins with an overview of current learning community trends in research and practice.

Today's Learning Communities

Thirty years into the modern learning community movement, there is still no single, agreed upon definition of these programs. Instead, practitioners and scholars have adopted and adapted several typologies since the 1980s (Association of American Colleges and Universities, 2007; Gabelnick, MacGregor, Matthews, & Smith, 1990; Inkelas, Soldner, Longerbeam, & Leonard, 2008; Lenning & Ebbers, 1999; Love & Tokuno, 1999; Shapiro & Levine, 1999; Snider & Venable, 2000). The quest for a common description may finally be ending, with the National Learning Communities Association's (LCA) provisional definition set for formal evaluation in 2019 (Huerta, 2017). The broad description is as follows:

> Learning communities represent an educational approach that involves the integration of engaged curricular and cocurricular learning and emphasizes relationship and community building among faculty or staff and a cohort of students in a rich learning environment. This educational approach may come in different forms but typically involves, incorporates, or includes at least one of the following:

> • A curricular structure characterized by a cohort of students participating in an intentionally designed, integrative study of an issue or theme through connected courses, experiences, and resources.

- A community of learners participating in a residential learning community that intentionally integrates learning through curricular and cocurricular education in a residential experience (http://www.lcassociation.org/about-us.html).

The LCA's creation marks a milestone in a movement that has chiefly relied on the work of a small staff at the Washington Center for Improving Undergraduate Education and volunteers from institutions and regions across the country (Huerta, 2017). The LCA is poised to join other entities and individuals in building on past research and assessment that have made the case for learning communities' improving student retention (Tinto, 2003), increasing student engagement (Zhao & Kuh, 2004), enhancing student learning (Hegler, 2004), amplifying positive outcomes of first-year seminars (Chism Schmidt & Graziano, 2016; Henscheid, 2004), and facilitating critical thinking and integrative learning (Lardner & Malnarich, 2008).

The national movement is now poised to foster new lines of inquiry, especially on emerging approaches to learning communities, and on impact to student subpopulations (e.g., Engstrom & Tinto, 2008; Huerta & Bray, 2013, Smyth, 2016; Weiss, Visher, Weissman, & Wathington, 2015). Henscheid (2015) and West and Williams (2017) also argue that the time is ripe for clarifying how many and what kind of learning communities exist. The future will also include raising the profile of learning communities as natural homes for degree maps, guided pathways, and other "momentum" strategies (Complete College America, 2018, p. 5) developed by Complete College America, the College Promise Campaign, Achieving the Dream (Waiwaiole & Elston, 2017), the John N. Gardner Institute for Excellence in Undergraduate Education (Koch, 2017), and others. Results of the survey reported in this volume point to the need for new work on understanding how the increasing interdependence of learning communities and first-year seminars may be reshaping and reenergizing both.

Results

Reach

While survey respondents reported that learning communities offered a high rate of return on investment for their institutions (costs vs. educational benefits, as discussed below), their reach into first-year student populations continues to be limited. Only 26% of institutions represented in the survey require most of their first-year students to participate in learning communities, and just 15% require learning communities for all first-year students. Four-year and private institutions are twice as likely as two-year and public institutions to require all first-year students to enroll in learning communities. Remarkably, more than a third of institutions with an incoming class of fewer than 500 require all first-year students to participate in learning communities. Institutions of all other sizes require learning communities for less than 10% of their first-year students.

This is likely more frequent at smaller institutions for at least a few reasons. First, smaller institutions tend to focus on the liberal arts, where there is greater emphasis on a broad general education. Second, with a smaller number of students, organizing the co-enrollment across sections is much more manageable. Third, managing the course-taking patterns of students at smaller institutions is easier because there likely are fewer courses and sections.

Difficulty in launching and sustaining learning communities may partially explain their limited reach. Another factor may be undercounting programs that would qualify as learning communities but are not labeled as such, scattered throughout general education, majors, residence halls, online, and elsewhere (Henscheid, 2015; West & Williams, 2017). For example, some learning community counts may not include degree programs in health care in which interdisciplinary and cohort learning and coordinated curricula are gold standards (Maharajan, Rajiah, Khoo, Chellappan, De Alwis, Chui, & Lau, 2017). Certificate and associate degree programs in career and technical education may not make standard learning community lists despite their heavy reliance on applied and integrated learning (Fitzgerald & Singmaster, 2017). Underreporting programs may also depress accounting for the number of students who participate in learning communities. Programs reported on for this survey tend to serve high-ability and academically vulnerable students and those in specific majors; this held across institutional type, control, and size. Interestingly, two populations also at relatively high risk of leaving college, students from low-income backgrounds and first-generation students, are unlikely to be required to participate (perhaps as a function of the difficulty in identifying these students). As noted above, untangling how many and what kind of learning communities exist and which students participate in them necessitates ongoing work.

Characteristics

Survey respondents were asked to identify characteristics of first-year learning communities enrolling the largest number of first-year students. As noted in Table 7.1, the most prevalent characteristic of learning communities was their link with first-year seminars. This held true across institutional type and control (Tables 7.2 and 7.3).

Table 7.1

Characteristics of First-Year Learning Communities (n = 227)

Characteristic	Freq.	%
One of the courses in the learning community is a first-year seminar.	116	51.1
Students are co-enrolled in two or more courses, but not all courses in the students' schedules.	111	48.9
Course content in the linked courses is connected by a common intellectual theme.	103	45.4
Students in the learning community participate in a common set of theme-based experiences outside of the course, such as discussion groups, a speaker series, or other educational programs.	93	41.0
Course content is intentionally coordinated by the instructors of the linked courses.	88	38.8
The learning community includes a residential component (i.e., a living–learning community).	86	37.9
One of the courses in the learning community is a developmental or remedial education course.	30	13.2
Students are co-enrolled in all courses in the students' schedules.	20	8.8
Other, please describe.	19	8.4

Note. The sum of the percentages is larger than 100% because respondents were asked to select all characteristics that apply.

Even as the prevalence of first-year seminars has decreased (see Chapter 6), their presence in learning communities has increased from 17.2% in 1994 to 41.0% by 2017 (Figure 7.1). The central role these courses now play for all curricular and cocurricular components of many learning communities takes one or more of the following forms (Henscheid, Skipper, & Young, 2014):

- sharing common readings, assignments, and projects;

- pulling together concepts from other courses;

- serving as a site to process concepts from other courses and focus on metacognition (learning about learning itself);

- serving as a site for faculty members from other courses in the link to visit and discuss connections;

- serving as a site to explicitly connect personal or social concepts with concepts learned in linked course(s);

- serving as a site to discuss skills, behaviors, and dispositions important to achievement in linked course(s);

- serving as a site for community building;

- serving as a site for career exploration related to learning community themes and topics; and

- serving as a site for service-learning connected to learning community themes and topics.

Strategies for making these connections successful are explored by Chism Schmidt and Graziano (2016), Friedman and Alexander (2007), Henscheid (2004), and Young and Hopp (2014).

Table 7.2

Characteristics of First-Year Learning Communities by Institutional Type (n = 227)

	Institutional type		
	Two-year	Four-year	Difference
Characteristic	%	%	(%)
One of the courses in the learning community is a first-year seminar.	45.9	52.1	−6.2
Course content is intentionally coordinated by the instructors of the linked courses.	43.2	37.9	5.3
One of the courses in the learning community is a developmental or remedial education course.	37.8	8.4	29.4
Course content in the linked courses is connected by a common intellectual theme.	32.4	47.9	−15.5
Students are co-enrolled in two or more courses, but not all courses in the students' schedules.	29.7	52.6	−22.9
Students in the learning community participate in a common set of theme-based experiences outside of the course, such as discussion groups, a speaker series, or other educational programs.	27.0	43.7	−16.7
Students are co-enrolled in all courses in the students' schedules.	16.2	7.4	8.8
Other, please describe.	10.8	7.9	2.9
The learning community includes a residential component (i.e., a living–learning community).	2.7	44.7	−42.0

Note. The sum of the percentages is larger than 100% because respondents were asked to select all characteristics that apply.

With a few notable exceptions, characteristics of learning communities are similar across institutions based on the number of first-year students they enroll (Table 7.4). A full 60% of respondents at institutions with the largest first-year student enrollments (more than 4,000 entering first-year students) reported that the primary characteristic of their learning communities was a residential component, compared with less than one quarter at institutions with the smallest entering classes (< 500). Faculty at institutions with the fewest first-year students were much more likely to report intentionally coordinating content across courses (46.2%) than instructors with the highest entering student enrollments (16.7%).

Administration

Across institutions, all learning communities report to academic units, either at the department level or in central administration. These programs share this reporting line with first-year seminars in all but one instance (at institutions with first-year student populations of 2,001-4,000). This shared reporting structure may facilitate linking first-year seminars and learning communities.

Return on Investment

Results of the survey suggest that institutional objectives for first-year students align well with objectives of learning communities. This mirrors previous findings regarding learning community impact on student academic success and retention, building a connection to campus, higher-order thinking skills, interaction with faculty, and development of social support networks (Cross, 1998; Kuh, 2008; Leskes & Miller, 2006; Malnarich, Pettitt, & Mino, 2014). Learning communities are second only to first-year seminars among those practices included in the Association of American Colleges and Universities' list of high-impact practices (HIPs) as the most frequently identified primary vehicle for meeting first-year objectives. Respondents asked to rate their institutions' return on investment also placed learning communities at or near the top of the list of HIPs.

Assessment

The story of learning community assessment told by this survey's respondents is discouraging when one considers the focus the movement has placed on determining these programs' impact (Huerta & Hansen, 2013). Most respondents from private institutions and those with the smallest first-year classes said their learning communities had either not been assessed since Fall 2013 or that respondents were unaware whether assessment had occurred. Less than half of respondents from two-year, four-year, public, and private institutions reported that learning community assessment is occurring. The story is somewhat brighter at institutions with the largest first-year enrollments, with 70% of respondents indicating assessment is occurring.

Table 7.3

Characteristics of First-Year Learning Communities by Institutional Control (n = 227)

	Institutional control		
	Public	**Private**	**Difference**
Characteristic	%	%	(%)
One of the courses in the learning community is a first-year seminar.	51.0	51.4	−0.4
Students are co-enrolled in two or more courses, but not all courses in the students' schedules.	50.3	45.9	4.4
Course content in the linked courses is connected by a common intellectual theme.	45.8	44.6	1.2
Course content is intentionally coordinated by the instructors of the linked courses.	38.6	39.2	−0.6
The learning community includes a residential component (i.e., a living–learning community).	37.9	37.8	0.1
Students in the learning community participate in a common set of theme-based experiences outside of the course, such as discussion groups, a speaker series, or other educational programs.	37.3	48.6	−11.3
One of the courses in the learning community is a developmental or remedial education course.	15.0	9.5	5.5
Students are co-enrolled in all courses in the students' schedules.	10.5	5.4	5.1
Other, please describe.	8.5	8.1	0.4

Note. The sum of the percentages is larger than 100% because respondents were asked to select all characteristics that apply.

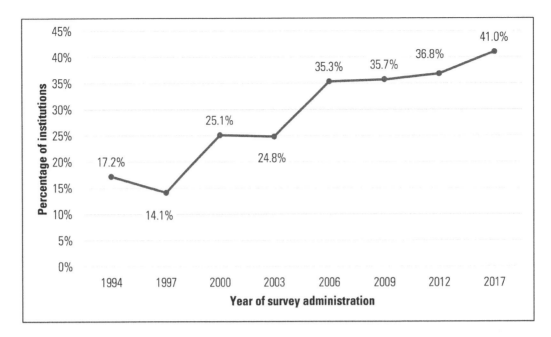

Figure 7.1. Percentage of institutions reporting first-year seminar is connected to a learning community. Figures for previous administrations of the National Survey of First-Year Seminars come from Padgett and Keup (2011), Tobolowsky and Associates (2008), and Young and Hopp (2014).

Table 7.4

Characteristics of First-Year Learning Communities by Number of Entering First-Year Students (*n* = 227)

	Number of entering first-year students				
	Less than 500	**501 – 1,000**	**1,001 – 2,000**	**2,001 – 4,000**	**More than 4,000**
Characteristic of the learning community	%	%	%	%	%
One of the courses in the learning community is a first-year seminar.	53.8	46.5	50.9	55.9	46.7
Students are co-enrolled in two or more courses, but not all courses in the students' schedules.	47.7	30.2	60.0	50.0	56.7
Course content is intentionally coordinated by the instructors of the linked courses.	46.2	27.9	49.1	41.2	16.7
Course content in the linked courses is connected by a common intellectual theme.	44.6	53.5	43.6	47.1	36.7
Students in the learning community participate in a common set of theme-based experiences outside of the course, such as discussion groups, a speaker series, or other educational programs.	40.0	32.6	40.0	50.0	46.7
The learning community includes a residential component (i.e., a living–learning community).	23.1	39.5	29.1	58.8	60.0
One of the courses in the learning community is a developmental or remedial education course.	9.2	20.9	14.5	8.8	13.3
Other, please describe.	9.2	9.3	7.3	2.9	13.3
Students are co-enrolled in all courses in the students' schedules.	7.7	7.0	3.6	17.6	13.3

Discussion and Conclusion

Chief among the interests of learning community advocates is building ever tighter links across curricular and cocurricular undergraduate experiences. Survey results reported here suggest that learning communities connected to first-year seminars are increasingly prime vehicles for coordinating the first college year. With the percentage of learning communities with embedded first-year seminars closing in on 50%, the timing is right to explore what more these programs can achieve together.

However, survey results also indicate several barriers to overcome as this combined HIP is considered. Learning communities at most institutions reach less than a quarter of first-year students, and a disappointingly low number of institutions assess their programs. In addition, the programs reported on here, as elsewhere, might not include campus initiatives aimed at integrating student learning that are not currently labeled as learning communities. Early alert, tied for first with learning communities as programs under consideration or under development, is another potential partnership that would benefit from greater clarity about learning communities.

As work on these communities continues, institutions would do well to prepare for the challenges Smith identified in 2001 that are still in effect. From the beginning, this work has involved recognizing student and faculty dissonance and discomfort when introduced to a different approach to teaching and learning, accounting for multiple student pathways into and through college, avoiding quick fixes to stay focused on true reform, and right-sizing expectations about what one first-year initiative, albeit an integrating one, can do. Overall, respondents to the 2017 NSFYE suggest that learning communities seem to be worth the sizeable lift they require.

References

Association of American Colleges and Universities. (2007). *College learning for the new global century: A report from the National Leadership Council for Liberal Education and America's Promise (LEAP).* Washington, DC: Author.

Barefoot, B. O., & Fidler, P. P. (1996). *The 1994 national survey of freshman seminar programs: Continuing innovations in the collegiate curriculum* (The Freshman Year Experience Monograph Series No. 20). Columbia, SC: University of South Carolina, National Resource Center for the Freshman Year Experience and Students in Transition.

Chism Schmidt, L., & Graziano, J. (Eds.). (2016). *Building synergy for high-impact educational initiatives: First-year seminars and learning communities.* Columbia, SC: University of South Carolina, National Resource Center for The First-Year Experience and Students in Transition.

Complete College America. (2018). *Promise with a purpose: College promise programs "built for completion."* Joint report of Complete College America, Promise Campaign, and Achieving the Dream. Available at https://completecollege.org/wp-content/uploads/2018/04/CCA015_PromisewithaPurpose_4.30.2018.pdf

Cross, K. P. (1998). Why learning communities? Why now? *About Campus, 3*(3), 4-11.

Dunlap, L., & Sult, L. (2013). Juggling and the art of the integrative assignment. *Learning Communities Research and Practice, 1*(1), Article 7. Retrieved from https://washingtoncenter.evergreen.edu/lcrpjournal/vol1/iss1/7

Engstrom, C. M., & Tinto, V. (2008). Learning better together: The impact of learning communities on the persistence of low-income students. *Opportunity Matters, 1,* 5-21.

Fink, J. E., & Inkelas, K. K. (2015). A history of learning communities within American higher education. *New Directions for Student Services, 149,* 5-15. San Francisco, CA: Jossey-Bass. doi:10.1002/ss.20113/

Fitzgerald, K., & Singmaster, H. (2017). Learning from the world: Best practices in CTE and lessons for the United States. *Techniques, 92*(3), 30-35.

Friedman, D. B., & Alexander, J. S. (2007). Investigating a first-year seminar as an anchor course in learning communities. *Journal of The First-Year Experience & Students in Transition, 19*(1), 63-74.

Gabelnick, F., MacGregor, J., Matthews, R., & Smith, B. (1990). Learning communities: Making connections among students, faculty and disciplines. *New Directions for Teaching and Learning, 41.* San Francisco, CA: Jossey-Bass.

Hegler, K. L. (2004). Assessing learning communities. *Assessment Update, 16*(6), 1-2, 7-8.

Henscheid, J. M. (Ed.). (2004). *Integrating the first-year experience: The role of first-year seminars in learning communities* (Monograph No. 39). Columbia, SC: University of South Carolina, National Resource Center for The First-Year Experience and Students in Transition.

Henscheid, J. M. (2015). It is time to count learning communities. *Learning Communities Research and Practice, 3*(2), Article 9. Retrieved from http://washingtoncenter.evergreen.edu/lcrpjournal/vol3/iss2/9

Henscheid, J. M., Skipper, T. L., & Young, D. G. (2016). National practices for combining first-year seminars and learning communities. In L. Chism Schmidt & J. Graziano (Eds.), *Building synergy for high-impact educational initiatives: First-year seminars and learning communities* (pp. 19-40). Columbia, SC: University of South Carolina, National Resource Center for The First-Year Experience and Students in Transition.

Huerta, J. C. (2017). The founding of the Learning Communities Association. *Learning Communities Research and Practice, 5*(1), Article 7. Retrieved from https://washingtoncenter.evergreen.edu/lcrpjournal/vol5/iss1/7

Huerta, J. C., & Bray, J. J. (2013). How do learning communities affect first-year Latino students? *Learning Communities Research and Practice, 1*(1), Article 5. Retrieved from https://washingtoncenter.evergreen.edu/lcrpjournal/vol1/iss1/5

Huerta, J. C., & Hansen, M. J. (2013). Learning community assessment 101—best practices. *Learning Communities Research and Practice, 1*(1), Article 15. Retrieved from https://washingtoncenter.evergreen.edu/lcrpjournal/vol1/iss1/15

Inkelas, K. K., Soldner, M., Longerbeam, S. D., & Leonard, J. B. (2008). Differences in student outcomes by types of living–learning programs: The development of an empirical typology. *Research in Higher Education, 49*, 495-512.

Koch, A. K. (2017). It's about the gateway courses: Defining and contextualizing the issue. *New Directions for Higher Education, 2017*(180), 11-17. doi:10.1002/he.20257

Kuh, G. D. (2008). *High-impact educational practices: What they are, who has access to them, and why they matter.* Washington, DC: Association of American Colleges and Universities.

Lardner, E., & Malnarich, G. (2008). A new era in learning-community work: Why the pedagogy of intentional integration matters. *Change, 40*(4), 30-37.

Lenning, O. T., & Ebbers, L. H. (1999). The powerful potential of learning communities: Improving education for the future. *ASHE-ERIC Higher Education Report, 26*(6), Washington, DC: The George Washington University, Graduate School of Education and Human Development.

Leskes, A., & Miller, R. (2006). *Purposeful pathways: Helping students achieve key learning outcomes.* Washington, DC: Association of American Colleges and Universities.

Love, A. G., & Tokuno, K. A. (1999). Learning community models. In J. H. Levine (Ed.), *Learning communities: New structures, new partnerships for learning* (Monograph No. 26, pp. 9-17). Columbia, SC: National Resource Center for The First-Year Experience and Students in Transition.

Maharajan, M. K., Rajiah, K., Khoo, S. P., Chellappan, D. K., De Alwis, R., Chui, H. C., & Lau, S. Y. (2017). Attitudes and readiness of students of healthcare professions towards interprofessional learning. *Plos ONE, 12*(1), 1-12. doi:10.1371/journal.pone.0168863

Malnarich, G., Pettitt, M. A., & Mino, J. J. (2014). Washington Center's online student survey validation study: Surfacing students' individual and collective understanding of their learning community experiences. *Learning Communities Research and Practice, 2*(1), Article 1. Retrieved from http://washingtoncenter.evergreen.edu/lcrpjournal/vol2/iss1/1

Padgett, R. D., & Keup, J. R. (2011). *2009 National Survey of First-Year Seminars: Ongoing efforts to support students in transition* (Research Report No. 2). Columbia, SC: University of South Carolina, National Resource Center for The First-Year Experience and Students in Transition.

Shapiro, N. S., & Levine, J. H. (1999). *Creating learning communities: A practical guide to winning support, organizing for change, and implementing programs.* San Francisco, CA: Jossey-Bass.

Smith, B. L. (2001). The challenge of learning communities as a growing national movement. *Peer Review, 3*(4), 4-8.

Smyth, T. J. (2016). Value added: Learning communities, experiential process and student engagement in lifelong learning in the culinary arts. *Learning Communities Research and Practice, 4*(2), Article 4. Retrieved from https://washingtoncenter.evergreen.edu/lcrpjournal/vol4/iss2/4

Snider, K. J. G., & Venable, A. M. (2000, May). *Assessing learning community effectiveness: A multi-campus approach.* Presented at the Association for Institutional Research Annual Meeting, Cincinnati, OH.

Tinto, V. (2003). *Learning better together: The impact of learning communities on student success* (Promoting Student Success in College, Higher Education Monograph Series, 1-8). Syracuse, NY: Syracuse University.

Tobolowsky, B. F. & Associates. (2008). *2006 National Survey of First-Year Seminars: Continuing innovations in the collegiate curriculum* (Monograph No. 51). Columbia, SC: University of South Carolina, National Resource Center for The First-Year Experience & Students in Transition.

Waiwaiole, E., & Elston, D. (2018). One question: Can you attend full-time, one time? *Change: The Magazine of Higher Learning, 49*(6), 23-31, doi:10.1080/00091383.2017.1398998

Weiss, M. J., Visher, M. G., Weissman, E., & Wathington, H. (2015). The impact of learning communities for students in developmental education: A synthesis of findings from randomized trials at six community colleges. *Educational Evaluation and Policy Analysis, 37*(4), 520-541. doi:10.3102/0162373714563307

West, R. E., & Williams, G. S. (2017). "I don't think that word means what you think it means": A proposed framework for defining learning communities. *Educational Technology Research and Development, 65,* 1569-1582. doi.org/10.1007/s11423-017-9535-0

Young, D. G., & Hopp, J. M. (2014). *2012-2013 National Survey of First-Year Seminars: Exploring high-impact practices in the first college year* (Research Report No. 4). Columbia, SC: University of South Carolina, National Resource Center for The First-Year Experience and Students in Transition.

Zhao, C., & Kuh, G. D. (2004). Adding value: Learning communities and student engagement. *Research in Higher Education, 45*(2), 115-138.

Chapter 8

New-Student Orientation

Buffy Stoll Turton
Miami University

Along with first-year seminars, new-student orientation programs are one of the oldest and most prolific practices for first-year student success. This chapter reviews data from the 2017 National Survey on the First-Year Experience (NSFYE) related to new-student orientation and discusses the implications of that data. Through the NSFYE data, I will explore the unique contributions of new-student orientation programs to first-year student transitions and how the orientation experience differs across institutional contexts.

New-student orientation functions to introduce new students to the university by teaching students—and often their family members—about the institution's culture and communities, norms and expectations, and processes and resources related to academic and student life. Orientation programs also commonly include academic advising and course registration, placement testing, student ID card distribution, and other tasks that facilitate new students' progression from newly admitted to fully matriculated members of their college or university community.

The 2017 NSFYE used the phrase *pre-term orientation* to describe orientation programs, which specifies a focus on those occurring before the start of a student's first semester at an institution. While the language behind pre-term orientation is discussed later in the chapter, I will generally use the more common terms *new-student orientation* or *orientation* to refer to this important component of the first-year experience (FYE).

Orientation: A Brief History

Though the history of orientation and transition programs can be traced back to the late 19th century, the term orientation in its earliest iterations referred to an amalgamation of experiences including first-year seminars, first-year lectures, and other elements we would now identify as parts of a broader FYE. The earliest program we would now describe as new-student orientation took the form of "Freshman Week," first offered in 1923 at the University of Maine. Through its "pre-college clinic" in 1949, Michigan State University offered a two- to four-day program several times throughout the summer so that attendance at each session could be kept small. The clinic included "testing, counseling, and some social and informational activities" (Drake, 1966, p. 10). This clinic was most similar to present-day summer orientation programs.

The pre-college clinic format grew in popularity through the 1960s and 1970s, echoing an evolution in the focus and function of orientation programs from university-centered instruction on institutional expectations—which could easily be accomplished en masse—to more student-centered approaches concerned with the experiences of individuals. As Drake (1966) described, this evolution situated orientation programs as "a means of communicating to students the essential goals of the college experience *and* of enhancing the students' clarification of their own goals" (p. 18, emphasis added). This shift toward understanding students' transition needs, including those identified by the students themselves, signaled the birth of modern approaches to new-student orientation.

As orientation programs became increasingly widespread, the role of orientation director emerged as a new area of responsibility on campuses. Orientation directors began to share ideas and best practices, first meeting as a group in 1948, and chartering the National Orientation Directors Association, or NODA (currently NODA: The Association for Orientation, Transition and Retention in Higher Education) in 1976 (NODA, n.d.). This cross-institutional communication coincided with an increased focus on assessing orientation programs and student transitions to college, which facilitated connections between orientation and student retention (Mack, 2010).

As they moved into the 1980s, orientation programs began to support students' social adjustment to college and build belonging by connecting students to the culture, values, and communities of their institutions. During this time, peer mentors were incorporated into orientation programming and more campus stakeholders, recognizing the importance of introducing students to their resources during this transition, also became involved (Mack, 2010). In addition, scholarly conversations about the purpose and outcomes of orientation became part of the emerging orientation profession, coinciding with the founding of the National Resource Center for The First-Year Experience and Students in Transition in 1986 (National Resource Center for The First-Year Experience and Students in Transition, n.d.).

That same year, Pascarella, Terenzini, and Wolfle (1986) published a foundational study of orientation as "an institutional intervention on student persistence/withdrawal behavior" (p. 156). The authors found that, even after controlling for background characteristics and initial institutional commitment, a two-day orientation program had a significant, positive impact on student persistence through the first year. The impact was realized indirectly through factors of social integration and increased institutional commitment. The researchers remarked that:

> The orientation experience impacted freshman persistence largely by facilitating a student's initial ability to cope with a new set of challenges in an unfamiliar environment. The process of applying this knowledge and developing initially successful integration into the social system of the institution was the factor which most directly influenced commitment to the institution and persistence. (p. 170)

These findings are important because they empirically established the contributions of orientation toward the broad institutional goal of retention. Additionally, the orientation study by Pascarella and colleagues (1986) focused on integrating new students actively into college and university life rather than simply instructing them on academic and conduct expectations.

In the 21st century, orientation programs have continued to evolve, adjusting to changes in student demographics, university structures, and influences such as technology and funding. Modern-day orientation programs must address the diverse transition needs of student populations including transfer, international, nontraditional, low-income, first-generation, LGBTQ+, and multicultural students; student veterans; students with disabilities; student athletes; commuter students; and family members. The work of facilitating new students' introductions to their college or university and supporting their academic and social transitions to higher education requires careful consideration of these students' diverse experiences and needs, as well as the institutional contexts to which they are transitioning.

Survey Data and Analysis

As data from the 2017 NSFYE show, today's orientation programs vary in form, focus, and content. Programs at four-year institutions look different from those at two-year schools; large and small institutions likewise take distinct approaches. These differences are often influenced by resources and institutional context; for instance, two-year programs focus less on developmental content, use peer leaders less frequently, and are more likely to be offered online than four-year programs. In addition, technologies such as online orientation boost potential for individualizing orientation and transition efforts, a factor that resonates with students of Generation Z (Seemiller & Grace, 2016) and satisfies institutional needs for maximizing efficiency of program delivery. Differences across program and institutional type are pertinent, though program design should be attuned to intersections between organizational resources and student needs and use purposeful and rigorous assessment to ensure program outcomes are being met.

In the first part of the NSFYE, respondents indicated which types of first-year success programs, initiatives, or courses were offered to their students; pre-term orientation was one of 22 available choices. Respondents who indicated offering pre-term orientation also responded to several questions about the characteristics of that program.

Institutions Offering New-Student Orientation Programs

Of 525 responding institutions, 396 (75.4%) reported offering orientation programs as a form of support for first-year students. As discussed in Chapter 2, orientation was the third-most common type of first-year success initiative, preceded by first-year academic advising (offered by 80.4% of institutions) and early-alert systems (79.0%). Four-year institutions were more likely (80.6%) to offer orientation programs than two-year colleges (58.5%; Figure 8.1).

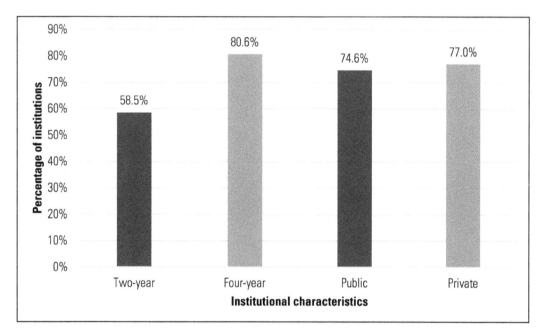

Figure 8.1. Institutions offering new-student orientation by institutional type and control (*n* = 396).

These data are somewhat surprising, as other recent surveys have indicated that new-student orientation is nearly ubiquitous across multiple types and sizes of institutions. In the NODA Databank 2017 survey, for example, 97.1% of respondents from two-year and four-year institutions in the United States and Canada (*n* = 237) indicated offering at least one type of orientation program (NODA, 2017). A 2012 study of four-year institutions conducted by the John N. Gardner Institute for Excellence in Undergraduate Education (JNGI) indicated that all respondents (*n* = 442) offered some type of pre-term orientation (Barefoot, Griffin, & Koch, 2012).

Several possible explanations for this unexpected result exist. As noted earlier, the NSFYE used the phrase pre-term orientation in its question-and-answer options. Though other surveys, particularly through JNGI (e.g., Barefoot et al., 2012), have successfully used the term, NSFYE respondents may have misunderstood the term or simply overlooked it on the list of 22 available choices. To gain more insight, the list of institutions that did not indicate having pre-term orientation was reviewed, and 25% of institutions on the list (32 of 128), including public, private, two-year, and four-year institutions of various sizes, were selected for further investigation. A search of these 32 institutions' websites found that 31 of them offered a summer, online, or welcome week orientation program for the upcoming year; in only one case was no mention of orientation found on the institution's website. This finding indicates the percentage of institutions offering orientation for new students is likely much higher than 75.4%. With this possible limitation in mind, the following analysis includes responses from those institutions that indicated offering pre-term orientation.

With regard to institutional size, those with fewer students were less likely to offer new-student orientation programs (Figure 8.2); the smallest institutions, with fewer than 500 first-year students, were least likely (68%) to offer it, and the largest institutions, with more than 4,000 new students, were most likely (93%). This relationship may reflect different institutional needs for structuring new-student transitions through coordinated efforts. Smaller schools may have more adaptable structures and common first-year experiences (e.g., courses, residence hall programs) through which to support new students' transitions.

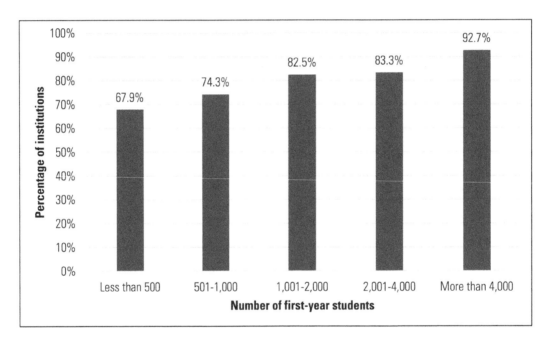

Figure 8.2. Institutions offering new-student orientation by institutional size (*n* = 396).

Participation in New-Student Orientation Programs

For each institutional type, it was most common for 91%-100% of incoming students to participate in orientation, though participation levels for two-year institutions were lower than those of other institutional types (see Figure 8.3). Only 26.9% of two-year institutions indicated participation at 91%-100%, while 67.6% of four-year institutions did so. It is important to acknowledge that two-year colleges are underrepresented in the NSFYE orientation data. Of those institutions that indicated offering pre-term orientation, only 18% are two-year, whereas two-year institutions make up about 35% of American colleges and universities (NCES, 2017). The survey responses in this chapter should be understood within that limitation, though comparisons to external sources throughout this chapter illustrate that NSFYE results are generally not atypical.

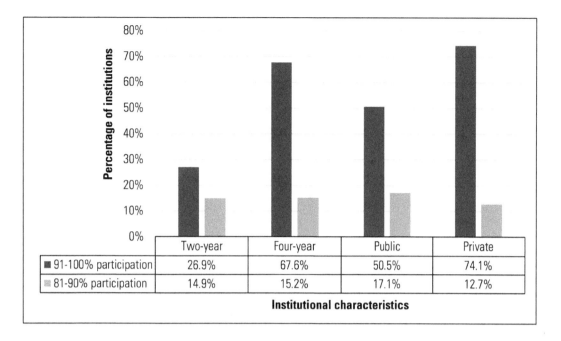

Figure 8.3. Participation rates of first-year students in new-student orientation, by institutional type and control (*n* = 376).

Low participation was uncommon across all institutional types and sizes; less than 10% of all respondents reported orientation participation at 50% or less. Of those, however, two-year institutions reported the lowest rates; 36% of two-year institutions reported participation rates lower than 50%, while 8.2% of other institutional types reported such low participation rates.

The NSFYE finding that two-year students participate in orientation at lower rates is consistent with other national surveys, including the Community College Survey of Student Engagement (CCSSE). In the 2011 CCSSE survey, 58% of respondents reported participating in an orientation program (Center for Community College Student Engagement, 2012), compared with 90% participation as reported by respondents to the 2007-2008 NODA Databank.

Participation in orientation for two-year institutions may be lower for several reasons. First, these institutions are much less likely to require participation in orientation; not requiring students to participate in orientation is associated with lower program attendance (see Figures 8.4 and 8.6). Orientation programs at two-year institutions also encounter unique challenges in meeting the diverse transition needs of their students who are more likely to be older than traditional college age, enroll part-time, be first-generation, and face competing commitments including employment and caring for dependents (Cuevas & Timmerman, 2014). Thus, students may lack availability to participate in orientation and may see it as less important than their other commitments.

In addition, orientation programs at two-year institutions report drastically lower funding than their four-year counterparts. In the 2017 NODA Databank report (NODA, 2017), two-year institutions (*n* = 23) reported an average operating budget of $31,523 for their orientation programs—less than 10% of that reported by four-year institutions (*n* = 221, average budget $337,150). Like the NSFYE, the Databank includes far fewer responses from two-year institutions. Even so, these figures indicate two-year institutions face formidable challenges in creating a culture of attendance at orientation without the resources and program infrastructure to serve the complex needs of their new students.

Private institutions were more likely to report the highest levels of orientation participation (91%-100%) than public institutions (74.1% vs. 50.5%). Larger universities indicated higher participation than smaller institutions; 71.4% of those with first-year classes of more than 4,000 students reported participation at 91%-100%, while this was true for 63.8% of institutions with classes smaller than 500 new students.

For all students and institutional types, new-student orientation provides a unique opportunity to learn about college and university life, build connections to institutional resources, and consider their own needs and goals. Students who do not participate in orientation risk being at a disadvantage in their academic and social transition to college, and may be less likely to be retained (Hossler, Ziskin, & Gross, 2009; Pascarella et al., 1986; Rode, 2000). In order to best support the transitions of new students and invest in their success, institutions of all types should aim to maximize student participation in orientation.

Achieving 100% participation can be challenging, particularly if the program is not required for all new students, as some may consider orientation inconvenient or unnecessary. Participation rates are likely influenced by a requirement to attend; the rates observed here clearly reflect the rates of institutions in this survey that require all first-year students to participate in orientation (Figure 8.4). In their study of institutional retention practices for the Lumina Foundation and the College Board, Hossler and colleagues (2009) observed a relationship between orientation participation and requirements to attend, which they linked to student retention. They found that "campuses with lower retention rates had lower participation rates in orientation programs and were less likely to have mandatory orientation policies" (p. 8). These observations further underscore the importance of orientation as an important program for student success.

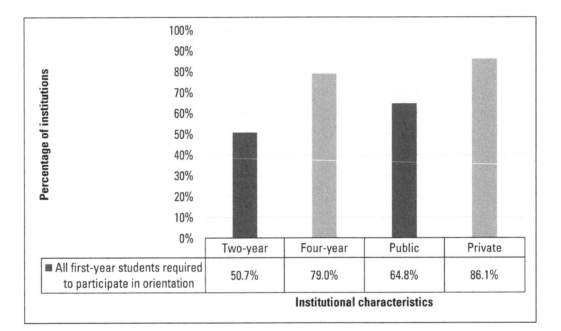

Figure 8.4. Percentage of institutions requiring all first-year students to participate in new-student orientation, by institutional type and control (*n* = 376).

Required Attendance

About three quarters of all responding institutions (73.9%) require all first-year students to participate in new-student orientation. Four-year institutions were much more likely to require orientation (79.0%) than two-year institutions (50.7%; Figure 8.4). Additionally, private schools were more likely to require attendance at orientation (86.1%) than publics (64.8%), and the smallest schools (less than 500 new students) were more likely (80.4%) to do so than the largest schools (more than 4,000 students; 65.7%; Figure 8.5). Also, 10.6% of responding institutions do not require any students to attend orientation; this includes 17.9% of two-year institutions and 9.1% of four-year institutions.

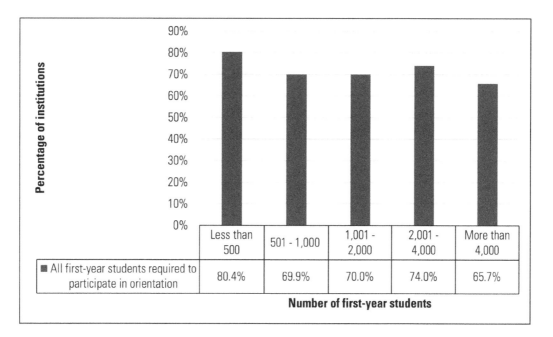

Figure 8.5. Percentage of institutions requiring all first-year students to participate in new-student orientation, by institutional size (*n* = 376).

These data also indicate that requiring participation in orientation may be on the upswing. In the 2007-2008 NODA Databank Survey of U.S. and Canadian institutions, 66% of respondents said they required first-year students to attend (Mann, Andrews, & Rodenburg, 2010), compared with 74.0% of institutions in the 2017 NSFYE.

Very few institutions—fewer than 4%—required attendance of select student populations, such as those eligible for federal or state equal opportunity programs (e.g., TRIO, Upward Bound), first-generation students, honors students, or international students. No responding institutions indicated a requirement for transfer students to participate in orientation programs, although more than 40% of 2007-2008 Databank respondents did so. This dramatic difference is surprising; while it is appropriate to recognize the transition needs of transfer students as distinct from first-year students, "it is important not to fall prey to the erroneous assumption that students with previous college experience require less direction, services, or attention" (Jacobs & Marling, 2014, p. 23).

It is possible that NSFYE survey respondents misunderstood this question, particularly if they intended to include transfer students with "all first-year students" in the answer choice. The NSFYE question asked, "Which students, by category, are required to participate in pre-term orientation?" It included all first-year students and transfer students as separate choices among 20 categories, but those categories may not be distinct on all campuses.

It is also interesting that very few schools (3.5%) reported requiring international students to participate in orientation, particularly since this group faces some of the most challenging transitions to American colleges and universities. It is possible that institutions indicating all students were required to attend included international students in that consideration. However, international students, like transfer students, have distinct transition needs that may not be met in a traditional first-year orientation for domestic students.

As new students' characteristics and transition needs continue to diversify, institutions of all types and sizes should carefully consider how to engage students—particularly special populations—in new-student orientation programs. Likewise, future administrations of the NSFYE should seek to clarify this area of inquiry. While the question's wording seems clear, perhaps the list of options could be reduced to ease potential confusion for respondents. Alternatively, this question could be broken into two parts—one that lists only first-year and transfer students as options, and another focusing on a select list of other special populations.

Connections Between Required and Actual Orientation Attendance

Because student attendance at orientation is key, it is helpful to consider insights from NSFYE data related to higher rates of orientation attendance. Survey results indicate these rates are linked to attendance requirements (Figure 8.6). The number of institutions reporting 81%-100% orientation attendance corresponds with the percentage of schools indicating a requirement to participate, regardless of the type of institution. The notable exception is large institutions (4,000+ entering students), where attendance at orientation exceeds requirements to do so. This relationship indicates that required attendance policies are likely effective across varying programs, types, and sizes of institutions.

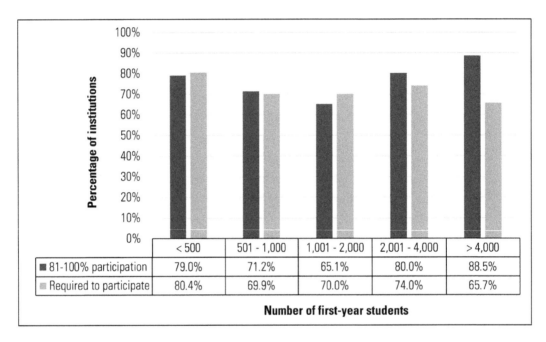

	< 500	501 - 1,000	1,001 - 2,000	2,001 - 4,000	> 4,000
■ 81-100% participation	79.0%	71.2%	65.1%	80.0%	88.5%
▦ Required to participate	80.4%	69.9%	70.0%	74.0%	65.7%

Number of first-year students

Figure 8.6. Relationship between required and actual orientation attendance by institutional size (*n* = 376).

Program Type

The survey asked institutions about the forms of new-student orientation offered on their campuses. The most common form was *on-campus pre-term activities*, offered by 85.4% of responding institutions (Figure 8.7). Outdoor adventure or wilderness experiences were the least common form, though it is notable that institutions with more than 4,000 new students were twice as likely as other institutions to use this model. In this section, I will focus the discussion on two types of orientation programs: on-campus pre-term activities and online orientation.

On-campus pre-term activities. This term in the NSFYE survey is somewhat unclear; the phrase could refer to several forms of transition experiences, including summer orientation, early arrival programs (e.g., focused on involvement/leadership), convocation, and summer bridge programs. It is particularly unclear how respondents distinguished orientation occurring in the days prior to fall semester (often referred to as a welcome week) from welcome week, which was included as a separate option for this question. This distinction is valuable, as these program experiences and outcomes differ significantly. Summer orientation typically engages smaller numbers of students over multiple sessions, while welcome week usually includes all new students and is generally less structured with fewer participation requirements. Just over half of respondents (52.7%) indicated offering both

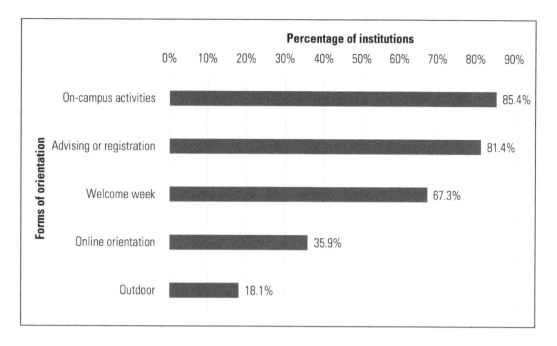

Figure 8.7. Forms of new-student orientation for all responding institutions (*n* = 376).

on-campus pre-term activities and welcome week. A clearer definition of on-campus pre-term activities would give more insight into these data.

Online orientation. Online orientation is the most recently developed orientation format, which may explain why we see the most variation across types of institutions that feature this program. Just over one third of responding institutions (36%) reported offering online orientation. For nearly all institutional types and sizes, this form of orientation was less common than on-campus activities, pre-term advising/registration, and welcome week (for two-year institutions, online orientation was more common than welcome week). Perhaps not surprisingly, two-year institutions were twice as likely as four-year institutions to use online orientation (59.7% vs. 30.7%; Figure 8.8). Public institutions were more than twice as likely as privates (46.3% vs. 20.9%) to offer online orientation, and larger institutions did so more frequently than smaller schools.

Online orientation programs can be a cost-effective approach for large populations of students, particularly when facilities or funding may not support an in-person program. Many students also find these online programs efficient, as they need not spend time and money traveling to an in-person orientation. Online formats may be especially useful to orient particular populations of students (e.g., transfers, distance learners) or to supplement an in-person program. The 2017 NODA Databank survey indicated online orientation for transfer students (offered by 28.2% of respondents) was more popular than for first-year students (24.1%). These numbers are significant increases from the 2007-2008 NODA Databank survey, in which 14.2% of respondents offered online orientation for transfer students, and 9.6% for first-year students. Data from the NSFYE indicated greater prevalence of online orientation programs compared with earlier estimates such as those in the NODA Databank. Based on the increasing percentage of institutions that report offering online orientation across the various data collection efforts, future administrations of the survey are likely to continue tracking this trend.

As more institutions consider offering online orientation, they should carefully consider how this format meets students' transition needs and desired program outcomes. Future versions of the NSFYE should also distinguish between orientation programs for online and in-person degree programs.

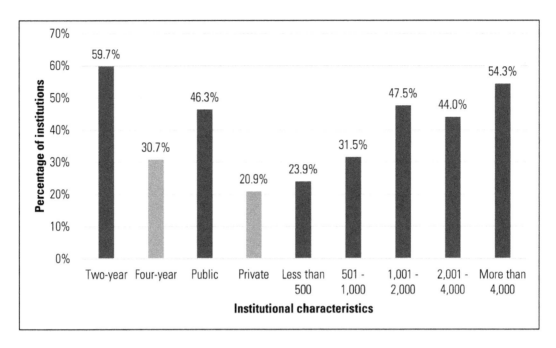

Figure 8.8. Institutions offering online orientation by institutional type and size (*n* = 376).

Orientation Activities

Survey respondents indicated which of 14 possible activities were included as part of their orientation program. The data illustrate convergence across all institutional types for the four most common orientation activities (Figure 8.9): introducing students to campus resources and services (94.9%), introducing students to campus facilities (87.8%), academic advising (86.2%), and course registration (80.9%).

By far, the least common program element for all institutional types was common readings. At least half of responding institutions included each of the other elements, while only 21.0% of campuses reported using a common-reading program. This figure raises questions about the extent to which common-reading programs are embedded in new-student orientation. Nearly twice as many respondents to a JNGI survey of retention initiatives at four-year institutions (43.0%; Barefoot et al., 2012) indicated including a common-reading program in orientation compared to 24.3% of four-year respondents on the 2017 NSFYE. A difference of a similar magnitude was present when comparing responses from two-year institutions in a separate JNGI study (Koch, Griffin, & Barefoot, 2014) to those on the 2017 NSFYE (8.0% and 4.5%, respectively). It is unclear whether these differences represent a shift away from embedding common-reading programs within new-student orientation or simply underlying differences in the samples across the three surveys. Regardless, the discussion of common readings in Chapter 4 suggests the prevalence of these initiatives may be holding steady within larger FYE efforts.

Other than the four most common program activities, components of new-student orientation for two- and four-year institutions look very different. Four-year institutions commonly included community-building activities, as well as sessions for family members, discussions on personal issues and challenges, health and wellness, and diversity and social justice. Figure 8.10 illustrates these differences in program components by institutional type.

Orientation programs at two-year institutions were likely shorter, more focused on academic elements, and less concerned with community building and topics related to student development. This may be because discussions about personal challenges may be difficult to create in a developmentally appropriate way for the varied contexts and experiences of students at two-year institutions. Nevertheless, new students' experiences outside the classroom are an important part of their transition and should be considered a priority relating to efforts to integrate new students to the campus community.

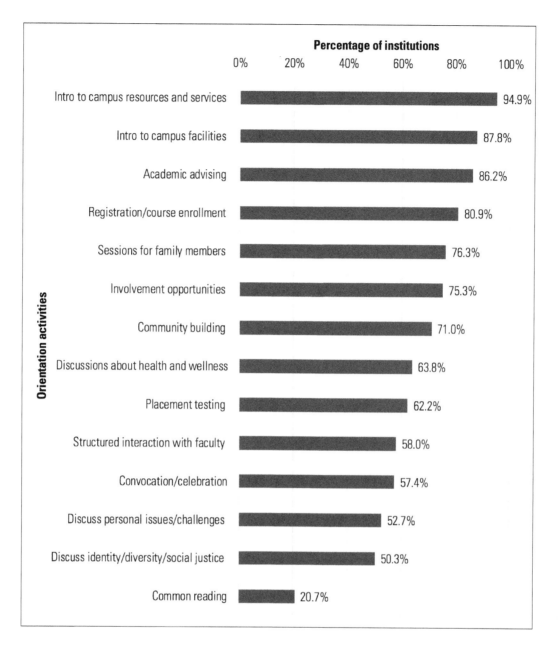

Figure 8.9. Orientation activities for all responding institutions (*n* = 376).

Considering the positive impact of new students' interactions with faculty members (Pascarella et al., 1986), orientation programs at all institutional types would benefit from including more faculty interaction in orientation. Faculty interaction was 10th most common on the list of 14 orientation activities; 58.0% of respondents reported structured faculty interaction as part of their orientation program. Private institutions and those with small first-year classes (less than 500) most frequently included faculty (70.3% and 68.1%, respectively), perhaps because these campuses are tighter-knit or take an "all hands on deck" approach to orientation. Large institutions (4,000+ students) and two-year schools were least likely to include faculty in orientation (34.3% and 29.9%, respectively). Though faculty availability during orientation season may pose a challenge, their involvement in socializing new students to the college or university should be considered a key component. Peer leaders are also key players in the orientation experience; though the NFSYE asks about roles of student leaders at orientation, future versions of the survey instrument should add "structured interactions with peer leaders" to this list of orientation activities as well.

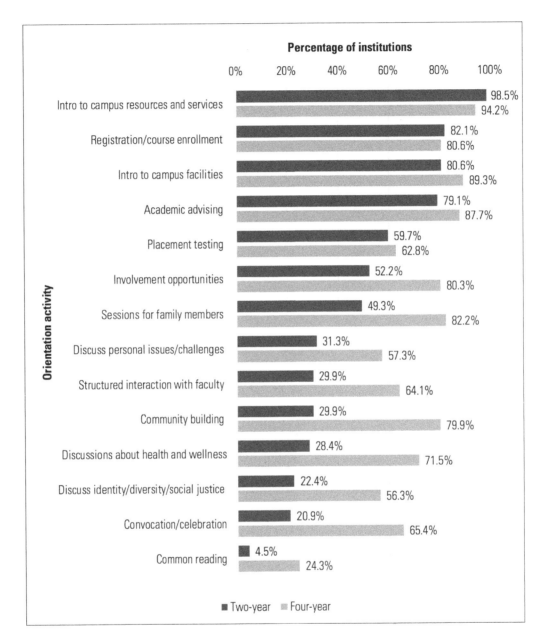

Figure 8.10. Orientation activities by institutional type (*n* = 376).

Undergraduate Students' Role

Undergraduate student leaders are a common presence at orientation, with more than 90% of institutions reporting their assistance with orientation in some way. Peer leader involvement in orientation programs can increase students' connections to one another and to the institution. In fact, numerous studies have illustrated the positive impact of peer leaders in higher education (Cuseo, 2010; Pascarella & Terenzini, 1991; Shook & Keup, 2012; Tinto, 1993).

The most frequent contributions made by undergraduate students were leading orientation activities (73.6%) and serving as peer mentors (73.3%). Undergraduate students were least likely to plan orientation logistics (35.7%). Two-year institutions were least likely to use undergraduate students in any capacity; 28.8% of respondents in this group indicated that undergraduate students do not assist with orientation, compared with 5.5% of four-year institutions. Additionally, two-year institutions were half as likely to use undergraduate students in leading activities or peer mentoring at orientation. Figure 8.11 illustrates the differences in how undergraduate students contribute to orientation programs at two- and four-year institutions. Differences were also seen in frequency of undergraduate student participation between public and private institutions. A higher percentage of private institutions indicated using undergraduate students in nearly every category, with the exception of delivering sessions (Figure 8.12).

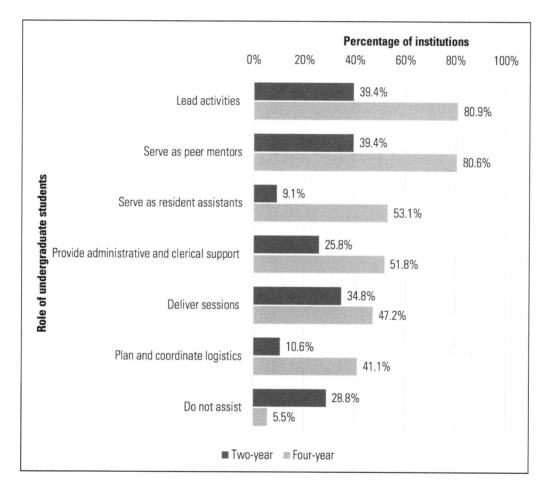

Figure 8.11. Roles of undergraduate students in orientation by institutional type (*n* = 375).

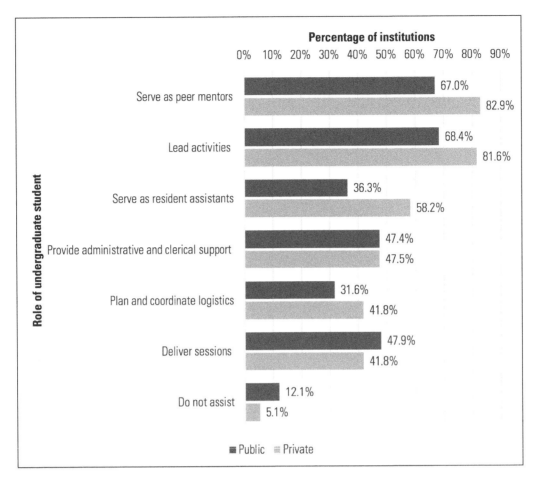

Figure 8.12. Undergraduate student contributions to orientation by institutional control (*n* = 375).

Administrative Home of Orientation Programs

More than half of responding institutions (57.3%) indicated their orientation program was housed in a student affairs central office. The second-most common response was "Other" (17.9%), of which the most common answer was offices reporting to student affairs. Several "other" answers also included dual reporting lines for orientation.

Though student affairs remains the most common home for orientation programs, these data indicate the administrative home for orientation is increasingly found in units elsewhere on campus. The 2007-2008 NODA Databank survey indicated that 73.5% of institutions housed orientation within student affairs. This percentage decreased to 60% in the 2017 Databank survey, a figure similar to NSFYE data (57.3%). The NSFYE and 2017 NODA Databank figures are similar on the number of institutions housing orientation in academic affairs (12.3% and 11%, respectively) and enrollment management (14.7% and 12%, respectively). The important takeaway here is not necessarily the unit of control, but the shift toward more multilateral leadership of orientation programs. The purpose and leadership of orientation is broadening in scope as the job of fostering new students' academic and social transitions to college becomes more complex.

Return on Investment

Survey respondents were asked to consider cost (staff time and resources) as well as educational benefits in gauging the return on investment (value) of their campus's approach to new-student orientation. Most institutions consider their orientation programs worthwhile; just over half (51.4%) rated the return on investment for their campus's pre-orientation at least 6 out of 7 on a 7-point Likert scale, though this still leaves significant room for growth. Fewer than 10% of respondents (8.8%) rated their campus's program at 3 or lower, and 6.4% felt they were unable to judge. Larger institutions rated their programs higher than average (Figure 8.13). Those with incoming classes of 2,001-4,000 students and 4,000+ students graded their programs highly for their return on investment at rates of 62.0% and 57.1%, respectively, and were most likely to rate their programs a 7, the highest perceived return on investment.

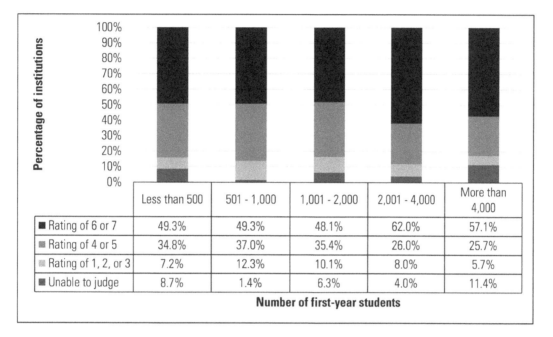

	Less than 500	501 - 1,000	1,001 - 2,000	2,001 - 4,000	More than 4,000
■ Rating of 6 or 7	49.3%	49.3%	48.1%	62.0%	57.1%
■ Rating of 4 or 5	34.8%	37.0%	35.4%	26.0%	25.7%
▨ Rating of 1, 2, or 3	7.2%	12.3%	10.1%	8.0%	5.7%
■ Unable to judge	8.7%	1.4%	6.3%	4.0%	11.4%

Number of first-year students

Figure 8.13. Perceived value of new-student orientation program by institutional size; rating of 1 is lowest, and 7 is highest (*n* = 375).

These data indicate campus leaders are generally supportive of their campus orientation programs, but may be thinking critically about the resources dedicated to them and the educational benefits that new students derive. Thus, we are reminded of the importance of examining the value of orientation—not only to satisfy others' curiosities but also to ensure that programs support and challenge today's diverse and dynamic student body in the most effective ways.

Program Assessment

Survey respondents were asked whether their orientation program had been formally assessed or evaluated since Fall 2013. Just over half (54.1%) of respondents indicated the program had been assessed in that time period, but fewer than one third (28.5%) reported no assessment efforts, and 17.3% were unsure. Of those institutions conducting orientation assessment, a survey instrument was by far the most common approach, used by 73.1% of respondents. Some campuses (36.3%) assessed programs by analyzing institutional data (e.g., GPA, retention rates, graduation), while others used direct assessment of learning outcomes (36.3%) and focus groups with orientation staff (34.3%) or students (28.9%). Program review, likely the most comprehensive assessment approach, was used by 31.8% of respondents (Figure 8.14). Major differences were not observed between institutional types.

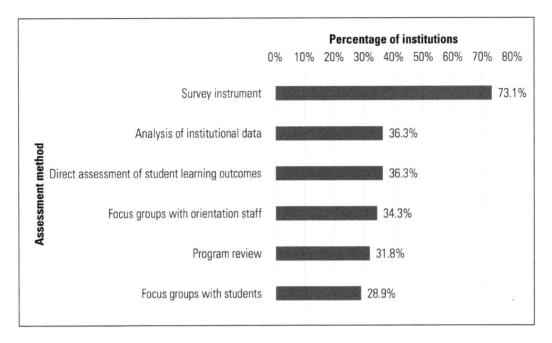

Figure 8.14. Most common assessment methods for new-student orientation (*n* = 201).

Program Outcomes

From a list of 27 common choices, respondents selected each outcome measured by their assessment process. Across all institutional types, student satisfaction was by far the most common outcome measured (77.1%; Figure 8.15). This differs from data gathered in a similar question from the 2017 NODA Databank survey in which 44% of respondents indicated measuring student satisfaction outcomes for first-year student orientation, 27% reported assessing learning outcomes, and 24% conducted needs assessments (NODA, 2017). The second-most commonly measured outcome for NSFYE was students' connection with the institution or campus (67.7%), followed by knowledge of institution or campus resources and services (60.2%). All other outcomes—including those related to academic adjustment, academic planning, social adjustment, health/wellness, diversity/intercultural competence, and career exploration—were measured by fewer than 40% of respondents.

Convergence across the most frequently measured outcomes reflects similarities across institutional types in the most common orientation activities: introduction to campus resources and services and introduction to campus facilities (see Figure 8.9). However, academic advising and course registration, included in about 80% of orientation programs, are less commonly measured. Outcomes related to academic orientation activities included introduction to college-level expectations (measured by 38.8% of institutions); academic planning/major exploration (30.3%); student–faculty interaction (27.4%); and introduction to a major, discipline, or career path (measured by 19.9%). This difference in academic activities and assessment of academic outcomes illustrates a gap in orientation assessment data related to students' academic transitions. Perhaps institutions measure academic outcomes using institutional data (e.g., GPA, retention) or student satisfaction, but these measures alone are likely insufficient to indicate orientation's impact on student academic transitions. Institutions of all types must also recognize the nonacademic transition experiences of first-year students; low rates of measuring outcomes related to personal exploration/development, health and wellness, and intercultural competence or diversity indicate missed opportunities or need for increased focus in these areas.

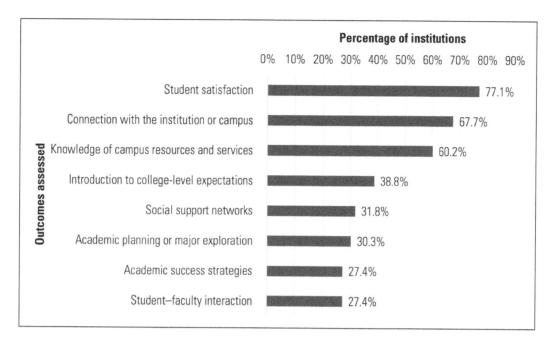

Figure 8.15. Most commonly measured orientation outcomes (*n* = 201).

Discussion and Implications

New-student orientation programs are a crucial step in the college transition for this population and their families. The data reviewed in this chapter signal several important implications for future practice and research in orientation, transition, and retention.

Lack of Common Language

First, a lack of consistent terminology makes it difficult to describe, discuss, and analyze orientation programs and activities. In the 1950s, orientations at U.S. colleges and universities—and the students they served—looked much the same. Over the past half-century, however, both college students and orientation programs have become more heterogeneous. Approaches to supporting student transitions have shifted to reflect student needs and institutional contexts, but the language has not kept up. The apparent misunderstanding of the survey term *pre-term orientation* by institutions in this study signals the lack of clarity for terminology around orientation programs. Whether the subject is pre-term orientation, pre-term advising, welcome week (considered orientation or not), summer orientation, or extended orientation, definitions and boundaries of these terms are not commonly understood, making the data much less reliable. Large-scale research is needed to review the full breadth of current models, analyze existing (and potentially develop new) terminology, and clarify directions for future scholarship and practice. Such an endeavor would require broad buy-in from practitioners and scholars alike and must allow for continued growth and diversification of new ideas and programs.

Future administrations of the NSFYE could contribute to clarity of these terms by defining orientation program types (e.g., pre-term orientation, welcome week, on-campus programs). The question asking respondents whether they offered pre-term orientation, for example, listed 22 answer options, more than half of which averaged responses below 50%; this could point to institutions finding the question too tedious for respondents to accurately review. Shortening the number of options could lead to more accurate results. Future administrations could also add new questions—while engaging orientation scholars and practitioners in shaping question-and-answer options—to learn more about characteristics of orientation programs (e.g., program length, program content, topics). These questions could help with data collection and analysis that would better interface with existing data-gathering efforts.

Mandatory Orientation Attendance

Across numerous important differences in orientation programs and practice, one theme is consistent: Orientation is effective at introducing new students to the postsecondary context and facilitating their academic and social transition to college and university life. However, students will not benefit from orientation if they do not participate. Requiring attendance is likely to broaden the reach and impact of orientation programs, which can positively impact student learning, satisfaction, and ultimately, persistence (Hossler et al., 2009; Pascarella et al., 1986; Tinto, 1993). Data from the NSFYE show that requiring students to attend orientation correlates with high levels of attendance (Figure 8.4) across nearly all institutional types and sizes.

Requiring participation should be carefully considered in order to make programs and resources accessible to all students (e.g., those with work schedules, those who are admitted later on a rolling timeline). This is especially important for two-year institutions, which historically are much less likely to require students to attend orientation than four-year schools and which, consequently, have much lower attendance. Sandoval-Lucero, Antony, and Hepworth (2017) remark that "community colleges have often failed to make the connection between orientation and student retention, success, and graduation" (p. 1641). Rather than seeing orientation as an inconvenience or barrier for two-year students, Sandoval-Lucero et al. (2017) say the imperative to serve the diverse needs of this population "builds the case for mandatory programs, to compel students who are balancing work, family, and school to participate in orientation that sets the tone for their success" (p. 1642). Two-year institutions that have recently mandated orientation programs report increased GPAs and boosts in retention rates measuring well into double digits (Boyd, Largent, & Rondeau, 2008; Center for Community College Student Engagement, 2012; Cuevas & Timmerman, 2014; Sandoval-Lucero et al., 2017). These results situate orientation as a particularly promising practice for two-year institutions and a key topic for future research and assessment.

When requiring participation in orientation programs, students' needs within the postsecondary context should be carefully considered; multiple or alternative forms of orientation or transition programs (e.g., online orientation, extended orientation) may be effective. Required programs also face increased scrutiny to deliver high-quality content and results. Thus, it is especially critical that these programs gain broad support from campuswide stakeholders and presenters, include interactions with faculty as well as peers and staff, facilitate both academic and social transitions, and evaluate their success based on stated goals (Council for the Advancement of Standards, 2012).

Rigorous, Purposeful Assessment

One of the most surprising NSFYE findings on orientation was that nearly half of all respondents reported that no program assessment had been conducted since Fall 2013. This figure is striking, particularly in the current age of higher education scrutiny. It is also pertinent to note that 17.3% of respondents did not know whether their orientation programs had been evaluated, suggesting that existing assessment data are not well-communicated on those campuses.

Assessment for all orientation programs is vital for success. As Schwartz and Wiese (2010) assert, "for the orientation professional, the ability to answer the questions of external and internal constituents with rigorous assessment and evaluation data is essential, providing a strong foundation for a better orientation program" (p. 218). Additionally, the Council for the Advancement of Standards (CAS; 2012) states that rigorous assessment for orientation must provide "evidence of program impact on the achievement of student learning and development outcomes" (p. 2).

Demands for accountability—from institutional leadership, new students and families, and accrediting bodies—are likely to grow, driven by the rising cost of higher education, expectations to demonstrate student learning, and the increasingly critical role of transition and retention initiatives (Mayhew, Vanderlinden,

& Kim, 2010; Schwartz & Wiese, 2010). Rigorous assessment must go beyond student satisfaction measures to evaluate student learning and behavioral outcomes and program impact, including ways that various student populations (e.g., transfer students, students of color) experience orientation differently (Mayhew et al., 2010). Institutional metrics (e.g., student matriculation after orientation, student persistence rates) as well as measures of student involvement, faculty interaction, and even first-year GPA could also be integrated into an orientation assessment plan that effectively illustrates the value of facilitating student transitions in a particular campus context. Benchmarking data from similar institutions may also be useful, and CAS outlines program standards and common expectations for orientation initiatives. To conduct effective and rigorous program assessment, staff who design and direct orientation may need additional training. In these cases, the NODA Core Competencies (NODA, 2016) are a valuable resource, providing "a common framework and foundation of skills" for orientation professionals in 12 foundational areas of practice, including research, assessment, and evaluation (NODA, 2016, p. 4).

Conclusion

Data from surveys such as the NSFYE aid both practitioners and scholars in understanding orientation initiatives on campuses nationwide and identifying areas of excellence and opportunity. Data analyzed here indicate that new-student orientation programs are widespread, well-valued, and should invest future efforts in conducting more rigorous assessment of clearly identified outcomes. Institutions also should consider requiring attendance at orientation programs, attending to the transition needs of various populations of new students (e.g., transfer, international, first-generation, non-traditional), and crafting orientation experiences to meet those needs. While collaboration and integration with other FYE programs will aid in reaching these goals, the unique timing, structure, and focus of orientation situates this particular FYE element to make a distinct impact on new-student experiences and an important contribution to first-year student success.

References

Barefoot, B. O., Griffin, B. Q., & Koch, A. K. (2012). *Enhancing student success and retention throughout undergraduate education: A national survey*. Brevard, NC: The John N. Gardner Institute for Excellence in Undergraduate Education. Retrieved from https://static1.squarespace.com/static/59b0c486d2b857fc86d09aee/t/59bad-33412abd988ad84d697/1505415990531/JNGInational_survey_web.pdf

Boyd, B., Largent, L., & Rondeau, S. (2008). *Community college orientation basics: How to structure a new student orientation program*. NACADA Clearinghouse of Academic Advising Resources. Retrieved from http://www.nacada.ksu.edu/tabid/3318/articleType/ArticleView/articleId/90/article.aspx

Center for Community College Student Engagement. (2012). *A matter of degrees: Promising practices for community college student success—a first look*. Austin, TX: The University of Texas at Austin, Community College Leadership Program.

Council for the Advancement of Standards in Higher Education (CAS). (2012). *CAS professional standards for higher education* (8th ed.). Washington, DC: Author.

Cuevas, C. J., & Timmerman, C. (2014). Orientation programs on the two-year campus (pp. 47-57). In B. Thibodeau (Ed.), *Orientation planning manual*. Minneapolis, MN: NODA: Association for Orientation, Transition, and Retention in Higher Education.

Cuseo, J. (2010). Peer power: Empirical evidence for the positive impact of peer interaction, support, and leadership. *E-Source for College Transitions, 7*(4), 4-6.

Drake, R. (1966). *Review of the literature for freshman orientation practices in the United States*. Fort Collins, CO: Colorado State University.

Grasgreen, A. (2014, March 26). Common reading canned. *Inside Higher Ed*. Retrieved from https://www.insidehighered.com/news/2014/03/26/after-abrupt-cut-purdue-faculty-call-restoration-common-reading-program

Hossler, D., Ziskin, M., & Gross, J. P. K. (2009). Getting serious about institutional performance in student retention: Research-based lessons on effective policies and practices. *About Campus, 13*(6), 2-11.

Jacobs, B. C., & Marling, J. L. (2014). The swirling, whirling world of transfer orientation: Meeting the needs of a dynamic student population. In B. Thibodeau (Ed.), *Orientation planning manual*. Minneapolis, MN: NODA: Association for Orientation, Transition, and Retention in Higher Education.

Koch, S. S., Griffin, B. Q., & Barefoot, B. O. (2014). *National survey of student success initiatives at two-year colleges*. Brevard, NC: The John N. Gardner Institute for Excellence in Undergraduate Education. Retrieved from https://static1. squarespace.com/static/59b0c486d2b857fc86d09aee/t/59bad37251a584437bccc737/1505416079925/ National-2-yr-Survey-Booklet_webversion.pdf

Mack, C. E. (2010). A brief overview of the orientation, transition and retention field. In J. A. Ward-Roof (Ed.), *Designing successful transitions: A guide for orienting students to college* (Monograph No. 13, 3rd ed., pp. 3-10). Columbia, SC: University of South Carolina, National Resource Center for the First-Year Experience and Students in Transition.

Mann, A., Andrews, C., & Rodenburg, N. (2010). Administration of a comprehensive orientation program. In J. A. Ward-Roof (Ed.), *Designing successful transitions: A guide for orienting students to college* (Monograph No. 13, 3rd ed., pp. 43-59). Columbia, SC: University of South Carolina, National Resource Center for The First-Year Experience and Students in Transition.

Mayhew, M. J., Vanderlinden, K., & Kim, E. K. (2010). A multi-level assessment of the impact of orientation programs on student learning. *Research in Higher Education, 51*(4), 320-345.

National Center for Education Statistics (NCES). (2017, November). *Number of degree-granting postsecondary institutions and enrollment in these institutions, by enrollment size, control, and classification of institution: Fall 2016*. Retrieved from https://nces.ed.gov/programs/digest/d17/tables/dt17_317.40.asp

National Resource Center for The First-Year Experience and Students in Transition. (n.d.). *About us*. Retrieved from https://sc.edu/about/offices_and_divisions/national_resource_center/about/index.php

NODA: The Association for Orientation, Transition, and Retention in Higher Education. (n.d.). *Mission*. Retrieved from https://www.nodaweb.org/page/Mission

NODA: The Association for Orientation, Transition, and Retention in Higher Education. (2016, August 3). *The NODA core competencies*. Retrieved from https://www.nodaweb.org/page/core_competencies

NODA: The Association for Orientation, Transition, and Retention in Higher Education. (2017, April 21). *NODA databank survey 2017*. Retrieved from https://www.nodaweb.org/page/Databank

Pascarella, E. T., & Terenzini, P. T. (1991). *How college affects students: Findings and insights from twenty years of research*. San Francisco, CA: Jossey-Bass.

Pascarella, E. T., Terenzini, P. T., & Wolfle, L. M. (1986). Orientation to college and freshman year persistence/ withdrawal decisions. *Journal of Higher Education, 57*(2), 155-175.

Rode, D. (2000). The role of orientation in institutional retention. In M. J. Fabich (Ed.), *Orientation planning manual*. Pullman, WA: NODA.

Sandoval-Lucero, E., Antony, K., & Hepworth, W. (2017). Co-curricular learning and assessment in new student orientation at a community college. *Creative Education, 8*, 1638-1655.

Schwartz, R., & Wiese, D. (2010). Assessment and evaluation in orientation. In J. A. Ward-Roof (Ed.), *Designing successful transitions: A guide for orienting students to college* (Monograph No. 13, 3rd ed., pp. 217-227). Columbia, SC: University of South Carolina, National Resource Center for The First-Year Experience and Students in Transition.

Seemiller, C., & Grace, M. (2016). *Generation Z goes to college*. San Francisco, CA: Jossey Bass.

Shook, J. L., & Keup, J. R. (2012). The benefits of peer leader programs: An overview from the literature. *New Directions for Higher Education, 2012*(157), 5-16.

Tinto, V. (1993). *Leaving college: Rethinking the causes and cures of student attrition* (2nd ed.). Chicago, IL: University of Chicago Press.

Chapter 9

First-Year Residential Programs

Catherine T. Sturm, Sara Reinhardt, and Kirsten Kennedy
University of South Carolina

Research examining the benefits of college students living on campus is longstanding and extensive. Chickering (1974) and Astin (1977) were the first researchers to study the effects of living in a residence hall on students. In *Commuting Versus Resident Students*, Chickering concluded that students living on campus were more likely to return to college in subsequent years, thus yielding higher first-to-second-year retention. He attributed this outcome to students' quantity and quality of involvement with the institution (e.g., cultural events, social activities, academic clubs) and interaction with peers. Chickering's work was monumental for two reasons: First, it was a national, longitudinal study that documented the benefits of living in a residence hall. Second, it allayed the common belief that dormitories were filled with students who abused alcohol and behaved badly.

Chickering's (1974) study was substantiated by Astin in 1977. The latter study encompassed more than 225,000 students from 1961 to 1974, from which the most important environmental factor in persistence to graduation was a student's living in a residence hall during their first year. Astin attributed persistence to graduation to students being involved in their collegiate lives, which happens more frequently and more intensely in a residence hall setting than for their non-residential counterparts. Since those watershed studies, many other researchers have backed Chickering's (1974) and Astin's (1977) work (Astin, 1993; Fidler & Moore, 1996; Heredon, 1984; Kanoy & Bruhn, 1996; Lenning & Ebbers, 1999; Osueguera & Rhee, 2009; Pascarella, 1993; Schudde, 2011; Thompson, 1993; Titus, 2006). Living in a residence hall is likely to indirectly affect student educational attainment, as measured by greater retention and graduation rates compared with non-residential students (Bronkema & Bowman, 2017). Students living in close proximity enhances their sense of belonging (i.e., social integration), leading to greater educational attainment (Mayhew et al., 2016).

The physical structure of residence halls also impacts educational attainment. Cross, Zimmerman, and O'Grady (2009) identify three basic building configurations: traditional, suite, and apartment. Traditional configurations comprise single, double, or triple rooms that share a common bathroom on the hallway. Suites typically have two rooms (single or double occupancy) and share a bathroom. Apartments have bedrooms (single or double occupancy) with a bathroom, kitchen, and common living space contained within the unit. Chambliss and Takacs (2014) found that traditional configurations are more conducive to socialization and making friends. Students, however, tend to prefer suite-style and apartment-style configurations because of the increased privacy. The conundrum for practitioners is how to balance what students prefer (suites and apartments) with the traditional-style configuration that best encourages socialization.

Bronkema and Bowman (2017) found that when students with higher high school GPAs lived in traditional configurations in college, their sense of community and college satisfaction was higher than their counterparts with lower GPAs. Additionally, Bronkema and Bowman discovered that first-year students living in first year-only residence halls have better educational outcomes than those assigned to mixed-classification halls.

Living in residence halls also has a positive impact on reducing high-risk behaviors, compared to living in a Greek-affiliated house, off campus, or at home with a family. DiBello, Benz, Miller, Merrill, and Carey (2018) found that students living off campus were 50% more likely to drink underage, 37% more likely to use tobacco, 50% more likely to smoke marijuana, and 60% more likely to use illicit drugs. In addition, students living off campus were 34% more likely to engage in unprotected sex and 28% more likely to have more sexual partners. DiBello et al. theorized that the rules and regulations of a residence hall may deter students from engaging in these high-risk behaviors.

Impact of Residential Programs and Initiatives

Respondents to the National Survey on the First-Year Experience (NSFYE) were asked about the percentage of first-year students reached by residential programs and initiatives on their campuses. Figure 9.1 presents this group disaggregated by institutional type (two- and four-year). A total of 240 institutions (5% identified with two-year institutions; 95% identified with four-year institutions) reported that their residential programs and initiatives reached at least some first-year students. Whereas nearly 49% of four-year institutions reported that 81% or more of their first-year students were reached by these programs, only 25% of two-year institutions reported equivalent evidence. By contrast, 58% of two-year institutions reported that 20% or less of their first-year students were reached by residential programs and initiatives, while only 7% of four-year institutions reported the same. These results were expected, since four-year institutions are more likely than their two-year counterparts to offer on-campus housing, which could potentially provide these residential programs and initiatives, to first-year students. Four-year institutions also are more likely to accommodate a more traditional student population enrolling as full-time, first-year students.

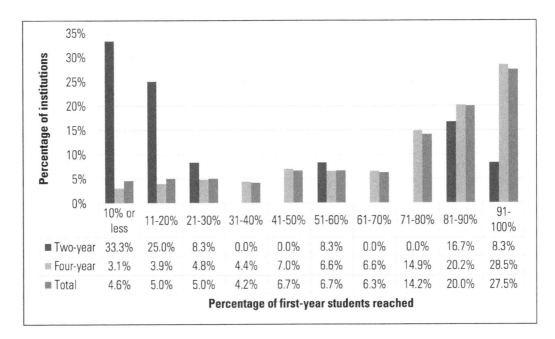

Figure 9.1. Percentage of first-year students reached by residential programs and initiatives, by institutional type (*n* = 240).

Figure 9.2 displays the results disaggregated by institutional control (public and private). Nearly 57% of private institutions reported 81% or more of their first-year students were reached by residential programs and initiatives, while only 38% of public institutions reported the same. Combining these results shows four-year institutions and private institutions were more likely to reach first-year students with residential programs and initiatives than two-year institutions and public institutions.

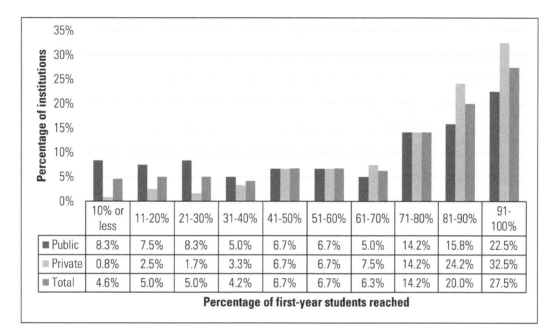

	10% or less	11-20%	21-30%	31-40%	41-50%	51-60%	61-70%	71-80%	81-90%	91-100%
■ Public	8.3%	7.5%	8.3%	5.0%	6.7%	6.7%	5.0%	14.2%	15.8%	22.5%
■ Private	0.8%	2.5%	1.7%	3.3%	6.7%	6.7%	7.5%	14.2%	24.2%	32.5%
■ Total	4.6%	5.0%	5.0%	4.2%	6.7%	6.7%	6.3%	14.2%	20.0%	27.5%

Percentage of first-year students reached

Figure 9.2. Percentage of first-year students reached by residential programs and initiatives, by institutional control (*n* = 240).

Categories of First-Year Students Required to Live on Campus

Respondents were asked to select categories of first-year students relevant to their institution who are required to live on campus. Results disaggregated by institutional type, displayed in Table 9.1, produced three frequently selected categories: (a) all first-year students are required to live on campus (with special exceptions; 55.0%); (b) no students are required to live on campus (35.4%); and (c) other, please specify (10.4%). Respondents selecting "other" reported additional categories such as: (a) first-time/full-time students who live at least 40 miles from the institution, (b) all first-year students are required except those who live with their parents/guardians, and (c) specific scholar or award recipients are required to live on campus. Four-year institutions were more likely to have a first-year on-campus requirement (57%) than two-year institutions (25%).

Results disaggregated by institutional control, displayed in Table 9.2, produced the same top three categories: (a) all students are required to live on campus (with special exceptions; 55.0%); (b) no students are required to live on campus (35.4%); and (c) other, please specify (7.5%). Private institutions were more likely to require all first-year students to live on campus (63.3%) than public institutions (46.7%).

Table 9.1

Categories of First-Year Students Required to Live on Campus by Institutional Type (n = 240)

| | Institutional type | | | | Difference |
| | Two-year | | Four-year | | |
Category of student	Freq.	%	Freq.	%	(%)
Percentages larger for two-year institutions					
Other, please specify	1	8.3	17	7.5	0.8
No students are required to live on campus.	8	66.7	77	33.8	32.9
Percentages larger for four-year institutions					
All first-year students are required to live on campus (with special exceptions).	3	25.0	129	56.6	−31.6
Honors students	0	0.0	2	0.9	−0.9
International students	0	0.0	2	0.9	−0.9
Learning community participants	0	0.0	3	1.3	−1.3
Provisionally admitted students	0	0.0	1	0.4	−0.4
Student athletes	0	0.0	2	0.9	−0.9
Students within specific majors, please specify	0	0.0	1	0.4	−0.4

Note. If *All first-year students are required to live on campus* was selected, respondents could not select other responses. Categories that reported 0% for both two- and four-year institutions are not presented in the table.

Table 9.2

Categories of First-Year Students Required to Live on Campus by Institutional Control (n = 240)

| | Institutional control | | | | Difference |
| | Public | | Private | | |
Category of student	Freq.	%	Freq.	%	(%)
Percentages larger for public institutions					
Learning community participants	3	2.5	0	0.0	2.5
Provisionally admitted students	1	0.8	0	0.0	0.8
Students within specific majors, please specify	1	0.8	0	0.0	0.8
No students are required to live on campus.	52	43.3	33	27.5	15.8
Percentages larger for private institutions					
All first-year students are required to live on campus (with special exceptions).	56	46.7	76	63.3	−16.6
Honors students	0	0.0	2	1.7	−1.7
Student athletes	0	0.0	2	1.7	−1.7
Equal percentages for both public and private institutions					
International students	1	0.8	1	0.8	0.0
Other, please specify	9	7.5	9	7.5	0.0

Note. If *All first-year students are required to live on campus* was selected, participants could not select other responses. Categories that reported 0% for both public and private institutions are not presented in the table.

Characteristics of First-Year Housing and Residential Life Programs

Respondents were asked two questions about the characteristics of first-year housing and residential life programs offered on their campuses: (a) Which of the following characteristics of your housing and residential life programs are intentionally and specifically dedicated to first-year students? (Select all that apply), and (b) Which of the following staff are specifically hired to provide support for first-year students? (Select all that apply). Figure 9.3 illustrates the overall results for each such program intended for first-year students. The three most frequently reported programs/initiatives intended for first-year students were: (a) specialized programming for first-year students (60.0%), (b) dedicated first-year residence halls (56.7%), and (c) first-year living–learning communities (49.2%).

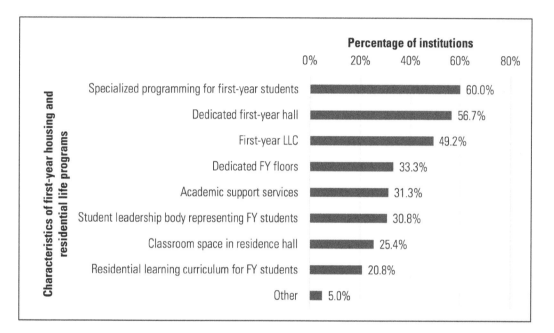

Figure 9.3. Specific types of housing and residential programs intended for first-year students (*n* = 240). The sum of the percentages is larger than 100% because of participants' ability to select more than one response. FY = first-year; LLC = living–learning community.

Specialized programming has the potential to provide purposeful learning opportunities and vital resources to boost the engagement and connectedness of first-year students living on campus. Residence halls and learning communities dedicated to first-year students are premier spaces that can potentially serve as the foundation for friendships, strengthen connections to campus, and provide extensive academic support, among other vital benefits.

We further examined the primary type of housing and residential programs intended for first-year students. When the programs were disaggregated by institutional type and control (Figure 9.4), more findings emerged. The results showed that 61% of four-year institutions and nearly 63% of public institutions provided specialized programming for first-year students. Private institutions were most likely to have dedicated residence halls (60.8%), followed by four-year institutions (59.2%). Finally, public institutions reported having first-year learning communities in place at the highest rate (59.2%), followed by four-year institutions (51.8%).

The second question focused on staff who are hired to support first-year students in residential programs. The three most frequently reported staff titles by respondents were: (a) student paraprofessional staff (71.3%), (b) professional live-in staff (68.8%), and (c) undergraduate academic peer educators (33.3%; Figure 9.5).

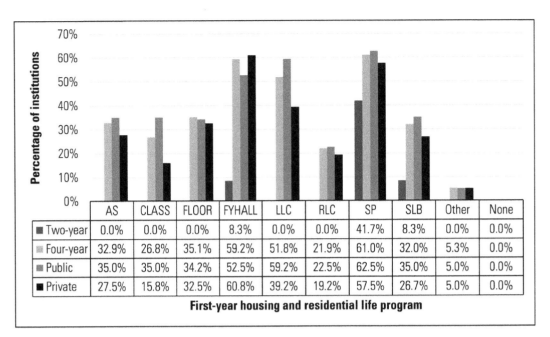

Figure 9.4. Housing and residential programs intended for first-year students by institutional type and control (*n* = 240). AS = Academic support services, CLASS = Classroom space in residence halls, FLOOR = Dedicated first-year floors, FYHALL = Dedicated first-year residence halls, LLC = First-year living–learning communities, RLC = Residential learning curriculum for first-year students, SP = Specialized programming for first-year students, SLB = Student leadership body representing first-year students.

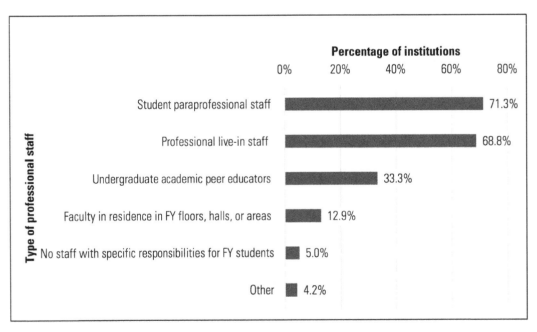

Figure 9.5. Specific types of professional staff hired to support first-year students (*n* = 240). The sum of the percentages is larger than 100% because of participants' ability to select more than one response. FY = first-year.

Return on Investment for First-Year Student Programming in On-Campus Residences

Respondents were asked to rate the return on investment for first-year student programming in on-campus residences. The Likert-type scale ranged from 1 to 7; respondents could also choose *unable to judge* as an option. For analysis, the scale was broken into three categories: low (1-3), medium (4), and high (5-7). Overall, more than half (59.2%; Figure 9.6) of responding institutions rated their return on investment as high, while 7.5% rated it low. Of two-year institutions, 33.3% indicated they were unable to judge the return on investment. Half of the two-year institutions rated the return as low (25.0%) or medium (25.0%); less than 17% rated the return as high. By comparison, participants at four-year institutions were much more likely to rate the return as high (61.4%). These results were expected, as two-year institutions typically offer fewer housing options and provide less residential programming than four-year institutions.

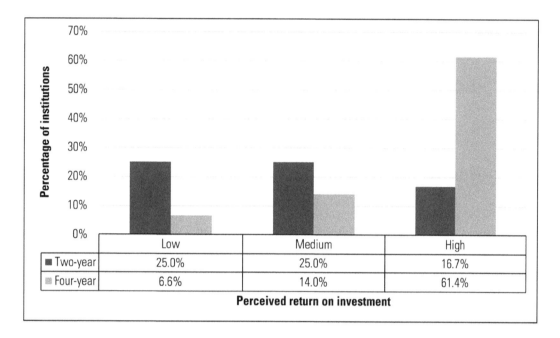

	Low	Medium	High
■ Two-year	25.0%	25.0%	16.7%
■ Four-year	6.6%	14.0%	61.4%

Perceived return on investment

Figure 9.6. Return on investment for first-year student programming in on-campus residences by institutional type (*n* = 240).

Assessing First-Year Student Residential Programs and Initiatives

In order to understand assessment measures for first-year residential programs, respondents were asked whether their programs had been formally assessed since Fall 2013. Overall, 35.8% of respondents indicated assessment had been conducted in that time period. Not surprisingly, no two-year institutions reported recent assessment of first-year residentials. Among four-year institutions, 37.7% of respondents had assessed their programs, while 32.9% were unsure whether their programs had been assessed.

The latter figure is substantial; it is possible that respondents did not know about assessment efforts either because of their institution's organizational structure (i.e., housing programs frequently are located in divisions outside academic or student affairs, such as auxiliary services) or because of the large and complex nature of many housing offices, which often include housing operations, residential life, and facilities, among other sub-units. When assessment of residential programs was broken down by institutional control, public institutions were more likely to assess their programs than privates (Table 9.3).

Table 9.3

Assessment of First-Year Residential Programs by Institutional Control (n = 240)

Assessment of programs	Institutional control				Difference (%)
	Public		Private		
	Freq.	%	Freq.	%	
Yes	50	41.7	36	30.0	12.0
No	32	26.7	44	36.7	−10.0
I don't know.	38	31.7	40	33.3	−1.6

Conclusion

For a first-year student, living on campus is important. Students who do so are more involved in their collegiate lives outside of class and develop supportive social networks, engage in high-risk behaviors less often, and are retained at a higher rate than their counterparts who do not live on campus. Being cognizant of the research, administrators responsible for first-year student living assignments should make the highest efforts in this area to provide the best possible academic and social start to college. Examples could include: (a) implementing a residential curriculum that focuses on first-year students and has the potential to reach a higher percentage of residents; (b) requiring first-year students to live on campus if housing is available; (c) connecting residents with professional live-in staff who can serve as mentors and assist daily with college student development, community integration, crisis management, and resource alignment; and (d) creating an assessment cycle for residential programs and gauging student satisfaction so program leaders can visualize the programs' impact, communicate efforts to internal and external audiences, and make adjustments where needed.

References

Astin, A. W. (1977). *Four critical years.* San Francisco, CA: Jossey-Bass.

Astin, A. W. (1993). *What matters in college? Four critical years revisited.* San Francisco, CA: Jossey-Bass.

Bronkema, R., & Bowman, N.A. (2017). Close campus friendships and college student success. *Journal of College Student Development, 58*(4), 624-630.

Chambliss, D. F., & Takacs, C. G. (2014). *How college works.* Cambridge, MA: Harvard University Press.

Chickering, A. W. (1974). *Commuting versus resident students.* San Francisco, CA: Jossey-Bass.

Cross, J. E., Zimmerman, D., & O'Grady, M. A. (2009). Residence hall room type and alcohol use among college students living on campus. *Environment and Behavior, 41,* 583-603.

DiBello, A. M., Benz, M. B., Miller, M. B., Merrill, J. E., & Carey, K. B. (2018). Examining residence status as a risk factor for health risk behaviors among college students. *Journal of American College Health, 66*(3), 187-193. doi:10.1080/07448481.2017.1406945

Fidler, P. P., & Moore, P. S. (1996). A comparison of effects of campus residence and freshman seminar attendance of freshman dropout rates. *Journal of The Freshman Year Experience & Students in Transition, 8*(2), 7-16.

Heredon, S. (1984). Recent findings concerning the relative importance of housing to student retention. *Journal of College and University Student Housing, 14,* 27-31.

Kanoy, K. W., & Bruhn, J. W. (1996). Effect of a first-year living–learning residence hall on retention and academic performance. *Journal of The Freshman Year of Experience & Students in Transition, 8*(1), 7-24.

Lenning, O. T., & Ebbers, L. H. (1999). *The power potential of learning communities: Improving education for the future.* Washington, DC: The George Washington University, Graduate School of Education and Human Development.

Mayhew, M. J., Rockenbach, A. N., Bowman, N. A., Seifert, T. A., & Wolniak, G. C., with Pascarella, E. T., & Terenzini, P. T. (2016). *How college affects students: Vol. 3. 21st century evidence that higher education works.* San Francisco, CA: Jossey-Bass.

Oseguera, L., & Rhee, B. S. (2009). The influence of institutional retention climates on student persistence to degree completion: A multilevel approach. *Research in Higher Education, 50,* 546-569.

Pascarella, E. T. (1993). Cognitive impacts of living on campus versus commuting to college. *Journal of College Student Development, 34,* 216-220.

Schudde, L. T. (2011). The causal effect of campus residency on college student retention. *Review of Higher Education, 34,* 581-610.

Thompson, J. (1993). The effects of on-campus residence on first-time college students. *NASPA Journal, 31,* 41-47.

Titus, M. A. (2006). No college student left behind: The influence of financial aspects of a state's higher education policy on college completion. *Review of Higher Education, 29,* 293-317.

Chapter 10

Discussion and Implications

Michael Dial
University of South Carolina

Stephanie M. Estrada
San Diego State University

Dallin George Young
National Resource Center for The First-Year Experience and Students in Transition

The presentation of results in the preceding chapters of this report provides broader and deeper insights into how campus environments have been created, structured, and coordinated to support student success in the first college year. Because of the breadth of information gathered through the 2017 National Survey on the First-Year Experience (NSFYE), comprehensive coverage of all the data is not practical. Therefore, we chose to highlight findings and provide an overview based on topics we found salient to contemporary conversations in higher education, viewed through our individual lenses.

To that end, this chapter begins with a discussion of a broad, integrative overview of implications of findings for the first-year experience (FYE) at institutions. This leads into a narrower discussion on the findings of two related and big-picture administrative aspects of an institutional approach to the FYE: assessment and perceived value of first-year programs. We then turn to consider two promising programmatic approaches for improving the student experience in the first year: peer education and early alert. Finally, the discussion concludes with an examination of specific implications of the survey's findings for two-year institutions.

Overall Implications for FYE

One of the NSFYE's key objectives was to gather information to increase our understanding of how first-year programs worked together to create environments to support student success. The survey and results presented in the previous chapters accomplished this in at least two ways. First, the survey updated and added to a history of research on a wide range of first-year student success initiatives. Collecting information on these individual programs in one volume allows readers to situate individual efforts among a comprehensive whole. Second, the survey provided information on the overall approach to the first year, allowing for analyses to be conducted about each institution's approach to offering first-year programs, while describing first-year objectives and illustrating ways these educational offerings are connected and coordinated.

To that end, the constellation of first-year programs presented in Chapter 2 revealed some interesting dynamics about the national picture of such offerings. As Figure 2.3 illustrates, some programs are offered at a wide variety of institutions, and their frequency is independent of whether any other (or at least a majority of other) first-year programs are offered. These frequently used programs include early alert, first-year advising, and student success centers; in Figure 2.3 they are represented as having no lines connected to other programs. There is evidence that some first-year programs are intentionally connected to others (e.g., first-year seminars connected to other high-impact practices [HIPs], learning communities that include first-year seminars, common-reading programs situated in orientation or first-year seminars), yet though those connections are not represented by the correlations represented by connecting lines in Figure 2.3. However, when institutions offer some of the less frequent first-year programs, they tend to offer a wider variety of them. This finding signals a wide-reaching attention to the first year. That is, these less frequent first-year programs come bundled and are used at a minority of institutions to provide, or at least potentially provide, comprehensive assistance for incoming students.

It would be easy to interpret the messaging in this report to suggest that having more first-year programs is better. Rather, the overall message we would suggest is to echo previous findings (Barefoot et al., 2005; Greenfield, Keup, & Gardner, 2013; Kuh & Kinzie, 2018; Young & Hopp, 2014) that institutions are better served with fewer programs that are well-designed and delivered as well as far-reaching (inclusive of and responsive to the demographic profile of incoming first-year students) than with more hastily designed and nonintentional curricular and cocurricular structures. In other words, a thoughtful, deliberate approach to creating and executing on the quality of practices is more desirable than simply adding more programs, courses, approaches, reforms, and technology that have been labeled *best, promising,* or even *high-impact* practices.

The results of the survey presented herein also raise interesting questions about how these first-year programs might work together at institutions to deliver on their promise to help all students succeed in college. Discrete first-year programs represent *activity systems* (Hatch, Crisp, & Wesley, 2016) aimed at achieving objectives, such as

* helping students enter the academic community of practice by socializing them to the values of the institution;

* teaching students how to operate in and navigate classrooms, residence halls, majors, and other operational realities of colleges and universities; and

* forging relationships with faculty, staff, and fellow students.

Findings show that, by and large, the objectives of individual first-year educational offerings included in this report are in line with what institutions say are overall goals for the first year.

First-year students move in and out of these different activity systems. Sometimes this happens overtly: A student may participate in an advising meeting, attend a first-year seminar, or engage in a living–learning community. Some instances are ad hoc and occasional, such as receiving academic coaching at a student success center or attending a convocation to discuss the book from a common-reading program. Other times, the activity system might happen more tacitly, and students may not be aware it is even taking place, such as with early-alert systems, gateway courses, or general education.

Taking all this into account, the questions then become:

* What experiences are first-year students having as they move in and out of these activity systems?

* In what ways could these different first-year programs work together to make the experience for students more cohesive and congruent?

Beginning with the premise that the answer to the latter question will result in improving the experiences in the former, we offer three suggestions to improve the coordination of first-year programs.

Work to align objectives, values, mission, and vision. This is a potential first step for collaboration and coordination, as it provides opportunities to find common ground, develop a shared language, and can also develop joint political capital throughout the process. On the campuswide level, it is helpful for institutions to identify common objectives for the first year. However, this must be done collaboratively, involving stakeholders representing key FYE programs. Moreover, the objectives should be accessible and achievable for all incoming students, including those from a wide variety of personal circumstances and backgrounds. Once campuswide objectives are in place, those in charge of individual first-year programs can find ways to tailor their work to align with objectives.

Align institutions' first-year activity, including structures, strategies, and communication. To achieve this, institutions can create organizational spaces to encourage collaborative discussion about the activities of key first-year programs on campus. They can also develop cross-functional teams made up of representatives from core FYE offices. To make such a structure efficient, these teams naturally involve a small number of representatives; to facilitate this step, individual programs can encourage faculty and staff to have collaborative conversations with others who work with first-year students. Including staff members from outside departments or offices can be achieved through existing structures (e.g., participating on working teams, serving on search committees, attending webinars, presenting on their work).

Finally, collaborate around aligning assessment and evaluative activity. This has the benefit of deepening the connection to institutional objectives while also providing greater understanding of the student experience, making decisions based on evidence over anecdote, and engaging in organizational learning around the first year. Additionally, when assessment results are disaggregated by student subpopulation, additional insights can be gained about students who are benefiting the most from these programs and those who may be falling behind. We recommend that any cross-functional and campuswide assessment effort include audits of available data on first-year students. We also recommend focusing assessment efforts on the campuswide first-year objectives for learning and development and moving the concern beyond simple first-to-second-year retention.

Assessment

Assessment has been linked to institutional integrity by helping to justify programs and specific educational activities that are effective in meeting learning outcomes, promoting sense of belonging, and increasing student success and retention. Through assessment, institutions can analyze data, collect feedback, and identify what is being done well and what is not working. This is all done to improve programs, remove those that are not achieving stated objectives, and introduce others that are more effective. With that said, and even with our knowledge of the value and insight that assessment brings, it is obvious that not all institutions assess their first-year programs consistently. Survey results showed that overall, only 34.6% of two-year institutions and 53.7% of four-year institutions included a specific focus on institutional assessment in the first year.

The NSFYE also asked respondents whether specific aspects of their first-year programming (i.e., first-year seminars, orientation, first-year advising, common-reading programs, early-alert systems, learning communities, and residential programs) had been formally assessed or evaluated within the three academic years prior to the survey administration. Respondents could select *yes, no,* or *I don't know* as their response. The data showed that some specific programs had only recently been assessed by a minority of respondents. For instance, only 17.6% of two-year institutions said their common-reading programs had been assessed since Fall 2013, compared with 28.5% of four-year institutions. Early-alert systems also came in at low rates, with only 36.6% of two-year institutions reporting assessment, while 29.8% of four-year institutions said the same. Additionally, 11.3% of two-year and 25.6% of four-year institutional respondents were unsure whether early-alert initiatives had been assessed during that period. While it is troubling that these programs had not been assessed more frequently in the recent past, it is also worrisome that so many respondents could not answer either way. This begs the question, Why do they not know?

One possibility is that the staff member answering the survey is not tasked with knowing this type of information off-hand. Another is that information on assessment may not be well-known within the institution. Because assessment can serve as a route to meaningful and purposeful decision making as well as justification for needed resources, clear communication through all appropriate channels is warranted so that respondents can give the most accurate representation of their practices. This could require something as simple as calling or emailing the appropriate staff member to find out whether a program has, in fact, been assessed.

Perceived Value of First-Year Programs

Institutional representatives were asked to rate the perceived return on investment, considering costs and benefits, for each of the first-year programs represented in the 2017 NSFYE. Figure 10.1 presents a side-by-side comparison of the overall ratings of the perceived benefits of the seven first-year programs in the survey. The mean rating for return on investment for all seven programs on a Likert-type scale of 1 to 7 was above 4.0, indicating most institutional respondents felt that benefits outweighed costs. The program with the highest mean rating was orientation ($M = 5.78$), followed by first-year advising ($M = 5.51$), first-year seminars ($M = 5.46$), residential programs ($M = 5.30$), early alert ($M = 5.16$), and learning communities ($M = 4.86$). Common-reading programs received the lowest overall mean rating ($M = 4.08$). Moreover, a review of Figure 10.1 shows that common readings had a far more even distribution of responses on the perceived rating than other first-year programs.

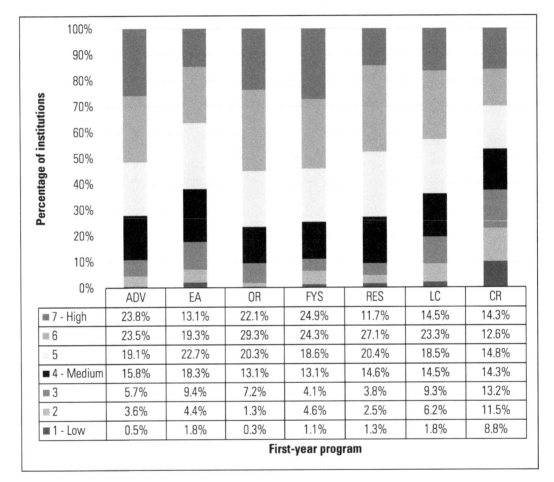

	ADV	EA	OR	FYS	RES	LC	CR
■ 7 - High	23.8%	13.1%	22.1%	24.9%	11.7%	14.5%	14.3%
■ 6	23.5%	19.3%	29.3%	24.3%	27.1%	23.3%	12.6%
5	19.1%	22.7%	20.3%	18.6%	20.4%	18.5%	14.8%
■ 4 - Medium	15.8%	18.3%	13.1%	13.1%	14.6%	14.5%	14.3%
■ 3	5.7%	9.4%	7.2%	4.1%	3.8%	9.3%	13.2%
2	3.6%	4.4%	1.3%	4.6%	2.5%	6.2%	11.5%
■ 1 - Low	0.5%	1.8%	0.3%	1.1%	1.3%	1.8%	8.8%

First-year program

Figure 10.1. Comparison of perceived return on investment of first-year educational activities. Responses of "Unable to judge" are not included in this presentation; therefore, percentages in the columns in the table will not equal 100%. The differences between the sum in each category and 100% represent the percentage of institutions responding that they were unable to judge the return on investment for the corresponding first-year program. ADV = First-year academic advising; EA = Early-alert systems; OR = New-student orientation; FYS = First-year seminars; RES = Residential programs or initiatives; LC = Learning communities; CR = Common reading.

These results point to a few observations. First, it should stand to reason that the survey respondents would rate these programs as having more benefits than costs on average; participants could only respond to the question about perceived value if they reported the presence of the program on their campuses. Thus, we might expect a different result for responses to these questions if institutions that had recently shuttered such programs, never had them, or even had them in the distant past could have provided an answer. This would be particularly interesting in the case of the first-year seminar, where there is evidence of a substantial decrease in the overall prevalence of the course among respondents. Second, the more institutionalized programs, particularly those with a more professionalized presence in higher education, were those with the highest means: orientation, first-year advising, first-year seminars, and residential programs.

The means and distribution of responses for learning communities and early-alert programs indicated slightly less confidence in the perceived value of these initiatives. Possible explanations for this include the reverse of what is true of the four highest-rated programs: They are less professionalized and less likely to have just one professional home on campus. Accordingly, administering these two programs tends to be more complex, requiring high levels of coordination.

The substantively different results for common-reading programs are worthy of discussion. These programs have come under scrutiny in popular opinion (see Flaherty, 2015; Jaschik, 2014; Randall, 2016, 2017; Skipper, 2014; Thorne, Wood, Plum, & Carter, 2013) and in the academy (Skipper, 2014). Additionally, as Krista Soria points out in Chapter 4, although a body of research on the structures, frequency, and impact of common readings is emerging, there remains a lack of information on the subject. Thus, these programs are likely not to be sheltered from scrutiny in the same way more institutionalized, professionalized, and well-researched programs might be. Additionally, common-reading programs are more visible and, thus, visibly expensive than other programs. There are costs for the procurement and distribution of books, and some speakers command notoriously high fees. Further, these programs are often one-off events or are at least perceived as such. Taking all these factors together might begin to explain the lower overall mean and the greater variability in perception about the return on investment for common-reading programs.

These results and analysis signal a few points for consideration. First, this further drives home the importance of good assessment of student success initiatives. For all programs, but especially those vulnerable to criticism and termination, evidence of effectiveness at the local level is important to be able to understand and communicate. Similarly, these findings point to the need for research on perceptions of cost versus perceptions of benefits for key institutional stakeholders.

One challenge researchers could face is parsing out the unique contribution of specific programs to outcomes. A key assumption with calls like this for increased assessment and research is that greater information about the benefits will shield a program from external pressures. However, more research is warranted to interrogate this assumption for these and other first-year programs. In other words, how much does perception of costs versus benefits protect a program against political fallout? Moreover, how much do history and institutionalization of a program protect it from the same?

Finally, research is warranted on the connection of how perceived value and institutionalization are related to the prevalence of a program on a national scale. More information is needed on the factors that lead to perceptions that certain first-year programs are capturing return on investment and how that drives their presence on campuses.

Peer Education

Peer-supported education remains a promising practice across the FYE. This should come as no surprise, as decades of research indicate peer groups as the primary forces influencing college student development (Astin, 1993; Chickering, 1969; Newton & Ender, 2010).

As one of the foundational experiences for many FYE programs, peer mentors figure heavily in the first-year seminar nationally. Just over half of all reporting institutions indicated that undergraduate students serve in these courses in some capacity. NSFYE respondents reported peer leaders serve as instructors' non-teaching assistants (53.3%), members of teaching teams (19.9%), and in a small number of cases (4.6%) are the primary instructors of the first-year seminar (Chapter 6).

Further, peer educators feature heavily in orientation programming by leading activities, serving as peer mentors to incoming students, helping with logistical planning, and providing administrative support (Chapter 8, Figure 8.12). Facets of peer-facilitated academic support (i.e., supplemental instruction, tutoring, peer-led team learning, peer mentoring) are part of the FYE at most institutions responding to the survey; these are listed under the umbrella of peer education as one of the primary FYE programs at just over a quarter of responding campuses (Chapter 2, Table 2.2). Peers also have a significant impact and influence on first-year students in residence life, where they are recruited and trained specifically for this task at 71.3% of responding institutions (Chapter 9, Figure 9.4). Even in the burgeoning programmatic service of early alert, a sizeable percentage (22.7%) of responding institutions use peer mentors in program delivery (Chapter 5, Figure 5.6).

While not groundbreaking, these results are a reminder of the positive potential of intentionally designed peer-to-peer interactions for first-year students on college campuses. It is notable that across all programmatic areas in the survey, four-year institutions report greater usage of peer-to-peer program delivery than their two-year counterparts (see Table 10.1). This may signal a need to design more intentional opportunities for peer-to-peer education in the two-year setting. Beyond the benefit to first-year students receiving support from their peers, recent scholarship points to immense personal gains for students who serve in peer leader roles. According to Keup (2016), these peer leaders benefit from this experience through

> development in their communication and leadership skills; integrative and applied learning; knowledge of campus resources; interaction with faculty, staff, and peers; critical thinking, problem solving, and higher order thinking skills; the ability to work under pressure; interpersonal skills; and an awareness and appreciation of diversity. (p. 32)

Table 10.1

Institutional Areas Offering Peer Education by Institutional Type

Institutional area	Two-year	Four-year
Overall institution (n = 525)	40.7%	68.9%
First-year seminar (n = 366)	36.4%	66.7%
Orientation (n = 375)	71.2%	94.5%
Residence life (n = 240)	25.0%	73.7%
Early alert (n = 383)	11.3%	25.3%

For both two-year and public, four-year institutions, peer-to-peer education offers tangible benefits for first-year students, peer educators, and institutions. In our current political climate, in which many states have not returned to pre-recession levels of public funding for higher education (Seltzer, 2018), effective use of peer education remains both a financially responsible approach to program delivery and more importantly, an effective means of delivering on the promise to support students in their personal development and degree attainment upon matriculation.

Early Alert

It is no surprise in a survey of this nature to see hallmark programs such as advising, orientation, and seminars rise to the top of a list of FYE programs adopted at a majority of institutions; these are also seen as primary programs for meeting FYE goals. These programs also have professional homes within national associations or organizations (i.e., the National Resource Center for The First-Year Experience and Students in Transition, NACADA, NODA).

Early-alert systems, facilitated at more than 70% of institutions (Chapter 2, Table 2.2), were identified by survey respondents as the second-most adopted FYE program. This confirms prior research indicating the widespread use of these programs (Barefoot, Griffin, & Koch, 2012; Habley, Bloom, & Robbins, 2012). Of particular interest to researchers, early alert was also the third highest-rated primary program used to meet FYE objectives (Chapter 2, Table 2.2). As one of the most utilized programs on campuses and one in which universities place significant importance in meeting the needs of first-year students, it is fascinating that no overarching organization has claimed early-alert programs within its realm. This could be because of early-alert programming's relative newness, but it may also be because it is housed in different programmatic areas at institutions nationwide (e.g., within advising, student success centers, FYE offices). Such a void of ownership results in practitioners lacking a one-stop resource for best practices and new innovations in early-alert programming. This may indicate the need for a professional association to take up this mantle or for a group of dedicated professionals to answer the call, bringing together their knowledge and skills to chart a path for early alert's future in the higher education landscape.

What is known is that most early-alert programs use some combination of attendance, academic performance, or behavior change as "red flags" (Cuseo, n.d.) to mark students' risk of attrition. Effective programs employ systems that allow faculty and staff to alert the appropriate service providers, who then contact students, connecting them to relevant campus resources, and when possible, following up with the referring agent. Thus, it goes without saying that faculty and staff must be trained to adequately monitor student performance and behavior, including attendance, within the confines of existing programs. In some cases, this may require curricular changes to allow students to exhibit academic proficiency or deficiency early enough in the semester to be recognized and flagged and for intervention to occur. Using personal outreach (e.g., phone, email, text message), these systems may provide added benefit at larger institutions (4,000+ students) by letting students know the university cares about their success. In doing so, university staff can make large institutions feel smaller and more connected.

Early alert presents potential responses to a number of challenges facing higher education. First, results of the NSFYE highlight the need for greater alignment between FYE programs to meet the needs of first-year students (Chapter 2). Early-alert programs could be key to creating formal, systemic networks across institutions, linking disparate offices and even divisions in the work of connecting first-year students to appropriate campus resources.

It may be useful to think of a number of FYE programs, specifically courses/learning communities and orientation/bridge programs, as environments where first-year students exist and can display red flags. Early alert, then, may be viewed as a bridge to FYE service providers or interveners. The communication loop required to operate these programs effectively has the potential to create supportive, collaborative, and student-focused networks within the context of FYE (Moschella, Bouknight, Dial, & Winfield, 2015). Future studies might explore and define best practices in early alert as a means of better aligning FYE programs with the intent to connect students to resources and services they need, when they need them, and when they are receptive to support.

Similarly, early alert may foster greater collaboration between academic and student affairs units at institutions, bringing faculty and administrators together as experts in their own realms of student success. Through these programs, student affairs professionals may be elevated as experts in academic support, navigation of campus policies and resources, and the general nature of student transitions. As partners in the work of connecting first-year students to appropriate campus resources and augmenting positive academic behaviors (e.g., attendance, study skills, time management), faculty and staff can approach collaboration with common language, aims, and outcomes.

Finally, it should be noted that technological advances have facilitated the quick pace of adoption of early-alert programming. Today, large-scale commercial vendors offer an array of sophisticated technology tools that connect to existing student information systems, identify local risk factors, track students through the alert and intervention process, and aid in assessment. Findings from this survey (Chapter 5), however, point to the immensely human nature of this work. While technology may help facilitate the process, it is not, in and of itself, the solution. On the referral side, faculty and staff should be trained to recognize students at potential crisis points in the first year. On the intervention side, practitioners must be able to diagnose individual student needs, help students develop relevant academic skills, and be knowledgeable enough to make appropriate referrals to campus resources. At a minimum, early-alert technology should be simple to use, cost-effective, and reasonably adaptable to changes as institutional needs evolve (Moschella et al., 2015).

The Two-Year Experience

Historically, the mission of two-year institutions has been to provide affordable and accessible education to everyone. In some cases, programs are in place that encourage students to begin their postsecondary education at two-year institutions by providing financial assistance. Tennessee Promise, for example, is a scholarship providing two years of tuition-free attendance at a two-year institution (community or technical college) in Tennessee to graduating high school seniors. Additionally, we are starting to see cities offering free tuition to community colleges in California and other places nationwide.

While two-year institutions are meant to serve everyone, they have served predominantly as the gateway to higher education for many fitting under the umbrella of nontraditional students. These students are more likely to be low-income, first-generation, older, and from underserved communities. Through the course of this report, it is obvious that some components of the FYE are not as prominent at two-year institutions. For example, data for the residential programs between two- and four-year institutions were not comparable. This is because most two-year institutions do not have on-campus housing for students and therefore do not have residential programs in place for the FYE. We know two-year institutions do invest in and value various components of the FYE (e.g., early alert, first-year advising), but moving forward, we should start to consider how the first-year experience differs from two- to four-year institutions.

If we normally look at the FYE through the lens of an 18-year-old student just out of high school (a more traditional student), we should start asking what that experience looks like for less traditional students. For example, someone who is a 30-year-old, full-time parent, full-time worker, and part-time student enrolled in courses for the first time at a two-year institution will see the FYE very differently. We must also keep in mind that once those students transfer from a two-year to a four-year institution, they will have missed out on the FYE at the latter because by the time they arrive, they may already be juniors and are trying to navigate the transition to a major rather than the first college year.

To really gauge how effective and important factors such as early-alert programs or first-year advising are to students in their first year, perhaps we should reevaluate the questions being asked. Could we be asking better questions? Are there programs we should be asking about at the two-year level that are more relevant to the FYE but have not been considered? There is a great possibility that we are missing out on crucial information about what the FYE looks like in the two-year context. Realizing two-year institutions' importance in higher education moving forward, it is necessary to delve deeper into the programming essential to the FYE and to the success of all the various types of students at the two-year level.

Conclusion

The results of the 2017 NSFYE have provided knowledge on critical curricular and cocurricular educational experiences aimed at supporting student success in the first year of college. The overall prosperity of students throughout their undergraduate education is contingent on a well-designed and delivered FYE. The results and analyses in this report can serve as guideposts and context for educators who are considering starting, improving, or integrating first-year programs. We echo the warning given in previous research reports on first-year seminars (Padgett & Keup, 2011; Young & Hopp, 2014): that administrators, faculty, and staff who wish to use this information as support for their decision making should consider their unique institutional environments when conceiving, adapting, or adopting new approaches to support student success. As Young, Chung, Hoffman, and Bronkema (2017) offered, "common practices are not always best practices" (p. 45).

References

Astin, A. W. (1993). *What matters in college? Four critical years revisited.* San Francisco, CA: Jossey-Bass.

Barefoot, B. O., Gardner, J. N., Cutright, M., Morris, L. V., Schroeder, C. C., Schwartz, S. W., … Swing, R. L. (2005). *Achieving and sustaining institutional excellence for the first year of college.* San Francisco, CA: Jossey-Bass.

Barefoot, B. O., Griffin, B. Q., & Koch, A. K. (2012). *Enhancing student success and retention throughout undergraduate education: A national survey.* Brevard, NC: The John N. Gardner Institute for Excellence in Undergraduate Education. Retrieved from https://static1.squarespace.com/static/59b0c486d2b857fc86d09aee/t/59bad-33412abd988ad84d697/1505415990531/JNGInational_survey_web.pdf

Chickering, A. W. (1969). *Education and identity.* San Francisco, CA: Jossey-Bass.

Cuseo, J. (n.d). *Red flags: Behavioral indicators of potential student attrition.* [White paper]. Retrieved from http://listserv.sc.edu/wa.cgi?A0=FYE-LIST

Flaherty, C. (2015, August 25). Duke U freshmen object graphic novel depicting lesbian relationships. *Inside Higher Ed.* Retrieved from http://www.insidehighered.com/print/news/2015/08/25/duke-u-freshmen-object-graph-ic-novel-depicting-lesbian-relationships

Greenfield, G. M., Keup, J. R., & Gardner, J. N. (2013). *Developing and sustaining successful first-year programs: A guide for practitioners.* San Francisco, CA: Jossey-Bass.

Habley, W. R., Bloom, J. L., & Robbins, S. B. (2012). *Increasing persistence: Research-based strategies for college student success.* John Wiley & Sons. San Francisco, CA: Jossey-Bass.

Hatch, D. K., Crisp, G., & Wesley, K. (2016). What's in a name? The challenge and utility of defining promising and high-impact practices. *New Directions for Community Colleges, 2016*: 9-17.

Jaschik, S. (2014, February 21). South Carolina lawmakers question books on gay topics. *Inside Higher Education.* Retrieved from https://www.insidehighered.com/quicktakes/2014/02/21/south-carolina-lawmakers-ques-tion-books-gay-topics

Keup, J. R. (2016). Peer leadership as an emerging high-impact practice: An exploratory study of the American experience. *Journal of Student Affairs in Africa, 4*(1), 33-52. doi:10.14426/jsaa.v4i1.143

Kuh, G. D., & Kinzie, J. K. (2018, May 1). What really makes a "high-impact" practice high impact? *Inside Higher Ed.* Retrieved from http://www.insidehighered.com

Moschella, E., Bouknight, J., Dial, M., & Winfield, J. (2015). Connecting students to success: A comprehensive approach to retention and persistence. In S. Whalen (Ed.), *Proceedings of the 11th National Symposium on Student Retention, Orlando, Florida* (pp. 160-171). Norman, OK: The University of Oklahoma.

Newton, F. B., & Ender, S. C. (2010). *Students helping students: A guide for peer educators on college campuses.* San Francisco, CA: Jossey-Bass.

Padgett, R. D., & Keup, J. R. (2011). *2009 National Survey of First-Year Seminars: Ongoing efforts to support students in transition* (Research Report No. 2). Columbia, SC: University of South Carolina, National Resource Center for The First-Year Experience and Students in Transition.

Randall, D. (2016). *Beach books: 2014-2016. What do colleges and universities want students to read outside of class?* New York, NY: National Association of Scholars.

Randall, D. (2017). *Beach books: 2016-2017. What do colleges and universities want students to read outside of class?* New York, NY: National Association of Scholars.

Seltzer, R. (2018, March 29). Tuition grows in importance. *Inside Higher Ed.* Retrieved from https://www.inside-highered.com/news/2018/03/29/state-support-higher-ed-increased-2017-so-did-tuition-revenue

Skipper, T. L. (2014, July 23). *The spring of our discontent: What's so bad about common reading?* [Web blog post]. Retrieved July 20, 2018, from http://tech.sa.sc.edu/fye/NRC_blog/?p=141

Thorne, A., Plum, C., Wood, P., & Carter, T. (2013). *Beach books: 2012-2013.* New York, NY: National Association of Scholars (NAS).

Young, D. G., Chung, J. K., Hoffman, D. E., & Bronkema, R. (2017). *2016 National Survey of Senior Capstone Experiences: Expanding our understanding of culminating experiences* (Research Reports on College Transitions No. 8). Columbia, SC: University of South Carolina, National Resource Center for The First-Year Experience & Students in Transition.

Young, D. G., & Hopp, J. M. (2014). *2012-2013 National Survey of First-year Seminars: Exploring high-impact practices in the first college year* (Research Report No. 4). Columbia, SC: University of South Carolina, National Resource Center for The First-Year Experience & Students in Transition.

Appendix A

Methods and Characteristics of Sample

Questionnaire Construction

The questionnaire was created and constructed by the National Resource Center for The First-Year Experience and Students in Transition with partnership from the John N. Gardner Institute for Excellence in Undergraduate Education. The 2017 National Survey on the First-Year Experience (NSFYE) was based in large part on two previous data collection efforts: the National Survey of First-Year Seminars (NSFYS), conducted by the National Resource Center, and the two-year and four-year National Surveys of Student Success Initiatives, conducted by the Gardner Institute. Selection of the sections on individual first-year programs was based, in large part, on two factors: (a) a substantive body of research and (b) professional efforts related to the first-year program. Estimates of these programs' prevalence indicated a wide distribution of the practice in higher education in the United States. The research team from the National Resource Center deliberated on the potential inclusion of specific modules investigating characteristics of a range of first-year programs and settled on the seven that were included in the 2017 administration. These decisions were communicated to and confirmed by the research team from the Gardner Institute.

Population

The population for the NSFYE were chief academic officers (CAOs), chief executive officers (CEOs), and/or chief student affairs officers (CSAOs) at regionally accredited, undergraduate-serving institutions of higher education listed in the *Higher Education Directory*. The CAOs, CEOs, and/or CSAOs were contacted via email and were asked to forward the invitation to participate if it would be more appropriate for another person on their campus to complete the survey. Giving contacts this instruction was designed to ensure that respondents would be those individuals who were the most knowledgeable about the first-year experience at each institution.

Survey Administration

Administration of the survey began on February 21, 2017. The first wave of invitations was sent to CAOs, or the CEOs if there was no listing for the CAO within the *Higher Education Directory*. If neither the CAO nor CEO was listed in the *Higher Education Directory*, the institution was omitted from the study. Non-verified or undeliverable email accounts were also omitted. The invitation served three main purposes: (a) to notify participants that the National Resource Center was conducting an administration of the NSFYE; (b) to provide detailed information about when they could anticipate receiving a link to the survey instrument; and (c) to confirm that the participant was the appropriate contact and representative who could accurately provide information about the first-year experience, and if not, request the correct campus contact information. The dissemination and administration of this survey was conducted using web-based survey technology developed and hosted by CampusLabs.

At survey launch, a total of 3,977 institutions were invited to participate. The institutions were emailed the survey link and given until April 21, 2017, to participate. Following the launch date, four follow-up reminders were sent to non-respondents. The first reminder email was sent to the CAO; the second reminder email was sent to the CEO; and the third reminder email was sent to all three institutional contacts (i.e., CAOs, CEOs, and CSAOs). The fourth and final email was sent to institutions that had participated in institutional improvement processes sponsored by the Gardner Institute. The deadline was extended to August 1, 2017, to allow the latter group sufficient time to participate. The survey link was officially disabled at noon EST on August 1, 2017.

Analyses

The analyses of the sample data were primarily conducted at the descriptive level. Comprehensive frequency distribution and sample percentages for each item reported throughout the research brief were tabulated for the sample in the aggregate (total) across institutional type, control, and size. Because of the potential for small cell counts throughout the analyses, differences by institutional characteristics throughout the report were conducted and reported in comparative form only. No claim is being made that the reported differences are statistically significant unless specifically stated.

Characteristics of the Sample

A total of 3,977 institutions were invited to participate in the 2017 NSFYE. The final number of campuses responding with information about their first-year experience efforts was 537, representing an effective response rate of 13.5%. This rate is substantially lower than expected from web-based education surveys, which normally are around 25% (Gunn, 2002; Wang, Dziuban, & Moskal, 2000), and less than the two previous online administrations of the NSFYS (Padgett & Keup, 2011; Young & Hopp, 2014). As a result, the low response rate presents a limitation in this research.

Table A.1 shows a comparison of the sample of all responding campuses to a national profile of institutions in the United States. The frequencies reported in this table demonstrate that four-year institutions are overrepresented in the sample of respondents. Similarly, the sample includes a greater proportion of campuses with more than 1,000 first-year students than the actual percentage nationally. Private, for-profit institutions were vastly underrepresented in the sample of responding institutions.

Because of the small number of private, for-profit responding institutions, comparisons between public and private institutions do not include private, for-profit institutions in the overall total for private institutions. We acknowledge important distinctions exist between private institutions that operate for profit and those that do not. However, there were so few responses from private, for-profit institutions that comparisons could not be made with any amount of confidence, and responses to many of the questions did not contain any representation from this sector.

Table A.1

Comparison of Institutional Characteristics for Responding Institutions

Institutional characteristic	National percentages	Percentages of all campuses responding to NSFYE (*N* = 537)
Control		
Public	37.7	58.1
Private, not-for-profit	38.3	40.8
Private, for-profit	23.9	1.1
Type		
Two-year	34.8	23.6
Four-year	65.2	76.4
Number of first-year students		
Less than 500 students	66.9	41.7
501 – 1,000 students	13.9	19.2
1,001 – 2,000 students	10.5	19.6
2,001 – 4,000 students	6.0	11.2
More than 4,000 students	2.7	8.4

Note. Figures for the national percentages are from The Integrated Postsecondary Education Data System by the National Center for Education Statistics, 2017.

References

Gunn, H. (2002, December). Web-based surveys: Changing the survey process. *First Monday, 7*(12). doi:10.5210/fm.v7i12.1014

Padgett, R. D., & Keup, J. R. (2011). *2009 National Survey of First-Year Seminars: Ongoing efforts to support students in transition* (Research Report No. 2). Columbia, SC: University of South Carolina, National Resource Center for The First-Year Experience and Students in Transition.

Wang, M. C., Dziuban, C. D., & Moskal, P. D. (2000). A web-based survey system for distributed learning impact evaluation. *The Internet and Higher Education, 2*(4), 211-220. doi:10.1016/S1096-7516(00)00021-X

Young, D. G., & Hopp, J. M. (2014). *2012-2013 National Survey of First-Year Seminars: Exploring high-impact practices in the first college year* (Research Report No. 4). Columbia, SC: University of South Carolina, National Resource Center for The First-Year Experience & Students in Transition.

Appendix B

Survey Instrument

National Survey on the First-Year Experience

This survey is intended to gather information regarding the first-year experience on your campus.

The *first-year experience* refers to any program, initiative, and/or educational activity specifically or intentionally geared toward first-year students. This goes beyond merely making educational activities available to first-year students. We are interested in learning about your school's first-year experience and the students it serves.

If this survey would be more appropriate for another person on your campus, please forward the email that contained the link to that individual. Examples of these individuals include directors of first-year programs, deans of "university colleges," or directors of assessment in new-student programs. Only one person from your campus can complete the survey.

The survey should take 30 minutes to complete. You may exit the survey at any time and return, and your responses will be saved. Your responses are important to us, so please complete the survey by Friday, April 21, 2017.

Because the survey may require gathering information from multiple people on campus, you can access a preview of the survey by following this link: [link to PDF of survey]

In particular, you will be asked about the following activities related to your institution's first-year experience:

- General information about your institution's attention to the first year
- First-year seminars
- Pre-term orientation
- First-year academic advising
- First-year learning communities
- Residential programs or initiatives
- Early-alert/academic warning systems
- Common-reading programs

In each of these sections, we will be asking questions about the following features:

- Students who participate
- Formats and characteristics
- Staffing and administration
- Assessment

To facilitate the accurate and timely completion of the survey, we recommend gathering the information prior to responding to the online questionnaire. Once the information has been gathered, the survey will take approximately 15-30 minutes to complete.

For the purposes of this survey, we offer the following definitions:

Campus or Institution: These terms, used interchangeably, refer to an individual campus that is either (a) an independent entity or (b) meaningfully distinct from other campuses in a system.

First-year students: Students in their first year at a campus. These students may have attained official standing beyond the first year based on accumulated credits prior to enrollment.

First-year program: Any educational offering **specifically or intentionally geared** toward first-year students. This goes beyond merely making educational activities available to first-year students. Some first-year programs may be a subset of a larger department or exist independently. For example, first-year advising may be a clearly defined specialty and focus area in a campus advising center. However, just assigning first-year students to advisors is not, in itself, a first-year program.

If you would like a copy of your responses, please print each page of your survey before moving on to the next page.

Thank you for your participation. It is greatly appreciated. We look forward to learning about your institution's first-year experience.

Respondent Information

Respondent First Name:_____

Respondent Last Name:_____

Respondent Email Address:_____

Institution Name:_____

Institution City:_____

Institution State: _____

Institutional Attention to the First Year

Institutional Efforts in the First Year

Q1. Which of the following campuswide objectives has your institution identified *specifically* for the *first year*? (Select all that apply.)

☐ Academic planning or major exploration

☐ Academic success strategies

☐ Analytical, critical-thinking, or problem-solving skills

☐ Career exploration and/or preparation

☐ Civic engagement

☐ Common first-year experience

☐ Connection with the institution or campus

☐ Developmental education, remediation, and/or review

☐ Digital literacy

☐ Discipline-specific knowledge

☐ Graduate or professional school preparation (e.g., premed, prelaw)

☐ Health and wellness

☐ Information literacy

☐ Integrative and applied learning

☐ Intercultural competence, diversity, or engaging with different perspectives

☐ Introduction to a major, discipline, or career path

☐ Introduction to college-level academic expectations

☐ Introduction to the liberal arts

☐ Knowledge of institution or campus resources and services

☐ Oral communication skills

☐ Personal exploration or development

☐ Project planning, teamwork, or management skills

☐ Retention or second-year return rates

☐ Social support networks (e.g., friendships)

☐ Student–faculty interaction

☐ Writing skills

☐ Other, please specify: _____

☐ Our institution has not identified campuswide objectives specifically for the first year.

Q2. Which of the following institutional efforts have included a *specific focus on the first year*? (Select all that apply.)

❒ Accreditation (e.g., Action Project or Quality Enhancement Plan focused on first-year students)

❒ Curricular or gateway course redesign

❒ Employment or job-placement study

❒ Graduation study

❒ Grant-funded project

❒ Institutional assessment

❒ Participation in a national survey of first-year students (e.g., NSSE, CIRP)

❒ Pathways programs or metamajors

❒ Program self-study

❒ Retention study

❒ Strategic planning

❒ Student services programming

❒ Other, please specify: _____

❒ Our institution has not engaged in any efforts with a specific focus on the first year.

Reach of First-Year Programs

Q3. Does your institution offer any of the following first-year student success programs, initiatives, or courses *specifically or intentionally geared toward first-year students*? (Select all that apply.)

❒ Common reading

❒ Convocation

❒ Developmental or remedial education

❒ Early-alert systems (i.e., systems that monitor student academic performance and may include direct outreach to students in academic or other types of difficulty)

❒ Experiential learning or learning beyond the classroom (not including service-learning)

❒ First-year academic advising

❒ First-year gateway courses

❒ First-year seminars

❒ General education

❒ Leadership programs

❒ Learning communities (i.e., curricular structures in which small cohorts of students are co-enrolled in two or more courses)

❒ Mentoring by campus professionals

❒ Peer education (e.g., supplemental instruction, tutoring, peer-led team learning, peer mentoring)

❒ Placement testing

❒ Pre-term orientation (including extended orientation and welcome programming)

❐ Residential programs or initiatives

❐ Service-learning

❐ Student success center

❐ Study abroad

❐ Summer bridge

❐ Undergraduate research

❐ Writing-intensive coursework

❐ Other, please specify:_____

❐ Our institution does not offer any programs specifically or intentionally geared toward first-year students.

Q4. Which of the following are the primary first-year programs by which the first-year objectives are met? (Please select up to 5.)

❐ Common reading

❐ Convocation

❐ Developmental or remedial education

❐ Early-alert systems (i.e., systems that monitor student academic performance and may include direct outreach to students in academic or other types of difficulty)

❐ Experiential learning or learning beyond the classroom

❐ First-year academic advising

❐ First-year gateway courses

❐ First-year seminars

❐ General education

❐ Leadership programs

❐ Learning communities (i.e., curricular structures in which small cohorts of students are co-enrolled in two or more courses)

❐ Mentoring by campus professionals

❐ Peer education (e.g., supplemental instruction, tutoring, peer-led team learning, peer mentoring)

❐ Placement testing

❐ Pre-term orientation

❐ Residential programs or initiatives

❐ Service-learning

❐ Student success center

❐ Study abroad

❐ Summer bridge

❐ Undergraduate research

❐ Writing-intensive coursework

Institutional Coordination of FYE

Q5. On your campus, how coordinated are first-year programs?

| | 1 | 2 | 3 | 4 | 5 | 6 | 7 |

1 – Totally decentralized, no coordination between any departments or units of first-year programs.

7 – Totally centralized, all first-year programs are coordinated by a single office or cross-functional team.

Q6. Does your institution have any of the following formal organizational structures to coordinate the first-year experience? (Select all that apply.)

❒ Cross-functional first-year team (e.g., team inclusive of curriculum and cocurriculum)

❒ First-year curriculum committee

❒ First-year program committee, task force, or advisory board

❒ First-year program office

❒ Other campuswide FYE coordination, please describe: _____

❒ Our institution does not have any formal organizational structures to coordinate the first-year experience.

Q7. Which of the following best describes the institutional division where the first-year program office is housed? *[Display if Q6 = First-year program office]*

❒ Academic affairs central office

❒ Academic department(s) (please list)

❒ College or school (e.g., College of Liberal Arts)

❒ Enrollment management central office

❒ Student affairs central office

❒ Other, please specify: _____

Individual FYE Programs

First-Year Seminar

[Display if Q3 = First Year Seminar]

Reach

Q8. What is the approximate percentage of first-year students who take a first-year seminar on your campus?

❒ 10% or less

❒ 11-20%

❒ 21-30%

❏ 31-40%

❏ 41-50%

❏ 51-60%

❏ 61-70%

❏ 71-80%

❏ 81-90%

❏ 91-100%

Duration

Q9. Approximately how many years has a first-year seminar been offered on your campus?

❏ 2 years or less

❏ 3-5 years

❏ 6-10 years

❏ 11-15 years

❏ 16-20 years

❏ More than 20 years

Formats of FYS

Q10. Select each type of first-year seminar that best describes the seminars existing on your campus: (Select all that apply.)

❏ **Academic seminar with generally uniform academic content across sections** – May be an interdisciplinary or theme-oriented course, sometimes part of a general education requirement. Primary focus is on academic theme or discipline, but will often include academic skills components, such as critical thinking and expository writing.

❏ **Academic seminar on various topics** – Similar to previously mentioned academic seminar except that specific topics vary from section to section.

❏ **Extended orientation seminar** – Sometimes called freshman orientation, college survival, college transition, or student success course. Content often includes introduction to campus resources, time management, academic and career planning, learning strategies, and an introduction to student development issues.

❏ **Preprofessional or discipline-linked seminar** – Designed to prepare students for the demands of the major or discipline and the profession. Generally taught within professional schools or specific disciplines such as engineering, health sciences, business, or education.

❏ **Basic study skills seminar** – The focus is on basic academic skills, such as grammar, note taking, and reading texts. This type of seminar might be targeted or even limited to academically underprepared students.

❏ **Hybrid** – Has elements from two or more types of seminars. (Please describe)

❏ **Other**, please describe

Q11. Which of the following first-year seminars has the highest student enrollment at your institution?

❑ Academic seminar on various topics

❑ Academic seminar with generally uniform content

❑ Basic study skills seminar

❑ Extended orientation seminar

❑ Hybrid

❑ Preprofessional or discipline-linked seminar

❑ Other

*You indicated that the first-year seminar type with the highest total enrollment on your campus is (Insert response from Q11). Please answer the following questions for **only** that seminar type.*

Students in Primary FYS

Q12. What is the approximate percentage of first-year students ***required*** to take the primary first-year seminar?

❑ None are required to take it

❑ Less than 10%

❑ 10-19%

❑ 20-29%

❑ 30-39%

❑ 40-49%

❑ 50-59%

❑ 60-69%

❑ 70-79%

❑ 80-89%

❑ 90-99%

❑ 100% - All first-year students are required to take it

Q13. Which students, by category, are required to participate in the first-year seminar? (Select all that apply.) *[Display if Q12 = any answer but "100%"]*

❑ First-generation students

❑ Honors students

❑ International students

❑ Learning community participants

❑ Preprofessional students (e.g., prelaw, premed)

❑ Provisionally admitted students

❑ Science, technology, engineering, and math (STEM) students

❑ Student athletes

❑ Students eligible for federal or state equal opportunity programs (EOP) (e.g., TRiO, Upward Bound)

❏ Students enrolled in developmental or remedial courses

❏ Students from low-income backgrounds

❏ Students on academic probation

❏ Students participating in dual-enrollment programs

❏ Students residing within a particular residence hall

❏ Students with at-risk factors such as GED, low ACT scores, etc., please describe: _____

❏ Students within specific majors, please specify: _____

❏ Transfer students

❏ Undeclared students

❏ Other, please specify:_____

Objectives and Topics

Q14. Select the three most important course objectives for the first-year seminar:

❏ Academic planning or major exploration

❏ Academic success strategies

❏ Analytical, critical-thinking, or problem-solving skills

❏ Career exploration and/or preparation

❏ Civic engagement

❏ Common first-year experience

❏ Connection with the institution or campus

❏ Developmental education, remediation, and/or review

❏ Digital literacy

❏ Discipline-specific knowledge

❏ Graduate or professional school preparation (e.g., premed, prelaw)

❏ Health and wellness

❏ Information literacy

❏ Integrative and applied learning

❏ Intercultural competence, diversity, or engaging with different perspectives

❏ Introduction to a major, discipline, or career path

❏ Introduction to college-level academic expectations

❏ Introduction to the liberal arts

❏ Knowledge of institution or campus resources and services

❏ Oral communication skills

❏ Personal exploration or development

❏ Project planning, teamwork, or management skills

❏ Retention or second-year return rates

❐ Social support networks (e.g., friendships)

❐ Student–faculty interaction

❐ Writing skills

❐ Other, please specify:_____

Q15. Select the three most important topics that compose the content of this first-year seminar:

❐ Academic integrity

❐ Academic planning or advising

❐ Academic success resources

❐ Academic success strategies (e.g., study skills, time management)

❐ Alcohol awareness and safety

❐ Campus activities and involvement

❐ Campus history and traditions

❐ Campus policies and community standards

❐ Campus resources

❐ Campus safety

❐ Campus tour

❐ Career exploration or preparation

❐ Commuter issues

❐ Course registration procedures

❐ Critical thinking

❐ Discipline-specific content

❐ Diversity issues

❐ Financial information, including financial aid and scholarships

❐ Financial literacy

❐ Global learning

❐ Health and wellness

❐ Information literacy

❐ Professional trends and issues

❐ Relationship issues (e.g., interpersonal skills, conflict resolution)

❐ Sexual assault and dating violence

❐ Social connections

❐ Writing skills

❐ Other, please specify: _____

Characteristics

Q16. What is the typical duration of a section of the first-year seminar?

❑ Half a term

❑ One quarter

❑ One semester

❑ One year

❑ Other, please specify: _____

Q17. How many credits does the first-year seminar carry?

❑ None

❑ 1 credit

❑ 2 credits

❑ 3 credits

❑ 4 credits

❑ 5 credits

❑ 6 or more credits

Q18. How is the first-year seminar credit applied? (Select all that apply.)
[Display if Q17 = any answer but "None"]

❑ As an elective

❑ Toward general education requirements

❑ Toward major requirements

❑ Other, please specify: _____

Q19. How is the first-year seminar graded?
[Display if Q17 = any answer but "None"]

❑ Letter grade

❑ Pass/fail

❑ No grade

❑ Other, please specify: _____

Q20. How many total classroom contact hours are there per week in the first-year seminar?

❑ 1 hour

❑ 2 hours

❑ 3 hours

❑ 4 hours

❑ 5 hours

❑ 6 or more hours

Q21. Do any sections incorporate online components?

❏ Yes

❏ No

❏ I don't know.

Q22. Are there any online-only sections?

❏ Yes

❏ No

❏ I don't know.

Q23. Which of the following pedagogical approaches are intentionally incorporated into the first-year seminar? (Select all that apply.)

❏ Educational experiences inside or outside the classroom that help students explore cultures, life experiences, and worldviews different from their own

❏ Educational experiences that develop students' ability to produce and revise various forms of writing

❏ Educational experiences that require collaboration and teamwork with other students

❏ Educational experiences that require students to engage in goal setting and planning

❏ Monitoring of student class attendance

Q24. Which of the following high-impact educational practices are connected to the first-year seminar with the highest enrollment of students? (Select all that apply.)

❏ **Common-reading experience** – First-year reading experience or summer reading program

❏ **Internships** – Experiential learning in which first-year students gain direct experience in a work setting

❏ **Learning community** – Linking a cohort of students in the first-year seminar to one or more other courses

❏ **Service-learning** – Nonremunerative service as part of a course

❏ **Undergraduate research** – Scientific inquiry, creative activity, or scholarship guided by a mentor from the faculty or research staff

Staffing - Instruction

Q25. Who teaches the first-year seminar? (Select all that apply.)

❏ Academic advisors

❏ Adjunct faculty

❏ Full-time, non-tenure-track faculty

❏ Student affairs professionals

❏ Tenure-track faculty

❏ Other campus professionals (please specify)

❏ Graduate students

❏ Undergraduate students

Q26. Is instructor training *offered* for first-year seminar instructors?

❐   Yes

❐   No

❐   I don't know.

Q27. Is instructor training *required* for first-year seminar instructors? [Display if Q26 = Yes]

❐   Yes

❐   No

❐   I don't know.

Q28. How long is the initial instructor training? [Display if Q26 = Yes]

❐   Half a day or less

❐   1 day

❐   2 days

❐   3 days

❐   4 days

❐   1 week

❐   2 weeks

❐   Other, please specify:_____

Q29. If undergraduate students assist in the first-year seminar, what is their primary role? (Select all that apply.)

❐   They teach independently.

❐   They teach as a part of a team.

❐   They assist the instructor, but do not teach.

❐   Undergraduate students do not assist in the first-year seminar.

❐   Other, please specify: _____

Administration

Q30. What campus unit directly administers the first-year seminar?

❐   Academic affairs central office

❐   Academic department(s) (please list)

❐   College or school (e.g., College of Liberal Arts)

❐   First-year program office

❐   Student affairs central office

❐   University college

❐   Other, please specify: _____

Q31. Is there a dean, director, or coordinator of the first-year seminar?

❒ Yes

❒ No

❒ I don't know.

Q32. If the dean, director, or coordinator has another role on campus, it is as a/an: (Select all that apply.)

❒ Academic affairs administrator

❒ Faculty member

❒ Student affairs administrator

❒ Other, please specify: _____

❒ The director doesn't have another role on campus.

Q33. In your opinion, considering both cost (staff time and resources) and educational benefits, what is the return on investment for your campus's approach to the first-year seminar?

1	2	3	4	5	6	7	UJ
Low			Medium			High	Unable to Judge

Assessment

Q34. Has your first-year seminar been formally assessed or evaluated since Fall 2013?

❒ Yes

❒ No

❒ I don't know.

Q35. What type of assessment was conducted? (Select all that apply.)

❒ Analysis of institutional data (e.g., GPA, retention rates, graduation)

❒ Direct assessment of student learning outcomes

❒ Focus groups with instructors

❒ Focus groups with students

❒ Individual interviews with instructors

❒ Individual interviews with students

❒ Program review

❒ Student course evaluation

❒ Survey instrument

❒ Other, please specify:_____

Q36. Select each student outcome that was measured: (Select all that apply.)

❒ Academic planning or major exploration

❒ Academic success strategies

❒ Analytical, critical-thinking, or problem-solving skills

- ❒ Career exploration and/or preparation
- ❒ Civic engagement
- ❒ Common first-year experience
- ❒ Connection with the institution or campus
- ❒ Developmental education, remediation, and/or review
- ❒ Digital literacy
- ❒ Discipline-specific knowledge
- ❒ Graduate or professional school preparation (e.g., premed, prelaw)
- ❒ Health and wellness
- ❒ Information literacy
- ❒ Integrative and applied learning
- ❒ Intercultural competence, diversity, or engaging with different perspectives
- ❒ Introduction to a major, discipline, or career path
- ❒ Introduction to college-level academic expectations
- ❒ Introduction to the liberal arts
- ❒ Knowledge of institution or campus resources and services
- ❒ Oral communication skills
- ❒ Personal exploration or development
- ❒ Project planning, teamwork, or management skills
- ❒ Retention or second-year return rates
- ❒ Social support networks (e.g., friendships)
- ❒ Student–faculty interaction
- ❒ Student satisfaction
- ❒ Writing skills
- ❒ Other, please specify: _____

Pre-term Orientation

[Display section if Q3 = Pre-term orientation]

Reach

Q37. What is the approximate percentage of first-year students who participate in orientation on your campus?

- ❒ 10% or less
- ❒ 11-20%
- ❒ 21-30%
- ❒ 31-40%
- ❒ 41-50%
- ❒ 51-60%

❐ 61-70%

❐ 71-80%

❐ 81-90%

❐ 91-100%

Students

Q38. Which students, by category, are *required* to participate in pre-term orientation? (Select all that apply.)

❐ All first-year students

❐ First-generation students

❐ Honors students

❐ International students

❐ Learning community participants

❐ Preprofessional students (e.g., prelaw, premed)

❐ Provisionally admitted students

❐ Science, technology, engineering, and math (STEM) students

❐ Student athletes

❐ Students eligible for federal or state equal opportunity programs (EOP) (e.g., TRiO, Upward Bound)

❐ Students enrolled in developmental or remedial courses

❐ Students from low-income backgrounds

❐ Students on academic probation

❐ Students participating in dual-enrollment programs

❐ Students residing within a particular residence hall

❐ Students with at-risk factors such as GED, low ACT scores, etc., please describe: _____

❐ Students within specific majors, please specify: _____

❐ Transfer students

❐ Undeclared students

❐ Other, please specify: _____

❐ No first-year students are required to participate in pre-term orientation.

Characteristics

Q39. Which of the following forms of pre-term orientation are offered at your campus? (Select all that apply.)

❐ On-campus, pre-term activities

❐ Online orientation

❐ Outdoor adventure/wilderness experience

❐ Pre-term advising or registration

❐ Welcome Week (i.e., on campus immediately preceding term)

❐ Other, please specify:_____

Q40. Which of the following activities does your campus's pre-term orientation program(s) include? (Select all that apply.)

❐ Academic advising

❐ Common reading (i.e., a book or article read before, and discussed during, orientation)

❐ Community building

❐ Convocations or other celebratory activities

❐ Discussion of personal issues and challenges

❐ Discussions about health and wellness on campus

❐ Discussions about identity, diversity, or social justice

❐ Introduction to campus facilities

❐ Introduction to campus resources and services

❐ Involvement opportunities

❐ Placement testing

❐ Registration or course enrollment

❐ Sessions for family members

❐ Structured interaction with faculty

❐ Other, please specify: _____

❐ None of the above

Administration

Q41. If undergraduate students assist in pre-term orientation, what is their primary role? (Select all that apply.)

❐ They deliver informational sessions.

❐ They lead orientation activities.

❐ They plan and coordinate logistical issues.

❐ They provide administrative and clerical support to professional orientation staff.

❐ They serve as peer mentors to the incoming students.

❐ They serve as resident assistants/mentors in the residence hall/living areas.

❐ Other, please specify: _____

❐ Undergraduate students do not assist in pre-term orientation.

Q42. Which of the following best describes the administrative division where the orientation program is housed? (Select all that apply.)

❐ Academic affairs central office

❐ Academic department(s) (please list)

❐ College or school (e.g., College of Liberal Arts)

❐ Enrollment management central office

❐ First-year program office

❐ Student affairs central office

❒ University college

❒ Other, please specify: _____

Q43. In your opinion, considering both cost (staff time and resources) and educational benefits, what is the return on investment for your campus's approach to pre-term orientation?

1	2	3	4	5	6	7	UJ
Low			Medium			High	Unable to Judge

Assessment

Q44. Has your orientation program been formally assessed or evaluated since Fall 2013?

❒ Yes

❒ No

❒ I don't know.

Q45. What type of assessment was conducted? (Select all that apply.)

❒ Analysis of institutional data (e.g., GPA, retention rates, graduation)

❒ Direct assessment of student learning outcomes

❒ Focus groups with orientation staff

❒ Focus groups with students

❒ Individual interviews with orientation staff

❒ Individual interviews with students

❒ Program review

❒ Student course evaluation

❒ Survey instrument

❒ Other, please specify: _____

Q46. Select each student outcome that was measured: (Select all that apply.)

❒ Academic planning or major exploration

❒ Academic success strategies

❒ Analytical, critical-thinking, or problem-solving skills

❒ Career exploration and/or preparation

❒ Civic engagement

❒ Common first-year experience

❒ Connection with the institution or campus

❒ Developmental education, remediation, and/or review

❒ Digital literacy

❒ Discipline-specific knowledge

❒ Graduate or professional school preparation (e.g., premed, prelaw)

❏   Health and wellness

❏   Information literacy

❏   Integrative and applied learning

❏   Intercultural competence, diversity, or engaging with different perspectives

❏   Introduction to a major, discipline, or career path

❏   Introduction to college-level academic expectations

❏   Introduction to the liberal arts

❏   Knowledge of institution or campus resources and services

❏   Oral communication skills

❏   Personal exploration or development

❏   Project planning, teamwork, or management skills

❏   Retention or second-year return rates

❏   Social support networks (e.g., friendships)

❏   Student–faculty interaction

❏   Student satisfaction

❏   Writing skills

❏   Other, please specify: _____

First-Year Academic Advising

[Display section if Q3 = First-year academic advising]

Reach

Q47. What is the approximate percentage of first-year students who participate in *first-year academic advising* on your campus?

❏   10% or less

❏   11-20%

❏   21-30%

❏   31-40%

❏   41-50%

❏   51-60%

❏   61-70%

❏   71-80%

❏   81-90%

❏   91-100%

Students

Q48. Which students, by category, are *required* to participate in first-year academic advising? (Select all that apply.)

❏ All first-year students are required to participate

❏ First-generation students

❏ Honors students

❏ International students

❏ Learning community participants

❏ Preprofessional students (e.g., prelaw, premed)

❏ Provisionally admitted students

❏ Science, technology, engineering, and math (STEM) students

❏ Student athletes

❏ Students eligible for federal or state equal opportunity programs (EOP) (e.g., TRiO, Upward Bound)

❏ Students enrolled in developmental or remedial courses

❏ Students from low-income backgrounds

❏ Students on academic probation

❏ Students participating in dual-enrollment programs

❏ Students residing within a particular residence hall

❏ Students with at-risk factors such as GED, low ACT scores, etc., please describe: _____

❏ Students within specific majors, please specify:_____

❏ Transfer students

❏ Undeclared students

❏ Other, please specify: _____

❏ No first-year students are required to participate in first-year advising.

Characteristics

Q49. What point on the following scale best describes your advising for first-year students?

	1	2	3	4	5	6	7	UJ
No first-year students are advised in a centralized advising unit/center (i.e., there is no centralized advising unit/center)							All first-year students are advised in a centralized advising unit/center	Unable to judge

Q50. Does your institution offer online-only first-year advising?

❐ Yes

❐ No

❐ I don't know.

Q51. For first-year academic advising, approximately how many students are assigned to each advisor?

❐ 1-50 students

❐ 51-100 students

❐ 101-150 students

❐ 151-200 students

❐ 201-250 students

❐ 251-500 students

❐ 501-1,000 students

❐ More than 1,000 students

Q52. At your institution, how frequently are first-year students *required* to meet with their assigned first-year academic advisor?

❐ Only once, during the first term

❐ Once during each term for the entire first year

❐ Two or more times each term for the entire first year

❐ First-year students are not required to meet with their first-year academic advisors.

❐ Other, please specify:_____

Q53. At your institution, first-year academic advisors are most likely to be:

❐ Faculty

❐ Graduate students

❐ Professional academic advisors (exclusive of graduate students)

❐ Undergraduate peer advisors

❐ Other, please specify:_____

Administration

Q54. Which of the following best describes the administrative division where first-year advising is housed?

❐ Academic affairs central office

❐ Academic department(s), please list: _____

❐ College or school (e.g., College of Liberal Arts)

❐ First-year advising office

❐ First-year program office

❐ Student affairs central office

❏ University college

❏ Other, please specify:_____

Q55. In your opinion, considering both cost (staff time and resources) and educational benefits, what is the return on investment for your campus's approach to advising?

1	2	3	4	5	6	7	UJ
Low			Medium			High	Unable to Judge

Assessment

Q56. Has your first-year academic advising been formally assessed or evaluated since Fall 2013?

❏ Yes

❏ No

❏ I don't know.

Q57. What type of assessment was conducted? (Select all that apply.)

❏ Analysis of institutional data (e.g., GPA, retention rates, graduation)

❏ Direct assessment of student learning outcomes

❏ Focus groups with advisors

❏ Focus groups with students

❏ Individual interviews with advisors

❏ Individual interviews with students

❏ Program review

❏ Student course evaluation

❏ Survey instrument

❏ Other, please specify: _____

Q58. Select each student outcome that was measured: (Select all that apply.)

❏ Academic planning or major exploration

❏ Academic success strategies

❏ Analytical, critical-thinking, or problem-solving skills

❏ Career exploration and/or preparation

❏ Civic engagement

❏ Common first-year experience

❏ Connection with the institution or campus

❏ Developmental education, remediation, and/or review

❏ Digital literacy

❏ Discipline-specific knowledge

❏ Graduate or professional school preparation (e.g., premed, prelaw)

❒ Health and wellness

❒ Information literacy

❒ Integrative and applied learning

❒ Intercultural competence, diversity, or engaging with different perspectives

❒ Introduction to a major, discipline, or career path

❒ Introduction to college-level academic expectations

❒ Introduction to the liberal arts

❒ Knowledge of institution or campus resources and services

❒ Oral communication skills

❒ Personal exploration or development

❒ Project planning, teamwork, or management skills

❒ Retention or second-year return rates

❒ Social support networks (e.g., friendships)

❒ Student–faculty interaction

❒ Student satisfaction

❒ Writing skills

❒ Other, please specify:_____

Learning Communities

[Display section if Q3 = Learning Communities]

Reach

Q59. What is the approximate percentage of first-year students who participate in *first-year learning communities* on your campus?

❒ 10% or less

❒ 11-20%

❒ 21-30%

❒ 31-40%

❒ 41-50%

❒ 51-60%

❒ 61-70%

❒ 71-80%

❒ 81-90%

❒ 91-100%

Students

Q60. Which students, by category, are ***required*** to participate in first-year learning communities? (Select all that apply.)

❐ All first-year students are required to participate

❐ First-generation students

❐ Honors students

❐ International students

❐ Learning community participants

❐ Preprofessional students (e.g., prelaw, premed)

❐ Provisionally admitted students

❐ Science, technology, engineering, and math (STEM) students

❐ Student athletes

❐ Students eligible for federal or state equal opportunity programs (EOP) (e.g., TRiO, Upward Bound)

❐ Students enrolled in developmental or remedial courses

❐ Students from low-income backgrounds

❐ Students on academic probation

❐ Students participating in dual-enrollment programs

❐ Students residing within a particular residence hall

❐ Students with at-risk factors such as GED, low ACT scores, etc., please describe:_____

❐ Students within specific majors, please specify:_____

❐ Transfer students

❐ Undeclared students

❐ Other, please specify: _____

❐ No first-year students are required to participate in first-year learning communities.

Characteristics

Q61. Which of the following are characteristics of first-year learning communities in which most first-year students participate? (Select all that apply.)

❐ Course content in the linked courses is connected by a common intellectual theme.

❐ Course content is intentionally coordinated by the instructors of the linked courses.

❐ One of the courses in the learning community is a developmental or remedial education course.

❐ One of the courses in the learning community is a first-year seminar.

❐ Students are co-enrolled in all courses in the students' schedules.

❐ Students are co-enrolled in two or more courses, but not all courses in the students' schedules.

❐ Students in the learning community participate in a common set of theme-based experiences outside of the course, such as discussion groups, a speaker series, or other educational programs.

❐ The learning community includes a residential component (i.e., a living–learning community).

❐ Other, please describe: _____

Administration

Q62. What campus unit(s) directly administer(s) the first-year learning communities? (Select all that apply.)

❒ Academic affairs central office

❒ Academic department(s), please list: _____

❒ College or school (e.g., College of Liberal Arts)

❒ Enrollment management central office

❒ First-year program office

❒ Housing or residence life

❒ Student affairs central office

❒ University college

❒ Other, please specify: _____

Q63. In your opinion, considering both cost (staff time and resources) and educational benefits, what is the return on investment for your campus's approach to first-year learning communities?

1	2	3	4	5	6	7	UJ
Low			Medium			High	Unable to Judge

Assessment

Q64. Has any aspect of your first-year learning communities been formally assessed or evaluated since Fall 2013?

❒ Yes

❒ No

❒ I don't know.

Residential Programs and Initiatives

[Display section if Q3 = Residential Programs and Initiatives]

Reach

Q65. What is the approximate percentage of first-year students on your campus who are reached by residential programs and initiatives?

❒ 10% or less

❒ 11-20%

❒ 21-30%

❒ 31-40%

❒ 41-50%

❒ 51-60%

❒ 61-70%

❒ 71-80%

❒ 81-90%

❒ 91-100%

Students

Q66. Which first-year students, by category, are **required** to live on campus? (Select all that apply.)

❒ All first-year students are required to live on campus (with special exceptions)

❒ First-generation students

❒ Honors students

❒ International students

❒ Learning community participants

❒ Preprofessional students (e.g., prelaw, premed)

❒ Provisionally admitted students

❒ Science, technology, engineering, and math (STEM) students

❒ Student athletes

❒ Students eligible for federal or state equal opportunity programs (EOP) (e.g., TRiO, Upward Bound)

❒ Students enrolled in developmental or remedial courses

❒ Students from low-income backgrounds

❒ Students on academic probation

❒ Students participating in dual-enrollment programs

❒ Students with at-risk factors such as GED, low ACT scores, etc., please describe:_____

❒ Students within specific majors, please specify: _____

❒ Transfer students

❒ Undeclared students

❒ Other, please specify:_____

❒ No students are required to live on campus.

Characteristics

Q67. Which of the following characteristics of your housing and residential life programs are **intentionally and specifically dedicated to first-year students**? (Select all that apply.)

❒ Academic support services (i.e., academic coaching, tutoring)

❒ Classroom space in residence halls

❒ Dedicated first-year floors

❒ Dedicated first-year residence halls

❒ First-year living–learning communities

❒ Residential learning curriculum for first-year students

❏ Specialized programming for first-year students

❏ Student leadership body representing first-year students (first-year community council, hall government)

❏ Other, please specify: _____

❏ We offer none of the listed programs or initiatives.

Q68. Which of the following staff are specifically hired to provide support for first-year students? (Select all that apply.)

❏ Faculty in residence in first-year floors, halls, or areas

❏ Professional live-in staff (e.g., hall directors, area coordinators) with specific responsibilities for first-year floors, halls, or areas

❏ Student paraprofessional staff (e.g., resident assistants) with specific selection, training, and responsibilities for first-year students

❏ Undergraduate academic peer educators (e.g., community academic advisors) for first-year students

❏ Other, please specify: _____

❏ We have no staff with specific responsibilities for first-year students or residences.

Administration

Q69. In your opinion, considering both cost (staff time and resources) and educational benefits, what is the return on investment for your campus's approach to first-year programming in on-campus residences?

1	2	3	4	5	6	7	UJ
Low			Medium			High	Unable to Judge

Assessment

Q70. Has any aspect of your first-year residential programs been formally assessed or evaluated since Fall 2013?

❏ Yes

❏ No

❏ I don't know.

Early-Alert Programs

[Display section if Q3 = Early alert]

Reach

Q71. What is the approximate percentage of first-year students on your campus who are reached by early warning/academic alert systems?

❏ 10% or less

❏ 11-20%

❏ 21-30%

❒ 31-40%

❒ 41-50%

❒ 51-60%

❒ 61-70%

❒ 71-80%

❒ 81-90%

❒ 91-100%

Students

Q72. Which types of first-year students are monitored through an early warning/academic alert system? (Select all that apply.)

❒ All first-year students

❒ Only students who volunteer or contract to have academic progress tracked

❒ First-generation students

❒ Honors students

❒ International students

❒ Learning community participants

❒ Preprofessional students (e.g., prelaw, premed)

❒ Provisionally admitted students

❒ Science, technology, engineering, and math (STEM) students

❒ Student athletes

❒ Students eligible for federal or state equal opportunity programs (EOP) (e.g., TRiO, Upward Bound)

❒ Students enrolled in developmental or remedial courses

❒ Students from low-income backgrounds

❒ Students on academic probation

❒ Students participating in dual-enrollment programs

❒ Students residing within a particular residence hall

❒ Students with at-risk factors such as GED, low ACT scores, etc., please describe: _____

❒ Students within specific majors, please specify: _____

❒ Transfer students

❒ Undeclared students

❒ Other, please specify: _____

❒ No first-year students are monitored through an early warning/academic alert system.

Characteristics

Q73. Please indicate the selection that best describes the early warning system that is most prevalent at your institution.

| | 1 | 2 | 3 | 4 | 5 | 6 | 7 | UJ |

An early warning tool that is entirely **technology-based** (such as a learner analytics platform that mines data to determine which students are at-risk and subsequently guides intervention)

An early warning system that is entirely **human-based and relies on faculty, staff, and/or fellow students** observing behavior and then notifying someone so outreach can occur (such as a faculty referral system)

Unable to judge

Q74. Which of the following characteristics describe your campus's early warning/academic alert system for first-year students?

- ❐ Monitoring and/or response occur only before midterm.
- ❐ Monitoring and/or response occur only at or after midterm.
- ❐ Monitoring and/or response are ongoing throughout the term.
- ❐ Monitoring and/or response are ongoing throughout the first year.
- ❐ Other, please describe: _____

Q75. Which employees at your institution participate in some aspect of early-alert/academic warning systems? (Select all that apply.)

- ❐ Academic advisors
- ❐ Academic support personnel
- ❐ Athletic department staff
- ❐ Counseling/health services staff
- ❐ Faculty/instructors
- ❐ Information technology staff
- ❐ Peer mentors
- ❐ Residence life staff
- ❐ Student affairs staff
- ❐ Other, please describe:_____

Q76. Which of the following describes the type of intervention that occurs? (Select all that apply.)

❐ Students are contacted by phone, letter, or electronic means.

❐ Students are contacted in person.

❐ Students are informed about opportunities to seek assistance.

❐ Students are required by individual faculty members, another unit, or the institution to obtain assistance.

❐ Students' families are notified (with student waiver of privacy rights).

❐ Other, please describe: _____

Administration

Q77. In your opinion, considering both cost (staff time and resources) and educational benefits, what is the return on investment for the early-alert/academic warning system on your campus?

1	2	3	4	5	6	7	UJ
Low			Medium			High	Unable to Judge

Assessment

Q78. Has any aspect of your early-alert program been formally assessed or evaluated since Fall 2013?

❐ Yes

❐ No

❐ I don't know.

Common Reading

[Display section if Q3 = Common Reading]

Reach

Q79. What is the approximate percentage of first-year students who participate in a first-year common-reading program on your campus?

❐ 10% or less

❐ 11-20%

❐ 21-30%

❐ 31-40%

❐ 41-50%

❐ 51-60%

❐ 61-70%

❐ 71-80%

❐ 81-90%

❐ 91-100%

Students

Q80. Which first-year students, by category, participate in a common-reading program on your campus? (Select all that apply.)

- ❏ Academically underprepared students (i.e., students with at-risk factors)
- ❏ All first-year students
- ❏ First-generation students
- ❏ Honors students
- ❏ International students
- ❏ Learning community participants
- ❏ Preprofessional students (e.g., prelaw, premed)
- ❏ Provisionally admitted students
- ❏ Science, Technology, Engineering, and Math (STEM) students
- ❏ Student athletes
- ❏ Students eligible for federal or state equal opportunity programs (EOP) (e.g., TRiO, Upward Bound)
- ❏ Students enrolled in developmental or remedial courses
- ❏ Students from low-income backgrounds
- ❏ Students on academic probation
- ❏ Students participating in dual-enrollment programs
- ❏ Students residing within a particular residence hall
- ❏ Students with at-risk factors such as GED, low ACT scores, etc., please describe:_____
- ❏ Transfer students
- ❏ TRIO participants
- ❏ Undeclared students
- ❏ Students within specific majors, please specify:_____
- ❏ Other, please specify: _____
- ❏ No first-year students participate in a common-reading program on campus.

Characteristics

Q81. Which of the following activities does your first-year common-reading program include? (Select all that apply.)

- ❏ Bringing speakers related to text to campus
- ❏ Campus programming throughout academic year
- ❏ Campus–community engagement
- ❏ Discussion groups
- ❏ Film adaptations of or films related to common-reading text
- ❏ Incorporation of text in English and writing courses

❏ Incorporation of text in first-year seminar

❏ Structured interaction with faculty

❏ Other, please specify:_____

Administration

Q82. What campus unit(s) directly administer(s) the common-reading experience? (Select all that apply.)

❏ Academic affairs central office

❏ Academic department – other

❏ Academic office, please specify: _____

❏ Campus activities/student programming board

❏ English or writing department

❏ First-year program

❏ Library

❏ Orientation office

❏ Residence Life

❏ Student affairs central office

❏ University college

❏ Other, please specify: _____

Q83. In your opinion, considering both cost (staff time and resources) and educational benefits, what is the return on investment for the common-reading program on your campus?

1	2	3	4	5	6	7	UJ
Low			Medium			High	Unable to Judge

Assessment

Q84. Has any aspect of your common-reading programs been formally assessed or evaluated since Fall 2013?

❏ Yes

❏ No

❏ I don't know.

No FYE programs

[Display section if Q3 = "Our institution does not offer any programs specifically or intentionally geared toward first-year students."]

Reasons for No FYE

Q85. Please indicate the reason why your institution offers no FYE programs or initiatives:

❏ Lack of expertise

❏ Lack of funding

❒ Lack of staff or faculty buy-in

❒ Limited time

❒ Not an institutional priority

❒ Other, please specify: _____

Past FYE Efforts

Q86. Has your institution had initiatives specifically geared toward first-year students in the past five years?

❒ Yes

❒ No

❒ I don't know.

Q87. If yes, which of the following student success programs, initiatives, or courses *specifically or intentionally geared toward first-year students* has your institution offered in the past five years?

❒ Common reading

❒ Convocation

❒ Developmental or remedial education

❒ Early-alert systems (i.e., systems that monitor student academic performance and may include direct outreach to students in academic or other types of difficulty)

❒ Experiential learning/learning beyond the classroom

❒ First-year academic advising

❒ First-year gateway courses

❒ First-year seminars

❒ General education

❒ Leadership programs

❒ Learning communities (i.e., curricular structures in which small cohorts of students are co-enrolled in two or more courses)

❒ Mentoring by campus professionals

❒ Peer education (e.g., supplemental instruction, tutoring, peer-led team learning, peer mentoring)

❒ Placement testing

❒ Pre-term orientation

❒ Residential programs or initiatives

❒ Service-learning

❒ Student success center

❒ Study abroad

❒ Summer bridge

❒ Undergraduate research

❒ Writing-intensive coursework

❒ Other, please specify: _____

Future FYE Efforts

Q88. Is your institution considering or developing any future student success programs, initiatives, or courses *specifically or intentionally geared toward first-year students*?

❏ Yes

❏ No

❏ I don't know.

Q89. If yes, please indicate which of the following student success programs, initiatives, or courses *specifically or intentionally geared toward first-year students* your institution is considering or developing: (Select all that apply.)

❏ Common reading

❏ Convocation

❏ Developmental or remedial education

❏ Early-alert systems (i.e., systems that monitor student academic performance and may include direct outreach to students in academic or other types of difficulty)

❏ Experiential learning/learning beyond the classroom

❏ First-year academic advising

❏ First-year gateway courses

❏ First-year seminars

❏ General education

❏ Leadership programs

❏ Learning communities (i.e., curricular structures in which small cohorts of students are co-enrolled in two or more courses)

❏ Mentoring by campus professionals

❏ Peer education (e.g., supplemental instruction, tutoring, peer-led team learning, peer mentoring)

❏ Placement testing

❏ Pre-term orientation

❏ Residential programs or initiatives

❏ Service-learning

❏ Student success center

❏ Study abroad

❏ Summer bridge

❏ Undergraduate research

❏ Writing-intensive coursework

❏ Other, please specify: _____

Survey Information

[Display section for all survey participants]

Q90. Does your institution offer any student success programs, initiatives, or courses specifically or intentionally geared toward the following transition points?

- ❏ Sophomore year
- ❏ Transfer
- ❏ Senior capstone
- ❏ None of the above

Q91. It is our practice to create a research report based on an analysis of the general information gathered from this survey. Would you like to be informed when this research report is made available?

- ❏ Yes
- ❏ No

Q92. The National Resource Center for The First-Year Experience and Students in Transition will be conducting a follow-up study to gather and analyze first-year seminar syllabi from a national sample of institutions. Please provide the contact information of the person on your campus in the best position to provide an example first-year seminar syllabus from your campus.

First name:_____

Last name: _____

Title: _____

Email address:_____

Q93. The National Resource Center for The First-Year Experience and Students in Transition will be conducting its national surveys on student transition programs on a four-year cycle. This includes the administration of the National Survey of Sophomore-Year Initiatives in Spring 2018 and the National Survey of Senior Capstone Experiences in Spring 2020. More information about these national surveys can be found at https://sc.edu/about/offices_and_divisions/national_resource_center/research/research_findings/

The National Resource Center will be conducting the National Survey of Sophomore-Year Initiatives in Spring 2018. To ensure the survey will be sent to the person on your campus in the best position to answer questions regarding sophomore-year initiatives, please provide this individual's contact information below:

First name:_____

Last name: _____

Title: _____

Email address:_____

Appendix C

List of Institutions Participating in the 2017 National Survey on the First-Year Experience[1]

Institution	City	State
Alderson Broaddus University	Philippi	WV
Allen County Community College	Iola	KS
Arkansas State University - Main Campus	Jonesboro	AR
Ashland University	Ashland	OH
Auburn University	Auburn	AL
Austin Peay State University	Clarksville	TN
Beacon College	Leesburg	FL
Bennett College	Greensboro	NC
Brazosport College	Lake Jackson	TX
Cabrini University	Radnor	PA
Caldwell Community College and Technical Institute	Hudson	NC
Caldwell University	Caldwell	NJ
California State University, East Bay	Hayward	CA
Cape Fear Community College	Wilmington	NC
Cardinal Stritch University	Milwaukee	WI
Centenary University	Hackettstown	NJ
Cincinnati State Technical and Community College	Cincinnati	OH
College of Charleston	Charleston	SC
College of Micronesia–FSM	Pohnpei	Micronesia
College of William and Mary	Williamsburg	VA
Comanche Nation College	Lawton	OK
Cornerstone University	Grand Rapids	MI
Cuyamaca College	Rancho San Diego	CA

Table continues on page 176

[1]This is a partial list (*n* = 135) of total respondents to the National Survey on the First-Year Experience (*N* = 537). Institutions could opt out of being publicly identified as a survey respondent.

Table continued from page 175

Institution	City	State
Durham Technical Community College	Durham	NC
East Carolina University	Greenville	NC
El Camino College - Compton Center	Torrance	CA
Fairleigh Dickinson University - Florham Campus	Madison	NJ
Fairmont State University	Fairmont	WV
Florida International University	Miami	FL
Florida National University - Main Campus	Hialeah	FL
Fort Hays State University	Hays	KS
Framingham State University	Framingham	MA
Fresno City College	Fresno	CA
Fullerton College	Fullerton	CA
Georgia State University	Atlanta	GA
Goucher College	Baltimore	MD
Governors State University	University Park	IL
Grand Rapids Community College	Grand Rapids	MI
Gustavus Adolphus College	St. Peter	MN
Hamilton College	Clinton	NY
Hardin-Simmons University	Abilene	TX
Harding University	Searcy	AR
Heidelberg University	Tiffin	OH
Hennepin Technical College	Brooklyn Park	MN
Hiram College	Hiram	OH
Holy Cross College	Notre Dame	IN
Illinois State University	Normal	IL
Immaculata University	Immaculata	PA
Indiana University Kokomo	Kokomo	IN
Indiana University–Purdue University Indianapolis	Indianapolis	IN
Jamestown Community College	Jamestown	NY
Jefferson Community and Technical College	Louisville	KY
Kansas State University	Manhattan	KS
Kennesaw State University	Kennesaw	GA
Kent State University at Salem	Salem	OH
Keuka College	Keuka Park	NY
Laboure College	Milton	MA
Lakeshore Technical College	Cleveland	WI
Lasell College	Newton	MA
Life Pacific College	San Dimas	CA
Macalester College	St. Paul	MN
Madonna University	Livonia	MI

Table continues on page 177

Table continued from page 176

Institution	City	State
Marietta College	Marietta	OH
Metropolitan State University of Denver	Denver	CO
Milwaukee Institute of Art & Design	Milwaukee	WI
Minnesota State University, Mankato	Mankato	MN
Monmouth University	West Long Branch	NJ
Monroe Community College	Rochester	NY
Mount Holyoke College	South Hadley	MA
Mount Saint Mary College	Newburgh	NY
Murray State College	Tishomingo	OK
Nash Community College	Wake Forest	NC
New Mexico Highlands University	Las Vegas	NM
North Iowa Area Community College	Mason City	IA
Northeast Iowa Community College	Calmar	IA
Northwest Missouri State University	Maryville	MO
Olivet College	Olivet	MI
Oregon College of Art and Craft	Portland	OR
Pace University-New York	New York	NY
Pacific Lutheran University	Tacoma	WA
Palo Verde College	Blythe	CA
Polk State College	Winter Haven	FL
Potomac State College of West Virginia University	Keyser	WV
Regis College	Weston	MA
Rio Salado College	Tempe	AZ
Rivier University	Nashua	NH
Sam Houston State University	Huntsville	TX
Seton Hall University	South Orange	NJ
Shepherd University	Shepherdstown	WV
Silver Lake College of the Holy Family	Manitowoc	WI
Southern Connecticut State University	New Haven	CT
Southern Illinois University Carbondale	Carbondale	IL
Southern Utah University	Cedar City	UT
Southwestern Assemblies of God University	Waxahachie	TX
St. Edward's University	Austin	TX
Stella and Charles Guttman Community College	New York	NY
Stockton University	Galloway	NJ
SUNY Canton	Canton	NY
SUNY Cortland	Cortland	NY
Tennessee Wesleyan University	Athens	TN
Texas Woman's University	Denton	TX

Table continues on page 178

Table continued from page 177

Institution	City	State
The College of Idaho	Caldwell	ID
The Evergreen State College	Olympia	WA
The University of Tampa	Tampa	FL
The University of Tennessee, Knoxville	Knoxville	TN
The University of Virginia's College at Wise	Wise	VA
Trinity Christian College	Palos Heights	IL
University of Alaska Southeast	Juneau	AK
University of Baltimore	Baltimore	MD
University of California, Berkeley	Berkeley	CA
University of California, Los Angeles	Los Angeles	CA
University of California, Riverside	Riverside	CA
University of Cincinnati - Main Campus	Cincinnati	OH
University of Great Falls	Great Falls	MT
University of Houston–Clear Lake	Houston	TX
University of Louisiana at Lafayette	Lafayette	LA
University of Mississippi	Oxford	MS
University of Nevada, Las Vegas	Las Vegas	NV
University of North Dakota	Grand Forks	ND
University of Oregon	Eugene	OR
University of Rhode Island	Kingston	RI
University of South Carolina Columbia	Columbia	SC
University of St. Thomas	St. Paul	MN
University of Washington	Seattle	WA
Upper Iowa University	Fayette	IA
Victor Valley College	Victorville	CA
Virginia Polytechnic Institute and State University	Blacksburg	VA
Wabash Valley College	Mt. Carmel	IL
Warner Pacific College	Portland	OR
Western Carolina University	Cullowhee	NC
Western Illinois University	Macomb	IL
Western Piedmont Community College	Morganton	NC
Western State Colorado University	Gunnison	CO
Winona State University	Winona	MN
Winston-Salem State University	Winston-Salem	NC

About the Editor

Dallin George Young is the assistant director for research, grants, and assessment at the National Resource Center for The First-Year Experience and Students in Transition at the University of South Carolina. He is responsible for the original research agenda of the National Resource Center and has overseen national and international administrations of Center surveys including the National Survey of First-Year Seminars, National Survey of Sophomore-Year Initiatives, National Survey of Senior Capstone Experiences, and the National and International Surveys of Peer Leaders. His research agenda focuses on outcomes of postsecondary education, the impact of professional standards in higher education, and assessment. His work in these areas has led to co-authorship of research reports, book chapters, and research articles as well as a number of presentations to the higher education community. Dallin holds a BA in liberal arts and sciences from Utah State University, an MA.Ed from Virginia Tech, and a PhD from the University of Georgia. Before joining the Center, he worked in administrative roles in student housing and student affairs assessment.